THE ARMENIAN MASSACRES 1894–1896

THE ARMENIAN MASSACRES 1894–1896

U.S. Media Testimony

Edited and with an Introduction by
ARMAN J. KIRAKOSSIAN

Foreword by BOB DOLE

WAYNE STATE UNIVERSITY PRESS   DETROIT

Copyright © 2004 by Wayne State University Press,
Detroit, Michigan 48201. All rights are reserved.
No part of this book may be reproduced without formal permission.

Library of Congress Cataloging-in-Publication Data

The Armenian massacres, 1894–1896 : U.S. media testimony / edited and with an intro. by Arman J. Kirakossian ; foreword by Bob Dole.
p. cm.
Includes bibliographical references and index.
ISBN 0-8143-3153-X
1. Armenian massacres, 1894–1896—Foreign public opinion, American. 2. Turkey—History—19th century—Sources. 3. Armenians—Turkey—History—Sources. 4. Armenia—History—1801–1900—Sources. I. Kirakosëiìan, A. Dzh. (Arman Dzhonovich)
DS194.A684 2004
956.6′20154—dc22

2003023289

⊗ The paper used in this publication meets the minimum requirements of the American National Standard for Information Sciences—Permanence of Paper for Printed Library Materials, ANSI Z39.48–1984.

The publication of this book is sponsored by the Tekeyan Cultural Association of the United States and Canada through a generous grant by Rouben and Nina Terzian of Montecito, California.

"Americans have . . . a special reason, over and above
their quick responsiveness to sentiments of humanity,
for feeling a warm interest in the condition
of the Armenian Christians."

—James Bryce, 1895

CONTENTS

Foreword *by Bob Dole* 11
Preface 13
Introduction 15

Unhappy Armenia
John J. O'Shea (*The Catholic World*, January 1895) 47

The Armenian Trouble
E. L. Godkin (*The Nation*, January 1895) 53

An Eye-Witness to the Armenian Horrors
(*The Catholic World*, May 1895) 56

Lord Salisbury and Armenia
(*The Nation*, August 1895) 58

The Evil of the Turk
(*The Outlook*, August 1895) 61

Turkey and the Armenian Crisis
Theodore Peterson, B.D. (*The Catholic World*, August 1895) 67

Why We Catholics Sympathize with Armenia
Rev. R. M. Ryan (*The Catholic World*, November 1895) 77

The Armenian Question
James Bryce (*The Century Magazine*, November 1895) 82

Rational Sympathy
(*The Nation*, November 1895) 92

The Armenian Massacres
Rev. Cyrus Hamlin, D.D. (*The Outlook*, December 1895) 95

Armenia, Past and Present
Rev. Henry Hyvernat, D.D. (*The Catholic World*, December 1895)   100

The Eastern Question
W. J. Stillman (*The Nation*, January 1896)   112

Aid for Armenia: An Appeal for Immediate Help
(*The Outlook*, January 1896)   116

The Armenian Resolutions
E. L. Godkin (*The Nation*, January 1896)   122

The Turks and the Armenians
Elbert Francis Baldwin (*The Outlook*, February 1896)   125

Why the Sultan Is Responsible for the Armenian Massacres
(*The Outlook*, February 1896)   136

The Massacres in Turkey from October 1, 1895, to January 1, 1896
(*The Review of Reviews*, February 1896)   140

Who Is Responsible? A Question from Armenia
(*The Review of Reviews*, April 1896)   146

The Sultan of Turkey by One Who Knows Him
(*The Review of Reviews*, April 1896)   149

What Must Be Done in Armenia?
(*The Review of Reviews*, April 1896)   151

An American Heroine in the Heart of Armenia: Dr. Grace Kimball and Her Relief Work at Van
Elizabeth B. Thelberg, M.D. (*The Review of Reviews*, April 1896)   155

Armenia's Impending Doom: Our Duty
M. M. Mangasarian (*The Forum*, June 1896)   164

Turkey in Extremis
E. L. Godkin (*The Nation*, September 1896)   176

The Constantinople Massacres
D. Kalopothakes (*The Nation*, October 1896)   179

CONTENTS

The Massacres at Van
(The Review of Reviews, October 1896)   185

The Eastern Ogre; Or, St. George to the Rescue, 1878 and 1896
W. T. Stead *(The Review of Reviews,* November 1896)   189

The Situation in Armenia
Grace N. Kimball, M.D. *(The Outlook,* November 1896)   205

The Immediate Future of Armenia: A Suggestion
W. K. Stride *(The Forum,* November 1896)   211

The Armenian Question
Lyman Abbott *(The Outlook,* December 1896)   225

The Armenian Refugees
M. H. Gulesian *(The Arena,* March 1897)   236

Armenia's Desolation and Woe
(The Review of Reviews, May 1897)   248

An Interview with Sultan Abdul Hamid
The Honorable A. W. Terrell *(The Century Magazine,* November 1897)   252

A Mother of Martyrs
Chalmers Roberts *(The Atlantic Monthly,* January 1899)   263

Germany and the Armenians
W. J. Stillman *(The Nation,* May 1899)   274

Contribution to the Armenian Question
Carl Albert Paul Rohrbach *(The Forum,* May 1900)   278

Notes   291
Bibliography and References on the Armenian Question, 1890s   299
Index   307

FOREWORD

The articles in this excellent compilation present a chilling picture of a ruthless, inhumane campaign to exterminate many thousands of Armenians and drive the remainder from their ancestral lands. Sadly, this brutality is not unique in modern history. While the preceding century will be remembered as the one that gave our civilization its most monumental democratic, economic, and technological advances, it is also the century of the Holocaust, the Armenian genocide, and, more recently, the genocides of Bosnia, Cambodia, and Rwanda.

The subject of this book is close to my heart, as it is for many people in the United States. Our country is home to hundreds of thousands of Armenian Americans, many of whom fought for our country's freedom and made significant contributions to its economic and cultural development. The Armenian-American community is largely comprised of descendants of the survivors of the Armenian massacres in the 1890s and the subsequent genocide.

As this volume demonstrates, the plight of the Armenians during this period was reported widely in the press in the United States and other Western democracies. The missionaries, public figures, and concerned journalists who authored these reports clearly cared for and sympathized deeply with the Armenian people. In the nineteenth century hundreds of American missionaries lived in the Ottoman Empire, where they provided social, educational, and moral support to all citizens, without regard to race or religion. Indeed, the Armenian population came to see the American presence in the Empire as one of the few rays of light in an otherwise increasingly hostile environment.

After the massacres of the 1890s, American Red Cross officials, civic-minded citizens, and missionaries made contributions to Armenian charities, conducted field work, and asked the Ottoman authorities to address the problem. Today, this spirit of aid and charitable giving continues as the U.S. government and other

Foreword

American entities, organizations, and individuals work to assist the people of the Republic of Armenia in building a peaceful, stable, and developed nation and Caucasus region. Above all, their goal is to unleash the productive energy of the Armenian people in the realization of a free, democratic, and prosperous future.

The stability and long-term development of Armenia and the South Caucasus ultimately depends upon a successful resolution of regional disputes and conflicts. A necessary first step for strong Armenian-Turkish bilateral cooperation is a historic rapprochement between these two great nations. Acceptance and understanding of the past can help to cultivate the seeds of mutual trust and reconciliation between the Armenian and Turkish peoples. My profound hope is that this book will contribute to this understanding by offering an uncensored description of one of the most tragic sequences of events in modern history.

BOB DOLE
Washington, D.C.

PREFACE

The author "conceived" this book when he was researching the U.S. policies and public opinion on the Armenian Question, as a necessary part of his work on his previous monographies, *Great Britain and the Armenian Question in the 1890's* (Yerevan, 1990) and *British Diplomacy and the Armenian Question, 1830's–1914* (Yerevan, 1999). The author also plans to release the second volume of the book, presenting the coverage of the Armenian Massacres of 1894–1896 in the British periodicals.

The original spelling and use of names and places have been preserved throughout the book. The author recognizes that this may be confusing to some readers. But he believes that the benefits of having unedited and uncensored text, published in the same form and format in which it originally appeared, far outweigh the expediency of converting all names and terms to a modern usage. *The footnotes appearing in the text are the original footnotes in the articles, while the author's comments are carried in the endnotes.*

The author expresses his sincere gratitude and appreciation to prominent Armenian-American benefactors Rouben Terzian (Chairman of Armenian National Alliance) and his wife Nina Terzian, who sponsored the publication of this book. The author also thanks Hasmik Haroutyunian and Haik Gugarats for their help in putting together this book, and owes a debt of gratitude to his family and friends, whose love, respect, and dedication to this project helped bring it to a successful conclusion.

Dr. Arman J. Kirakossian
Washington, D.C.

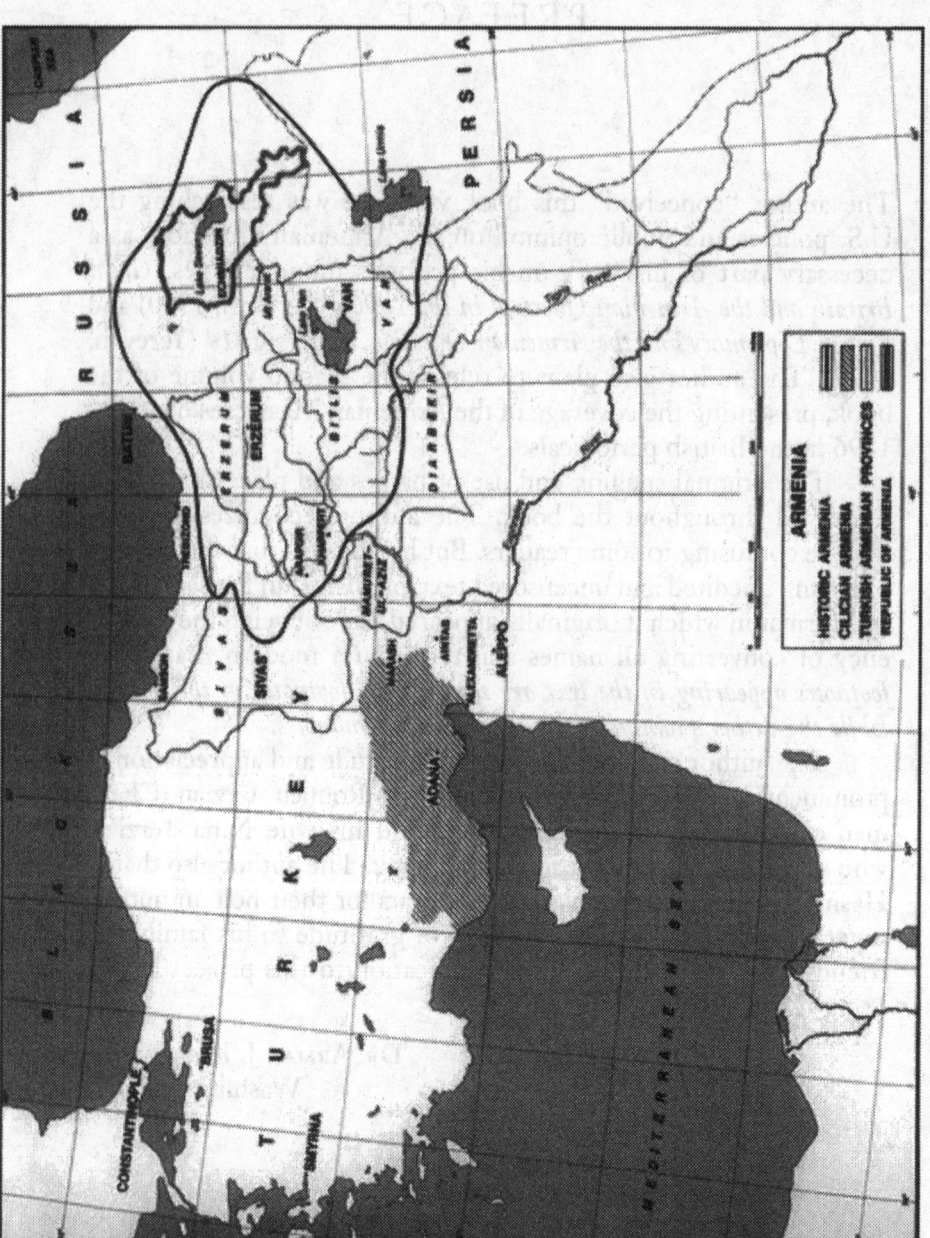

From Robert Mirak, *Torn Between Two Lands: Armenians in America 1890 to World War I* (Cambridge: Harvard University Press, 1983).

INTRODUCTION

The Ottoman Empire and the European Powers

By the middle of the nineteenth century, the Ottoman Empire, then the largest territory in the Near East, turned into a battleground and a prize for competing interests of the major European powers. As they vied for political and economic domination of Turkey, each of those powers sought to advance its own interests and agenda in the Ottoman Empire, as well as to check the efforts by other powers to do likewise.

The period of Western influence and domination, from the end of the eighteenth to the middle of the nineteenth centuries, brought immense changes on every level of society. To some extent, these changes were due to the actions or interventions of the European powers. The accelerated transformation of the traditional structure of the Ottoman Empire under the pressure of the European governments thereafter was a result of the so-called Tanzimat period, which started with the first Tanzimat edict, the Hatt-e-Sherif of Gülhane in 1839, and ended with the dissolution of the first Ottoman parliament by Sultan Abdul Hamid II in 1878.

The Ottoman reforms were an attempt to safeguard the integrity of the Empire in a world that was becoming dominated by the European powers and Western civilization. The reform efforts of Tanzimat were not guided by any long-term strategy to modernize the society but, rather, determined by the political events of the day. Confronted with the deteriorating external and internal security situation and with the integrity and sovereignty of the state at stake, the Ottoman reforms were a classic example of what was called "defensive modernization."[1] They were gestures of propitiation to qualify for loans and other benefits and at the same time ward off intervention and occupation.

The main effort of the Ottoman reformers was directed toward military modernization and administrative centralization.

The purpose of these intertwined designs was to restore and maintain the authority of the government both at home, against the national liberation movements and Western ideology, and abroad, against increasingly powerful enemies.

In their efforts to exploit the situation and acquire dominance, the European powers invoked the already irrelevant principle of preserving the status quo of the Empire, which played into the hands of the Sultan's absolutist government as it pursued its reactionary domestic policies. The European powers used the precarious state of the Christian nations in the Ottoman Empire to put pressure on and interfere in the domestic affairs of the Sublime Porte to win new political and commercial concessions. Not only did this not alleviate the plight of the minorities, it led to the deterioration of their condition.

From the early years of the nineteenth century, the Ottoman Empire faced yet another threat to its territorial integrity. In addition to the foreign powers advancing on its borders, there were now local leaders and movements in many parts, seeking autonomy or even independence. The attempts of the imperial Ottoman government to restore the authority of the capital ignited resistance. In the central provinces of the Empire, the Sultan was gradually able to restore and strengthen his authority. In the remote provinces, however, this proved to be a more difficult task.

The impact of the European influence was naturally stronger and more immediate on the Christian peoples of the Ottoman Empire. During the nineteenth century, the Christian minorities in the Empire pursued three difficult and ultimately irreconcilable objectives. The first of these was equal citizenship in the Ottoman state, that is to say, equal rights for the Christians and the Muslim majority. The idea of equal citizenship was urged on the Turks by the European powers. The second objective, pursued with increasing energy by more and more Ottoman Christians, was that of independence, or at least autonomy within a national territory of their own. The third aim was the retention of the privileges and autonomies that the Millets (religious-political communities) had had under the old order, including the right to maintain and enforce their own religious laws, control their own educational systems in national languages, and, generally, to maintain a distinct culture.[2]

INTRODUCTION

The Second Tanzimat period started with the Hatt-e-Hümayun of 1856. In this edict the Sultan confirmed the reform measures of the Hatt-e-Sherif of Gülhane and the Tanzimat in general, with a strong emphasis on religious liberty and equality for his non- Muslim subjects. The status of non-Muslim minorities was stipulated according to a legal status of citizenship with general individual rights. The edict eliminated on paper all distinctions between Muslim and Christian or any other non-Muslim subjects. It granted freedom and security to all, in terms of law and taxation, property, and education in civil or military schools, and it allowed all to enroll in the military or the civil service. Non-Muslim subjects were now eligible for military service, from which they had hitherto earned exemption by paying a special toll tax.

From the middle of the century onward the spirit of reforms within the Ottoman Empire was losing its vigor. The economic reforms, however, were not fully implemented and, therefore, did not lead to significant changes in economic and social development of the Empire. Nor did the reforms address the concerns of the non-Turkish peoples. Mistrustful of the true intentions of the Ottoman government, the Christian population still preferred to seek foreign aid from the European powers, especially from Russia, in its quest for autonomy and, in the end, full independence.

In 1875 the Sublime Porte declared bankruptcy, being unable to service its external debt; the interest payments reached an astronomical figure of 6 billion francs. The European powers further increased their control over the Empire's finances, edging out competitors in the market. The country's weak industrial base stagnated under the double pressure of the authorities' mismanagement and the foreign competition. A law passed in 1874 allowed foreign citizens to receive licenses for industrial production, which, coupled with the previously granted concessions (or "capitulations") to the foreign commercial interests, gave them an absolute edge over any local producer.

The European governments took advantage of the increasing economic and political weakness of the Ottoman Empire to advance their objectives and interests there. All were eager to control the East-West commercial routes passing through the Empire. The competition between Great Britain and France, in particular, increased after the opening of the Suez Canal in 1869, although the

French defeat in the Prusso-French War of 1870–1871 significantly strengthened the British positions in the Eastern Mediterranean. Russia tried to play one European nation against another as it extended assistance to the Christian peoples in the Ottoman Empire to restore its former positions in the Balkans.

As for the bulk of the Muslim population, they were outraged by this emancipation of the "infidels," which struck right at the roots of their traditional conceptions of the absolute superiority of Islam and the inferiority of all other religions. The Christian peoples were inferiors who, in view of their disparate beliefs, could never be regarded as equals, or accepted as such, morally or socially, in such a secular community as the principles of Tanzimat envisaged.[3] This opposition provoked throughout the Empire a widespread spirit of negative reaction, and was expressed in the ideology of pan-Islamism, a common front of the Muslim people against the common threat of the Christian Empires and minorities.

Significantly, this was seen as achieving a solidarity and unity of all Muslims—a group defined by its religion, or community, rather than by its Turkishness or any other ethnic, linguistic, or territorial affiliation. A limited and controlled pan-Islamism became official Ottoman policy. It was useful both at home, where it helped the Sultan in his appeals to the Muslim subjects for loyalty against subversives of all kinds, and abroad, where it served to win support among the non-Ottoman Muslims and especially among the Muslim subjects of the European countries.

The visible decline of Ottoman power during the Balkan crisis of 1875–1878 raised new hopes for non-Muslim peoples of the Empire. The Bulgarian crisis of 1876, followed by the defeat of the Ottoman Empire and the involvement of the European powers in its internal affairs, seemed to be positive signs for non-Muslims. While the European powers, especially Britain, were following a policy of settling the minority problems in the Balkans at the expense of the Ottomans, they were at the same time supporting the Empire as a "would-be bulwark" against the expansionist ambitions of Russia. This contradiction was due to the fact that events in the Balkans were no longer a matter only for the European balance of power but also for the European public, now supportive of the nationalist movements and pushing their governments to intervene.

INTRODUCTION

The Ottoman elite in Istanbul saw itself beset by external conspiracies and internal treason.

The thirty-two-year reign (1876–1908) of Sultan Abdul Hamid II is usually referred to as a period of absolutist or despotic rule. The Sultan dissolved the parliament and suspended the Ottoman constitution in 1878. He cracked down on any kind of opposition to his rule, built up a repressive network of intelligence services, and muzzled the critical journalists and novelists who had just started to spread their ideas to the literate public.

After parceling out the European provinces, the European interference drifted from the Balkans into the Anatolian heartland of the Ottoman State. But "the former 'sick man of Europe,' back within his Islamic frontiers, now aspired to be the Strong Man of Asia . . . to antagonize Europe and the civilized world of the West more than ever before." As Lord Kinross mentioned in *The Ottoman Centuries. The Rise and Fall of the Turkish Empire*, "for within those frontiers there still thrived a large Christian minority which he increasingly mistrusted and treated as an obstacle to all his designs, the Armenian people."[4]

Armenia and the Armenian Question

By the end of the eighteenth century, Armenia was divided between the Ottoman Empire (Western Armenia) and Persia (Eastern Armenia). Geographically situated between East and West, at the confluence of the permanently warring imperialist tides of its powerful neighbors or invading hordes, Armenia had lost its national independence five hundred years earlier.

As a result of the Russo-Persian war of 1826–1828, Eastern Armenia was annexed by Russia in a treaty of Turkmenchai, and the khanates of Yerevan and Nakhichevan made up the Armenian Province. The Armenian economy received a boost of energy. In major industrial and trade centers of South Caucasus, such as Baku, Tiflis, and Batumi, the Armenian commercial elite played a leading role. Administrative and judicial reforms carried out by the Czarist government in Eastern Armenia, and formation of the Yerevan province in 1849, introduced centralized rule, promoting the industrial development of the country. Preferential tariffs were set up to stimulate the development of trade relations. Nevertheless, Armenia and the South Caucasus remained a backward, predominantly agricultural region. The czarist regime barred Armenians from access to government and court offices, and strove to eliminate the national culture.

In the second half of the nineteenth century, Western Armenia remained under the Ottoman rule. Divided between a large Armenian Gregorian (Apostolic) group and smaller Protestant and Catholic communities, the total Armenian population in six of the eastern provinces of the Ottoman Empire and various towns and provinces amounted to around three million people. Most of them were peasants in areas dominated by the Turcoman and Kurdish tribes. Over the centuries, they had migrated along the major east-west trade routes of Anatolia, so that by the early nineteenth century there were also important Armenian settlements in many of the major Anatolian towns and in Constantinople itself. Despite social, ethnic, and religious persecution, as well as harassment by the local Ottoman authorities and Muslim tribes, the Armenian peasantry had until the latter part of the nineteenth century remained politically quiescent. Like their brethren in the business communities of the cities, they had earned a reputation for sobriety and thrift.

Nonetheless, as a race loyal to their religion, language, and culture, the Armenians were a people of strong national pride. They felt themselves to be European, and as time went on came to benefit from a Western education, not only in Europe, but also in the East at the hands of the American Protestant missionaries.

To prevent the insurrection movement of the Armenians, the Ottoman government did everything it could to hinder their national consolidation. Measures were taken to put an end to the semi-independent existence of some Armenian provinces and to arouse fanaticism in the Muslim population. Repressive measures were initiated against the press, as well as literary and educational organizations; corruption and violence became common. The 1860s witnessed a rise in the Armenian liberation movement, with insurrections in Van and Zeytun in 1862 and Mush in 1863.

The Russo-Turkish War of 1877–1878 ended with a Russian victory, as the Russian troops in the Balkans reached the walls of Constantinople and occupied Western Armenia on the Caucasian front. The outcome of the war and the successful national liberation struggle of the Balkan nations inspired the Armenians to take on the task of national liberation and reunification of the two Armenias, ostensibly under the Russian protectorate. The foreign policies of Czarist Russia, carried out under the cloak of "protection" of the Christian peoples of the Ottoman Empire, happened to coincide with the national aspirations of the Armenian people.

The Armenian Question was initially addressed in Article 16 of the Russo-Turkish preliminary San Stefano Treaty of 1878, which stated that

> as the evacuation by the Russian troops of the territory which they occupy in Armenia, and which is to be restored to Turkey, might give rise to conflicts and complications detrimental to the maintenance of good relations between the two countries, the Sublime Porte engages to carry into effect, without further delay, the improvements and reforms demanded by local requirements in the provinces inhabited by the Armenians, and to guarantee their security from Kurds and Circassians.[5]

The provision was beneficial as far as Armenia was concerned because Russia was designated the official protector of the Armenian people, and at the same time allocation of a larger part of Western Armenia to Russia would provide the Armenian people with an opportunity to consolidate national resources and achieve a measure of economic and cultural development.

The treaty, however, was signed in a period of acute international crisis, as Russia faced a strong resistance from Austria-Hungary and Great Britain. Great Britain, in fact, made serious preparations for war. In February 1878 six battleships appeared in the Dardanelles and anchored off the Prince Islands in the Sea of Marmora, while reserves were built up in Malta. The British General Staff had devised a plan of attack in the area of the Straits and the Caucasus, including disembarking troops on the Black Sea coast. The Armenian territory was to be used as well, with forces in Alexandretta attacking from the south. Austria-Hungary was also strongly opposed to the spread of the Russian influence in the Balkans and to the prospect of the Slavs' statehood, and made an effort to prevent a concerted action of Serbia, Montenegro, Bosnia and Herzegovina, as well as Bulgaria, for independence.

Thus, Russia found itself up against the Anglo-Austrian coalition, but the Czar's government was not ready to go to war again.

On May 18, 1878, a secret Anglo-Russian agreement was signed, which stripped Russia of half the advantages it had gained under the Treaty of San Stefano. Russia was to give up the Alashkert Valley and Bayazid; it agreed that the protection of the Armenian Christians was to be guaranteed jointly by the European powers, not by Russia solely, and, at the same time, Russia undertook not to stretch its borders further into Asiatic Turkey. The British Government then entered into secret negotiations with the Porte. Greatly dismayed by their recent defeat, the Turkish authorities once again took London's promises of friendship and cooperation as sufficient grounds for determining their line of policy. On June 4, 1878, Grand Vizier Savfat Pasha and Ambassador Layard signed the Anglo-Turkish (Cyprus) Convention, providing for Britain to lead the island of Cyprus, thus extending its influence over the Eastern Mediterranean. Britain was to defend Ottoman Turkey and particularly its Asiatic frontier. The document did not refer to Armenia as a separate territorial unit and the problem of the reforms was touched upon only in respect to the Christians in Asiatic Turkey.[6]

Great Britain and Austria-Hungary demanded that an international congress be held with the aim of preventing Russia from fully enjoying the fruits of its victory in the war. The Berlin Congress, which modified the provisions of the San Stefano Treaty, also deprived Russia of its monopoly over the Armenian Question. The Armenian delegation in Berlin requested the appointment of a Christian governor-general—as there had been in a part of Lebanon (Mutassarifiya) since its autonomy in 1861—to serve their interests in the Eastern provinces. Though this met with no response, the European powers acknowledged the needs of the Armenians for local improvements and reforms in their provinces and for guarantees of their security against the Circassians and Kurds.

In the Treaty of Berlin the provision that most concerned the Armenians was Article 61, which read: "The Sublime Porte undertakes to carry out, without further delay, the amelioration and reforms demanded by local requirements in the provinces inhabited by the Armenians, and to guarantee their security against the Circassians and Kurds. It will periodically make known the steps taken to this effect to the Powers, who will superintend their application."[7] The substitution of Article 16 of the San Stefano Treaty with Article 61 of the Berlin Treaty effectively removed the exclusive Russian right to address the problems of Western Armenia, thus leaving the Armenian Question under the will and control of all the European cabinets. The Armenian Question was transformed from being an internal Ottoman matter to a subject of international relations, and was subsequently used by the European powers as an instrument of intervention in the Empire's internal policy.

At the same time, nothing would prevent the Sublime Porte from addressing the problem as it saw fit. The Berlin Treaty left the larger part of Western Armenia under Turkish domination, with tragic—if not fatal—results for the population of Western Armenia, which was facing a real possibility of annihilation.

The Armenian Massacres, 1894–1896, and Policy of European Powers

Realizing that the Armenian Question was being used as an instrument in the foreign policies of major powers, the government of Sultan Abdul Hamid II began to address the issue by increasing the persecution of the Armenian element of the Empire. Among the measures used were inciting Muslim fundamentalism, spreading anti-Armenian propaganda, permitting robberies and murders, forced conversion of Armenians to Islam, stricter censorship, settling Muslim refugees from the Balkans in the Armenian-populated villages and lands, unleashing the Kurdish tribes, and creating an irregular Kurdish cavalry. The Kurds spread fear through the open avowal that their official task was to suppress the Armenians, and that they were assured of legal immunity for any acts of oppression against the Christian population. The Sultan prohibited circulation of Armenian newspapers in the inner provinces of the Empire. The teaching of Armenia's history and geography was forbidden throughout the Empire, books on these subjects were confiscated and burned, and authors and teachers were commonly tried as criminals. All these measures had as an objective the physical extermination of ethnic Armenians.

Under the terms of the Cyprus Convention, the British government sent consuls to the Armenian provinces. The reports filed by the consuls confirmed the injustices endured by the Armenians in Turkish courts and the gross discrimination against them in the assessment and collection of taxes and tithes by the corrupt Turkish and local authorities. When the British approached the Porte with objections to the treatment of the Armenians, it was met with a smokescreen of verbiage.

The 1880s and 1890s brought a new phase in the national liberation movement of the Armenian people when the first Armenian political parties were created. Armed resistance against the policies of oppression increased in Western Armenia, with rebellions in Zeytun (1878, 1884), Van (1886), Vaspurakan, and Alashkert, and a peaceful rally in Constantinople (1890). Responding to antigovernment demonstrations in Sasun, the Sultan's regime organized a massacre of local Armenians in August and September 1894, which resulted in the deaths of more than 10,000 Armenians.[8]

British officials tried to keep the details of the Sasun massacre from spreading throughout England by preventing leaks of the British consuls' reports on the local situation and the unbearable condition of the Armenians. But news of the Sasun events swept into the British press in November 1894, causing a public outcry against the Sultan. The British public also blamed the British government for its failure to act on behalf of the Armenian people.

The British government nonetheless called for united action by the European powers, stressing that such an action was the "one and only safe and guaranteed instrument." Prime Minister Lord Rosebery, speaking at the traditional banquet of the Lord Mayor of London on November 9, 1894, emphasized the need to improve Britain's relations with Russia and France by reaching an agreement on Egypt and the Armenian Question. The Russian government was thus given an opportunity to intervene in Western Armenia, but the Czarist officials were not interested in getting involved there.[9]

The establishment of independent states by the Slavic people in the Balkans in the aftermath of the Russian military victories of 1877–1878 was a progressive development, although it came as a result of the Czarist government's expansionist policies. Russia has exercised its traditional policy of claiming patronage of the Christian peoples, pushing the Sultan to implement reforms for his Christian subjects. Yet, after the Congress of Berlin, when the Russian military victories were effectively reversed by the European powers, Russia had tried to avoid confrontation in the Near East and in the 1890s was shifting its expansion efforts from the Near

East to the Far East. Possessing no independent capacity to capture and hold them, Russia would work to keep the straits closed and preserve the status quo in the Black Sea by supporting the territorial integrity of the Ottoman Empire. The Russian policies coincided with the Turkish interests, and, despite the noisy rhetoric from Russia, the Czarist government chose not to intervene on behalf of the Armenian Christians, although Russia, in concert with the European powers, had demanded from the Porte reforms to guarantee the safety of the Christian population of the Ottoman Empire.

Under pressure from the European powers, the Sultan was forced to create a commission to investigate the Sasun pogroms, with representatives of Great Britain, France, and Russia. In April 1895 the British drafted a reform package for Western Armenia, which provided defacto autonomy of the region under the auspices of the European powers.

When France and Russia endorsed the demands for a reforms package, the draft was presented to the Sublime Porte on May 11, 1895. The reforms package consisted of the following proposals: reduction of the number of provinces (vilayets); appointment of a governor in consent with the Powers; a general amnesty and release of political prisoners; return of the refugees to Western Armenia; reforms of the judicial system and penitentiaries; abolishment of tortures; compensation for the victims of the Sasun massacres; the appointment of a High Commissioner for the observation and implementation of the reforms; and the establishment of a Parliamentary Commission.[10]

Nevertheless, the powers of the Triple Alliance expressed dissatisfaction with the unilateral proposal by the British, Russian, and French governments. The Austro-Hungarian Foreign Minister proposed the establishment of a commission of six powers to implement reforms in Western Armenia.[11] The British Ambassador in Germany reported that the Sultan had attempted to sow discord among the powers by appealing to the Kaiser to curb the British and Russian actions.[12]

The Sasun massacre was unwelcome news to the German diplomats, who could not risk being seen as condoning the anti-Armenian activities of Sultan Abdul-Hamid because of public opinion in Germany. Yet the Kaiser did not want to condemn the Sultan's government because that might endanger the German influence in the Ottoman Empire and its expansion plans in the Near East. Liberation of the Christian peoples in Asiatic Turkey would lead to the collapse of the Ottoman Empire, and Germany supported the Empire's territorial integrity and opposed the creation of an independent Armenia. The German diplomacy continued to support the Sultan's government, and formally took part in the collective diplomatic appearances of the powers in Constantinople only to allay the domestic public opinion.

As a German ally, Austria-Hungary was mostly interested in exerting its influence in the Balkans, and perceived Russia as a major obstacle for its policies. The Russo-Austrian rivalry in the Balkans was caused by identical goals of domination, but their competing interests also promoted stability in the region. Austria-Hungary continued to support the territorial integrity of the Ottoman Empire, fearing that establishment of new states or expansion of the existing Slavic states in European Turkey would damage the existence of the multiethnic Austro-Hungarian Empire. The Austro-Hungarian government nominally expressed its solidarity with the British proposals on the Armenian Question to promote the rights of the Christian subjects, calculating that this position would not alienate the Sultan.

In turn, Italy was sensitive to the position of Germany and Austria-Hungary, its allies in the Triple Alliance, and feared that the collapse of the Ottoman Empire would alter the balance of power in the Balkans and the Mediterranean. Italy's formal position on the Armenian Question was to demand that the Sultan implement reforms and ensure the safety of the Christian population of the Empire.

The Sultan's response was announced on July 3. The Porte rejected nearly all the European proposals, objecting to the appointment of a Commissioner and a Control Commission, reforms in the judiciary, gendarmerie and the police, return of the refugees, amnesty, compensation for the victims of the massacres, and protection of the rights of the Armenians in other provinces. The Sultan retained his right to veto the appointment of the governor. Thus, the Sultan almost totally rejected the reforms package presented by Britain, France, and Russia.[13]

Following the Sultan's response, the European powers did not follow up on their proposals for reforms. The Russian foreign minister told the British ambassador in St. Petersburg that Russia had not intended to give the Sultan an ultimatum to implement the reforms package and would not approve any measures to force the reforms package.[14] The French backed the Russians, as the two countries worked to check the British and German influence in the Ottoman Empire. Also, the Ottoman Empire was an important commercial partner of France, with more than 2.5 billion francs, or 10 percent of the French foreign capital, invested in Turkey. Because the collapse of the Ottoman Empire could lead to heavy losses for French investors, France supported the status quo and had a very careful approach to the Armenian Question.

The French government chose to downplay the agitated public opinion on the Armenian Question, and the issue was discussed in the National Assembly for the first time only on November 3, 1896. The Chamber of Deputies overwhelmingly adopted a resolution supporting the government's position without reservations (402 deputies voted in favor, with only 90 deputies opposing the resolutions). The resolution stated that the Armenians and their behind-the-curtain British supporters were partly to blame for the Turkish authorities' brutality and that the anti-Armenian policies were the result of the bad conditions in the political, financial, and administrative management of the Turkish government. The resolution suggested that financial and political support of the Sultan's government could help diffuse the crisis and stop the massacres, and that the French government should continue its time-honored tradition of supporting the territorial integrity of the Ottoman Empire.[15]

Constrained by the positions of other powers, the Liberal cabinet of Lord Rosebery hesitated to undertake an independent British action. In June the cabinet discussed the possibility of using the Mediterranean Fleet, posted at Beirut (three hundred miles away from Western Armenia), against Turkey, but did not reach any conclusions. At any rate, Lord Rosebery's cabinet resigned in June, and Queen Victoria asked Lord Salisbury of the Conservative Party to form the next government.

The return to power of Lord Salisbury raised the hopes in the British public that the leader of the Conservative Party could find a way out of the Near Eastern crisis and stop the Armenian massacres. Salisbury made an effort to reach an Anglo-Russian understanding on the Armenian Question. Simultaneously, he wanted to force the Sultan to acquiesce to the British occupation of Egypt and increase the British position in the Ottoman Empire vis-à-vis Russia. Thus, he was playing a double game by using the Armenian Question as an instrument to increase its influence in the Near East by professing friendship with Germany and Russia. In fact, Lord Salisbury endorsed the position of his predecessor by demanding that the Porte punish the perpetrators of the Sasun massacres and implement the reforms as provided for in the Treaty of Berlin. The instructions on the Armenian Question received by the British diplomatic missions in Turkey were no different from those sent by Lord Rosebery.[16]

Sultan Abdul Hamid was extremely concerned with the proactive British position on this issue. In a note sent to the British embassy, he stated that the reforms were acceptable and there was reason to believe they could be implemented. The Sultan requested British support in getting the Armenians to halt the propaganda and provocations that supposedly delayed the implementation of the reforms. The Sultan committed to commencing the reforms within a week.[17]

On July 16, 1895, the commission investigating the events in Sasun concluded its task after hearing testimonies of more than two hundred witnesses. The European members of the commission presented a collective report on the evidence, which concluded that a real indiscriminate massacre of the Armenian population was perpetrated by the Turkish regular troops in the Sasun region. The investigation did not find any evidence of "rebel" activities by the Armenians.[18]

On August 15, 1895, Queen Victoria presented the Queen's Speech at the State Opening of Parliament, which included the government's statement on the Armenian Question. Her speech stated that the British government was waiting for the Sultan's response to the reform proposals put forward jointly by the British, Russian, and French ambassadors. Condemning the Sultan's government, the Prime Minister said in his remarks that the Porte would be faced with serious consequences if it did not accept the proposals of the three great powers on the reforms in Western Armenia. Lord Salisbury expressed his regret that the Russian and French governments did not agree on the necessity of working out enforcement measures for the proposals. During a later speech in Dover, Lord Salisbury referred to Turkey as a "demoralizing centre that will spread the disease to the healthy parts of Europe, close to the Turkish territories,"[19] and predicted an imminent collapse of the Ottoman Empire.

On September 17, 1895, the Armenian population in Constantinople held a peaceful rally to protest delays in implementation of the reform measures. The government responded promptly by organizing a pogrom, with a death count of more than six thousand Armenians.[20] The Sultan's government announced the reforms on October 20, 1895. Not only were those reforms not implemented, but massacres of the Armenian population started all over the Ottoman Empire. The government skillfully took advantage of the disagreements among the European powers. More than 300,000 Armenians were massacred in the Ottoman Empire from 1894–1896.

Following the savage campaign and drawing on various sources, it is possible to conclude that the massacres were mass-scale and organized, and were carried out by Muslim fundamentalists, police, and regular troops, as well as the Kurdish cavalry, which had been specially created in 1891 by the Sultan for this specific purpose. In 1895 and 1896 the massacres started almost simultaneously in all provinces. A rifle shot or trumpet sounds from the Muslim quarter of cities would usually signal the beginning of the pogrom.[21] The pogroms in the cities were usually preceded by the savage attacks on the Armenian-populated villages by the Kurdish cavalry. Mobs of Kurds, Circassians, and Lases would storm the cities and, together with the local Turkish population, troops and gendarmes would conduct a massacre of the Armenian population and loot their property.[22] The local authorities were instructed to kill the male population primarily. The only victims of the pogroms were Armenians: the Greeks and Jews were almost unaffected. The massacres of the Armenians were organized, and regular troops and gendarmes took part in murders and looting. The pogroms would end as suddenly as they had started, usually after a horn signal.[23] In many cities the municipality would later force the Armenian representatives to sign a document "admitting" guilt for inciting the pogroms.²⁴

During the massacres, Sultan Abdul Hamid protested cynically to the British ambassadors the "rumors of the massacres," describing them as fairy tales and assuring the European nations that his troops were merely protecting the eastern provinces of the Empire from the infringement of the Armenian revolutionaries. The Sultan's government isolated Western Armenia by instituting a strict censorship, barring journalists, businessmen, and tourists from visiting Armenian-populated regions.²⁵

British officials condemned the Turkish authorities for their actions; at the same time, the British diplomacy worked in concert with other European powers to work out a unified approach to the problem. On November 5, 1895, the ambassadors of six European powers told the representatives of the Porte that they continued to receive troubling reports from their consular agents in the provinces. The foreign powers' diplomatic representatives warned that the anarchy spreading in the provinces was of serious concern, and, although the unrest had no connection with the Armenian propaganda, it threatened the lives of all the Christians. The ambassadors stated that they would ask their respective governments to take appropriate measures if the Porte did not take steps to reduce the violence. They requested that the foreign minister inform them of the steps the Ottoman government intended to take to stop the riots and massacres.²⁶

The outwardly forceful intervention of the European powers inspired great hopes among the Armenians of the Ottoman Empire, who had already been agitated by the massacres. The Armenian population of the Zeytun region rose in rebellion against the Sultan's rule on November 24, 1895, and held out against the regular Turkish troops until February 1, 1896, when the Sultan requested help from the European powers in mediating the conflict. The Armenians of Zeytun succeeded in organizing a defense, leaving the attacking troops with more than 13,000 casualties. But the indifference of the European powers demolished the hopes of the Armenians in Cilicia for liberation from the Sultan's rule, and forced them to accept the conditions of the Porte.²⁷

In February 1896 British Prime Minister Robert Salisbury

made a speech at the Nonconformist Unionist Association, in which he essentially discounted the possibility of providing help to the Armenians of the Ottoman Empire. Salisbury rejected "interference in the Armenian affairs not only in present but also in the future," and stated that his country had never undertaken any obligations in this regard. In reporting on the speech, the *Spectator* weekly referred to it as "the latest excuse of Great Britain." What Salisbury meant was that, under the provisions of the Treaty of Berlin, the Armenian Question was to be addressed equally by all the European powers, and Britain was not obligated to do more on this issue than any other power would. Lord Salisbury rejected even the obligations accepted by the British government under the Cyprus Convention. In his speech he professed his belief that the Sultan had done everything possible to implement reforms in Western Armenia. The Prime Minister stated that it was impossible to intervene militarily to protect the suffering Armenian population, noting "in an open sea we could succeed over five or six sultans."[28] On April 30, he said in a speech before the House of Lords that "our ships could not reach the top of the Taurus mountains."[29]

On August 26, 1896, a group of thirty Armenians armed with revolvers and dynamite bombs seized the Central Bank of the Sultan's government, threatening to blow themselves up in the building if the Sultan did not accept urgent measures restoring law and order and implementation of the reforms. The European embassies promised to fulfill the Armenians' demands and provide a safe passage to the group holding the bank building. The Turkish secret police had been warned in advance of the plot to seize the bank, but the Sultan had chosen not to prevent the attack in order to inflame the anti-Armenian sentiment among the Muslim mob in the capital and score an anti-Armenian point in the European public opinion.

On August 28, the Armenians holding the bank sent a messenger to the Sultan, demanding a guarantee that their demands would be implemented if they left the bank. But the European representatives persuaded the group to leave the building and board a British ship, with a promise to press the Sultan to implement reforms in Armenia. With the situation resolved and the Armenian activists having left the capital, the authorities unleashed armed bands of Kurds and Lases, who acted alongside the fanatical Muslim mob to massacre the Armenian population. The authorities appropriated a large number of carts to transport dead bodies, while the police and the army were ordered to put down any resistance and render assistance to the mob. The witnesses to the tragedy described brutal and indiscriminate killings of anyone who even looked Armenian, with "rivers of blood flowing down the streets." The mass-scale massacres and robberies took place without interruption for two days. The number of victims was never ascertained, but the European embassies estimated the number of killed at five to six thousand people. According to the official report sent to the Palace, more than 8750 people were killed, not including those thrown into the sea.[30]

During the August pogroms, the European embassies in the capital appealed to the Sultan every day with requests to put down the massacres. The foreign embassies refused to hold fireworks and pompous receptions in honor of the Sultan's birthday. The Sultan, nonetheless, refused to give in to the pressure and was not swayed by the protests, since he counted on the disagreements among the powers to help him have his way in Turkey.[31]

The European embassies undertook efforts to transport thousands of Armenian refugees to safety: some twelve thousand Armenians found shelter in Bulgaria, about one thousand in Alexandretta, and hundreds emigrated to Marseilles, Athens, and Piraeus.[32]

On October 20, Lord Salisbury sent a circular to the governments of the European powers stressing the need for joint actions to address the Armenian Question, emphasizing that each nation had its own interests in the Ottoman Empire. He proposed that a European conference be held to discuss a settlement of the Eastern crisis. After two months of hard diplomatic discussions, the European cabinets finally agreed to organize a conference of ambassadors of the great powers in Constantinople. On February 2, 1897, the ambassadors ended the discussion of the draft of general reforms in the Ottoman Empire, focusing on seven areas: establishment of a Supreme Council; establishment of a commission of control over the implementation of reforms in the provinces; supervision of finances; reforms of the judiciary; reforms of the police; establishment of municipal governments; and freedom of speech.[33]

Nevertheless, this draft was soon largely forgotten because of the Greek-Turkish War that broke out in 1897, with the European powers siding with the Porte on the issue of the Crete. In Constantinople the ambassadors of the great powers came to the conclusion that "during the current crisis the demand of the implementation of the reforms will be useless."[34]

The Constantinople Conference of the representatives of the European governments revealed once again that the powers did not want to jeopardize their already strained relations with the Porte. They would put forward the Armenian Question and make threats only in conjunction with other demands to the Sultan that would diminish his sovereign rights. The Sultan, meanwhile, would organize new pogroms of the Armenian population, which would be a bargaining chip between the Ottoman government and the European leaders.

Coming to power in the early twentieth century, the regime known as the Young Turks inherited the anti-Armenian policies of Sultan Abdul-Hamid II. In its desire to free itself of the problems of the Armenian reforms and to resolve—in its own way—the Armenian Question, the reactionary Young Turk regime adopted a tougher and more inhumane approach. As a result of the Genocide, mass-scale massacres, and deportation of the Armenian population perpetrated by the Young Turk government during World War I, Western Armenia finally lost its indigenous population.

The United States and the Missionary Movement in the Near East

At the close of the nineteenth century the Near East was not in the focus of the U.S. foreign policy. Unlike Europe, the United States established a presence in the Ottoman Empire without any political objectives. Nevertheless, the presence of American missionaries there prepared the ground for a strong American engagement in the region. The United States conducted a policy of "custodianship" toward the Christian population of the Ottoman Empire, focusing on cultural, philanthropic, and commercial areas of cooperation. For the Christian peoples, the United States was the country that sent out missionaries, teachers, and doctors to help them. While the Sultan's government mistrusted the work of American missionaries among the local ethnic minorities, it saw in the United States a potential ally in the economic development of the country.

The United States sold agricultural equipment and other machinery to Turkey. In 1900 U.S. exports to Turkey amounted to $500,000, while the imports of Turkish products (rugs, fruits, walnuts, opium, wool, leather) were almost $7 million.[35]

To assist the missionary activities and protect commercial interests, U.S. consulates were established in Alexandretta, Beirut, Erzerum, Harput, Jerusalem, Sivas, Smyrna, and Baghdad. Unlike their European counterparts working in the Near East, the American consulates worked in an easygoing, simple, and passive mode. The U.S. diplomacy worked hard not to get involved in political controversies, and their traditional role was defending the interests of the American citizens and organizations.

American missionary activities in the Ottoman Empire were aimed at converting the Eastern Christian nations to Protestant Christianity, and would sometimes result in the spread of pro-American feelings. The missionary movement was initiated in 1819, during the administration of President James Monroe. The Congregationalist- and Presbyterian-dominated American Board for Foreign Missions sent Rev. Pliny Fisk and Rev. Levi Parsons to scout possibilities for missionary activities in the Near East. Initially, the main target group of the missionaries were the Muslim majority of the population, and, despite the obvious difficulty of the task, they did not give up.

Consequently, the missionaries started to target the local "decadent" Christian faiths: the Armenians, Greek Orthodox, Nestorians, Copts, and others. The missionaries perceived the conversion of the local Christian faiths to Protestantism as a first step to spreading Western Christianity in the Muslim world. The American missionaries founded churches in cities and villages, visited isolated areas on a regular basis, and published and distributed the Protestant Bible and other Christian literature. The most important tool in meeting the missionaries' goal, however, turned out to be the missionary schools, hospitals, and clinics.[36]

By 1900 there were 162 American missionaries in the Ottoman Empire, including their family members and doctors. They, in turn, employed more than nine hundred locals. Their school network included four theological schools with twenty-two students; forty boarding schools and seven colleges with 2,700 students; and a 15,000-strong student body in the primary schools.[37] The main

American colleges in the Ottoman Empire were the Robert College, Constantinople Women's College, Central Turkish College (Ayntab), Euphrates College (Harberd), Central Turkish College (Marash), Anatolian College (Marzvan), American Protestant College (Beirut), and International Women's College in Smyrna. These schools, generally of lower quality than their counterparts in the United States, also included preparatory classes. The first U.S. college in the Empire was the Robert College, founded in 1860 by well-known missionary Cyrus Hamlin.[38] Out of 297 students, Greeks and Armenians comprised 74 percent, Bulgarians 13 percent, and Turks only 5 percent in the 1899–1900 academic year. The College graduated its first Turkish student in 1903.[39] Opened in 1871 as a preparatory school for women, the Constantinople Women's College was incorporated as a college by the Massachusetts Legislative Assembly in 1890, mostly because of the efforts of its principal, Mary Miles Patrick. Originally housing three students, the school had 146 students in 1900.[40]

The U.S. government gave priority to the activities of the American missionaries in the Ottoman Empire, allocating almost half a million dollars a year to the American school network there. One result of the missionaries' work was a mass-scale resettlement of Armenians to the United States. Fleeing from ruthless persecution by the Sultan's government, more than 12,500 Armenians emigrated to the United States from the Ottoman Empire from 1891 to 1898.[41]

U.S. Foreign Policy and the Armenian Question

At the close of the nineteenth century, U.S. and British colonial interests clashed in many parts of the world. Most notably, the two powers clashed during the Anglo-Venezuelan conflict of 1895–1896, when Britain occupied the disputed land area between Venezuela and British Guyana. Citing the Monroe Doctrine, the U.S. government served as a mediator in the conflict. In a note to the British government, presented on July 20, 1895, U.S. Secretary of State Richard Olney stated that occupation of any Venezuelan territory by Great Britain would be a violation of the Monroe Doctrine and would result in a war.

The U.S. government used the Armenian massacres of 1894–1896 as a pretext for interfering in European affairs and attacking

British policies. Secretary of State Olney stated that the United States would get involved in European affairs if the European powers failed to honor mutual commitments, or if the Christian population in any part of the world would lose its protector.[42] In his State of the Union address in 1895, U.S. President Grover Cleveland heavily criticized the British for their involvement in the Venezuelan conflict and their handling of the Armenian Question. He singled out Great Britain as one of the culprits of the Armenian tragedy, which shared responsibility for Sultan Abdul Hamid's orgy of violence.[43]

The U.S. threats over the Anglo-American disagreements in Central America were a factor in limiting British involvement in the Orient. In case of a war in Europe, the unfriendly position of the United States would have threatened the British colonial domination. According to the *Spectator*, the Sultan realized that the Anglo-American disagreements effectively neutralized the British threat to his empire. On one hand, the weekly wrote that only the United States was capable of effectively pressuring the Sublime Porte as it was not involved in "petty European disputes."[44] But the same paper had earlier predicted that the United States would not help "the people living in misery, without home or means of survival in the mountains of Armenia."[45] The New York-based *Nation* magazine seemed to share this opinion when it wrote that the protection of the rights of the Christian subjects of the Ottoman Empire would be impossible with a naval intervention, as the U.S. Navy could bomb Constantinople only with the assistance of the European navies.[46]

The U.S. leadership viewed the Armenian Question as a way to threaten the Sultan and increase the U.S. influence among the Christian subjects of the Empire. At that time, the White House and the Senate held more debates on Armenia than on Venezuela.[47]

In his State of the Union address in December 1893, President Cleveland discussed U.S.-Turkish relations, which had been recently affected by the arson and looting of Anatolian College in Marzvan by a fanatical Muslim mob. The President pointed out an "unusual indifference," with which the Sultan's government treated the event. He accused the Turkish authorities of complicity, demanded punishment for the culprits and compensation for the damages.[48] Cleveland informed Congress that he had instructed his

Minister in Turkey, Alexander Terrell,[49] to demand that the Sublime Porte treat the ethnic Armenians with American citizenship "without undue severity."[50]

Neither President Cleveland nor Secretary Olney gave much weight to the reports of the Sasun massacre of 1894, which were published in the media and were also presented by Terrell. Secretary Olney, for example, stated, "the media reports of the massacre of Armenians are greatly exaggerated."[51] The President, in turn, stated that the United States was not a signatory to the Berlin Treaty and would not intervene in the affairs of the Ottoman Empire.[52] At the same time, the U.S. government acted to show that it would participate in joint efforts of the European powers on Armenia. On December 3, 1894, Senator Newton Blanchard of Louisiana labeled "the indiscriminate massacre of thousands of men, women, and children" a "blot upon civilization of the age, meriting the severest condemnation of mankind."[53] On the same day, the Senate passed a resolution calling on the White House to work in concert with the European powers to demand an immediate cessation of the massacres, provide full information regarding cruelties to American citizens or to those declaring their intention to become naturalized citizens, and, further, report "any diplomatic steps taken by the United States."[54] In his statement for the record, Senator George Frisbie Hoar called on the President to develop a coherent policy for ensuring the punishment of the people implicated in organizing the mass-scale massacres of the Armenians, referring to them as "bandits" and "enemies of humanity."[55]

President Cleveland's first response to the massacres of 1895 was to protect the lives of Americans in Turkey. In his annual message to Congress, the President noted that the "reported massacres of Christians in Armenia and the development there and in other districts of a spirit of fanatic hostility to Christian influences naturally excited apprehension for the safety of the devoted men and women who, as dependents of the foreign missionary societies in the United States, reside in Turkey under the guarantee of law and usage and in the legitimate performance of their educational and religious mission."[56] Minister Terrell was explicitly told not to involve the United States in the Armenian issue as long as the American citizens were safe. Terrell strongly advised the Porte to safeguard all Americans in Turkey by stationing armed, uniformed militia at missionary establishments throughout the Empire.

Terrell said in 1895 that "the so-called reforms would, when announced, be followed by a massacre of Armenians and a period of great danger to our missionaries." In a letter to a leading American missionary in Turkey, Terrell wrote,

> A residence in the southern portion of the United States at the close of our late Civil War had prepared me to anticipate the fearful era through which we are passing here. I had seen the resentful violence of a proud, dominant race, caused by enforced reforms for a subject race. It was known here that at least one of the great powers would not consent to the use of force to make the reforms proposed for the benefit of the Armenian race effective. And so, on the 21st of October, when very many persons were rejoicing over the decree then issued, which proposed to arm and make officers of a race that had for centuries been subjugated and denied privileges, I demanded and obtained on that day telegraphic orders to every civil and military chief in the Ottoman Empire to protect American missionaries. Once before, in anticipation of the reforms, like orders were obtained at the Porte by myself, such frequent repetition being deemed necessary to impress officials in the interior.[57]

In general, Terrell spoke approvingly of Sultan's actions to protect U.S. citizens during the Armenian massacres.[58] Nevertheless, following reports of missionaries' sufferings during the Turkish government-sponsored atrocities, the U.S. Senate passed a resolution demanding that the Sultan issue immediate compensation for the damages.[59] Moreover, the congressional debates on this issue, which took place in late January 1896, forced President Cleveland to take stronger actions. With the determination of the Congress to assist the President in defense of the Americans, the President dispatched the U.S. Navy cruisers *San Francisco* and *Marblehead* to the Turkish waters, as a show of force against further outrages.

In his annual message of December 7, 1896, President Cleveland was trying to assure Congress that "our government at home and our minister in Constantinople have left nothing undone to protect our missionaries in the Ottoman territory, who constitute nearly all the individuals residing there who have a right to claim our protection on the score of American citizenship."[60]

On March 19, 1897, Minister Terrell was given an audience

with Sultan Abdul Hamid II, and had a long discussion with him. Terrell's long-winded and articulate praise for the Turkish Sultan is indicative of the official U.S. position on the Armenian Question. U.S. government leaders, including President Cleveland, Secretary of State Olney, and Terrell, praised and supported the Sultan with an aim of securing the growing U.S. interests in the region. During the Middle East crisis of 1895–1897, they viewed the Armenian Question as a tool to extract maximum benefits. The U.S. government was interested in the fate of the missionaries, not of the Armenian people. Nevertheless, in his article entitled "An Interview with Sultan Abdul Hamid," he wrote that the Sultan "is to a certain degree responsible for the massacre that plagued his Empire." He also writes that he had informed the Secretary of State of his opinion, and that his concerns were not addressed yet.[61]

The United States started to consider "the Turkish affairs" a priority during the administration of President McKinley in 1898, when he considered sending a U.S. fleet to Turkish waters to demand compensation for the damages incurred by the missionaries during the massacres of 1894–1896. Following the massacres, the missionaries had called on their government to demand restitution for their lost property. As early as 1898, President McKinley told the famous business magnate and philanthropist William Dodge, who was interested in supporting the U.S.-run colleges and missions in the Middle East, that he wanted to pressure the Ottoman Empire. The President, nevertheless, noted that such coercive measures would not be possible at the time as the situation in Cuba tied up the American Navy. In the spring of 1898 President McKinley asked U.S. Ambassador in Turkey Oscar Strauss to head a mission to Constantinople with the objective of compelling the Sultan's government to pay compensation. According to Strauss' report, McKinley "lost sleep" over the risk associated with the persistent demands of the missionaries, who thought "the only way to compel Turkey is to send in the ships to shake the windows in the Sultan's palace." Strauss warned the President that the "jealous" European powers would not allow the United States to "interfere in this center of European disturbance without a risk of confrontation." President McKinley promised not to send any ships to Turkey without Ambassador Strauss' demand.[62]

Before his departure to the United States in December 1899,

Ambassador Strauss wrote to Secretary of State William R. Day that his efforts to extract a promise of compensation from the Sultan were successful. Due to Strauss' preparatory work, Ambassador Lloyd Griscom did receive $95,000 from the Sultan's government, although he dispensed threats, employed diplomatic tricks, and had to call in U.S.S. *Kentucky*. To justify his actions and hide the payment of compensation to the United States for the damages incurred by the missionaries, Abdul Hamid stated that the money was meant to pay for the battleship built by a Philadelphia shipbuilding company.[63]

American Public Opinion and the Armenian Massacres

The Armenian massacres of 1894–1896 raised a wave of protests in the United States. The *New York Herald, New York Times, Christian Register, Daily News, Boston Herald,* and *Chicago Tribune* all published front-page articles, reports, and editorials by leading public figures, featuring maps of Armenia, photo reports about the life of Western Armenians, and comprehensive reports and editorials on the Armenian Question. The newspapers criticized Minister Terrell for his deference to the Sultan. The minutes of his audience with the Sultan were published and were the subject of unfavorable judgment by the American public. In particular, it was noted that he observed the tradition of the Protestant missionaries in Turkey, who followed the Sublime Porte's official policies so that their missionary activities were not threatened.[64]

Immediate reaction came from the outraged Armenian communities in the United States. The Armenian newspapers in Boston and New York covered the events in Turkey and protested the pogroms of Armenians organized by the Sultan's government. All factions united in protest marches, petitions to Congress, mass public meetings, and declarations. In November 1894 a rather militant rally of several hundred agitated citizens of Worcester, Massachusetts, including the mayor and the city's most prominent bankers, attorneys, and clergy, drafted a statement addressed to President Cleveland. And a petition signed by the ministers of the Congregational and Methodist churches in Marlboro, New Hampshire, called on Congress to "secure investigation by an accredited representative of our government into the recent massacre of Christian Armenians . . . and to secure redress for and prevent any such brutalities."

INTRODUCTION

In January 1895 the Young Men's Baptist Social Union of Boston remonstrated "against the recent atrocious crime against Armenian Christians." Even the State Grange of Delaware united in prayer, urging Congress to enact federal "legislation to prevent cruel and barbarous treatment of the Armenian Christians by Turkish soldiers."[65] Furthermore, Armenian-American philanthropic societies and committees were formed in the United States to provide material and monetary assistance to the Armenian population of the Ottoman Empire.[66] These organizations sponsored rallies and public meetings on the Armenian issues in Boston, New York, Philadelphia, Chicago, Providence, and other cities. A protest rally held in New York City on December 18, 1894, drew a large attendance. It was held to protest the massacre in Sasun, and the keynote speaker was well-known American Orientalist William Word, who accused the Sultan's government of masterminding the pogroms of Armenians. Another speaker, Edwin Bliss,[67] told the audience of the massacres in Bitlis, Van, and Mosul, and demanded that the U.S. government intervene to protect Armenians from the Turkish oppression.[68]

The Friends of Armenia Society, based in Boston, carried out a lot of work. In late 1894 Samuel Barrows, editor of *Christian Register* magazine, and Henry Blackwell of the *Woman's Journal* visited Secretary of State Walter Gresham on behalf of the society to request the U.S. government's support in helping to resolve the Armenian Question. The Secretary of State explained that the official position of noninterference was due to the fact that the United States had not been a signatory to the 1878 Berlin Treaty.[69] The same delegation was received at the White House by President Cleveland, and expressed gratitude for his (alleged) sympathizing with the Armenian Question.[70]

The Friends of Armenia held a meeting on February 24, 1895, to elect the nation's foremost crusader for human rights, Julia Ward Howe, as its chairman. Alice Blackwell, Henry Blackwell, Professor Peabody, and Henry Allen were also in attendance.[71] M. Gulesian, a well-known public figure and an author of articles on Armenian issues, was elected secretary of the group.[72]

In the summer of 1895 the Friends of Armenia joined forces with other organizations to form United Friends of Armenia. This group helped coordinate rallies all over the country, protesting inhumane policies of the Sultan's government and the indifference of other governments toward the Armenian Question.[73]

In June 1895 Patriotic Federation of Armenians was founded in New York under the chairmanship of M. Gabrielian, stating as its goal "the coordination of the efforts" to organize liberation of Western Armenia from the Sultan's yoke with "the support of Europe."[74] The Federation held rallies in New York and carried out an educational campaign about Armenia. M. Gabrielian and Ayvazian also gave lectures and made public statements.[75]

A club founded by the Armenian students in Boston in 1895 dedicated itself to educating Armenian-Americans about Armenian history.[76] Protestant church organizations, led by the American Board and the Evangelical Alliance, whipped up a systematic public outcry against the Turks even more vehemently than in 1894. From September to December, weekly sermons denounced the "unspeakable Turks" and called for a total condemnation of the "Red Assassin." Religious journals like the *Independent, Outlook, Christian Register, Congregationalist, Baptist Philadelphian, Commonwealth, Christian Herald,* and *Lend A Hand* demanded "deeds not words"[77] to address the situation.

Decrying the "brutal murders" by "Moslem savages" of Armenian men, women, and children "for no other or better reason than because of their devotion to the Christian religion," the Ohio General Assembly petitioned Congress to adopt "such measures as will show to all the world our abhorrence of such atrocities as have been committed in Armenia and extend to them such protection and material aid as is within the power of this Government."[78]

America's popular outburst against the atrocities was expressed in many ways, including a humanitarian crusade to assist the Armenians in the Ottoman Empire. A handful of missionaries and doctors struggled with the long lines of sick, injured, and malnourished in the refugee camps. Relief efforts had commenced after the Sasun massacres when local Armenian relief committees were organized in New York by Bishop Alonzo Potter and Archbishop Michael Carrigan. By December 1895 the New York Armenian Relief Committee had organized the National Armenian Relief Committee under the leadership of Supreme Court Justice David Brewer and the Reverend Frederick Greene.[79]

The American Red Cross, National Armenian Relief Committee, and Evangelical Alliance joined efforts to raise funds for the Armenian population of Turkey. Clara Barton, the President of the

National Chapter of Red Cross, stressed the importance of expediting the fund-raising efforts. The New York-based *Outlook* magazine called on its readers to donate money in support of the persecuted people, while the staff of the magazine made a $250 donation. In the same issue, there was a letter from a doctor at the American medical mission in Aintab, Dr. Caroline Hamilton, who wrote about the assistance rendered to the wounded Armenians.[80]

A rally held in Boston in 1895 passed a resolution, drafted by Cyrus Hamlin, calling on the United States government to support the American public in its efforts to assist the Armenian population of the Ottoman Empire.[81] The governor of Massachusetts was also present and delivered remarks on the events in Turkey.[82] The speakers at the rally demanded that the United States put pressure on the Sublime Porte to stop the massacres of Armenians.[83]

In 1896 the New York-based *Review of Reviews* published an article by missionary Grace Kimball, who expressed gratitude for the funds collected for the starving population of Van. Among the organizations that donated funds were the British Women's Relief Committee, an American school in Smyrna, the *Christian Herald* journal, and the International Commission on Investigation of the Sasun events.[84]

American missionaries and Armenian relief workers performed virtual miracles at a great personal risk. Dr. Grace Kimball fed about 1500 persons daily and saved hundreds from dying of typhus in the area around Lake Van. At the age of seventy-four, Clara Barton left for Constantinople to supervise the relief work and deal with the Porte. Upon arrival, she promised the Turkish Foreign Minister that she would not discriminate in her relief efforts, write a book while in Turkey, or commit surreptitious deeds. Only then was she permitted to enter the Ottoman Empire. The Red Cross mounted five expeditions into the desolated interior, two of which were headed by physicians. The objective of each was to distribute food, medicine, and tools to begin the massive reconstruction of the devastated towns and villages of Armenia.[85]

Edwin Bliss wrote with pride that the United States and Great Britain were among the first to alleviate the suffering of the Armenian Christian population. Armenian Relief Committees were set up all over the Empire to distribute food and medical supplies.[86]

The Armenian Patriarch in Constantinople also used the good offices of the American missionaries, sending money to his flock in the Eastern part of the Empire.[87] Phillip Currie, the British Ambassador in Turkey, called the American missionaries courageous, brave, and dedicated people.[88]

Conclusion

This volume contains thirty-five articles published between 1895 and 1900 in American periodicals, including *Catholic World, Nation, Outlook, Century Magazine, Review of Reviews, Forum* of New York, and the Boston-based *Arena* and *Atlantic Monthly*. The authors of the articles are American diplomats, missionaries, journalists, religious and public figures, scientists, writers, and British and German politicians, as well as prominent American Armenians.

Reprinted more than a century after their original publication, these articles are highly informative and present rich details on the Armenian people, the Armenian Church, the Ottoman Empire, the history of Western Armenia, the massacres of the Western Armenians in 1894–1896, and the policies of the United States and the European powers, as well as the public opinion in these countries on the Armenian Question.

The reader must keep in mind that the presented articles are characteristic of the public attitudes and perceptions in late nineteenth-century America; they reflect "the spirit of the times," so to speak. The positions and perceptions of the late nineteenth century are absolutely different from the principles and values applied to international affairs nowadays. So is the U.S. foreign policy. At the time, United States foreign policy in the Middle East was cautious and usually deferred to European diplomacy in this area, considering it a region of greater importance to Europe. So the American public, including the authors of the articles, were highly critical of the European powers' actions in the Ottoman Empire, calling for a more active and decisive involvement, including a military intervention, to defend the Christian Armenian population. The governments of both Europe and the United States were the subjects of criticism and scrutiny because of their perceived complacency, even as American policy began to display a greater interest in the affairs of the Ottoman Empire.

INTRODUCTION

The sympathetic attitude towards the Armenians and other Oriental Christians in the United States was due to religious feelings that ran deep among a large segment of Americans: namely, the perceived need to defend Christianity against Muslim encroachment, and the widespread negative image of Islam in the West. Compounding these attitudes were the activities of the Christian missionaries in the "enemy camp" (the predominantly Muslim nations in the East), which contributed to the developing public opinion on this subject. An important factor influencing public opinion was the perception of Sultan Abdul Hamid II as the ultimate anti-Christian, pan-Islamic Ottoman ruler. Negative opinion of Abdul Hamid was also strong in the European countries, especially Britain, in the wake of the Bulgarian and Armenian massacres.

The American assistance to the victims of the Armenian massacres, including the activities of the American Red Cross and other U.S. organizations, reflected the widespread public support for the Christian Armenians. The organizations of the nascent Armenian-American community were also crucial in this effort.

These factors have to be considered when reading the articles, as they explain the negative and even insulting remarks in the text about Muslims and Turks. Notwithstanding the language that is now justifiably deemed insensitive and offensive, these articles present a great picture of the charitable efforts and humanity of the American public.

Importantly, they show that American involvement in the Armenian Question and Armenia itself has a long history. The Armenian memories of the noble and selfless efforts by the American missionaries, public figures, and common citizens at the end of the nineteenth century were rekindled when there was an outpouring of humanitarian aid and sympathy toward the victims of the catastrophic earthquake in northern Armenia in December 1988. American doctors, philanthropists, and relief workers delivered much-needed help to Armenia. Then, after the long-sought independence was established in 1991, the Armenian-American community spearheaded the American efforts to assist Armenia as it strives to become a free, secure, and prosperous nation. The Armenian people will always remember the helping hand extended by the American people at the critical junctures of its history.

Unhappy Armenia

John J. O'Shea

Authentic confirmation of the first sinister reports of renewed outrage in Asiatic Turkey has been received. These reports may have been exaggerated, or they may not approach the truth as to the real extent of the tragedy. But the details which are beginning to leak out leave no room for doubt that a fresh illustration of the unfitness of Turkey for civilized community has been furnished in the outbreak.

Three times in the course of the fast-expiring century had the hand of the western civilization been stretched out perforce to rescue Christian populations from the brutal grasp of the Ottoman power. And now it seems likely enough, that a fourth essay must be made in order to finish the work. If only one tithe of the story of recent outrage be true, not all the perfumes of Arabia can wash the hand of Turkey clean enough to be suffered any longer to hold the reins of power over one inch of Christian territory, one soul professing the Christian faith.

For more than four centuries the experiment of trying to reconcile the Oriental barbarism which Turkey represents with the social life and the Christian systems of Eastern Europe and trans-Caucasia has been going on. Again and again has it been proved and decreed a failure, but a reprieve has come on every occasion when justice had drawn its sword, owing to the selfishness and the international distrust of the European powers. It is entirely owing to the *non placet* of England that the Christians of Armenia are still groaning under the iron heel of Turkish rule. For every drop of Armenian blood shed in the recent massacres, for every outraged maid and mother whose wrong and slaughter cry to Heaven for vengeance, the late Lord Beaconsfield,[90] England's cynical prime minister, is entirely responsible before God.

"Statesmanship" has committed many crimes in its day; but the policy which condemned those Christian populations in the East to a continuance of servitude to Turkish rule, after the revelations made about it in Bulgaria, deserves to be execrated as monumental Machiavellianism. Nor will the world ever forget the irony of it, when it is recalled that it was England, in whose name the iniquity was committed, which first, through the fiery eloquence of Mr. Gladstone,[91] caused the world to stir in behalf of the oppressed Bulgarians. Mr. Gladstone's noble work at the time of the Bulgarian massacres can never be forgotten. But equally will it be remembered that it was his rival, Disraeli, Lord Beaconsfield, who stepped in, when the sword of Russia had severed Armenia from the Turkish Empire, and insisted that it should be restored to the scoundrelly pashas. This was done with the sole purpose of preventing the weakening of the Turkish power; there was no attempt at cloaking the purpose. Disraeli was not hypocritical enough to pretend otherwise. He, who was so utterly impartial himself in the matter of religion, could see nothing wrong in compelling Christians to live under the system whose *raison d'etre* is hatred of Christianity. And so the new map of Asia which Russia had made by her conquests in the Caucasus had to be torn up and the miserable province doomed to sink back into the foul and degrading slavery from which it had fondly hoped to gallantry of Skobeloff[92] had for ever freed it.

In the most solemn manner, in the face of the world, the Sublime Porte undertook, as an alternative to the withdrawal of the Armenian territory from its jurisdiction, that it should have a complete reform in its government. The demands of the Armenian population it undertook to satisfy; their just grounds of complaint it undertook to remove. Under these conditions, and no other, did Russia consent to surrender the fruits of her costly victories in Asia Minor. Substantially, then, the Porte has exercised since then a trusteeship only over Armenia. It has stood in a fiduciary capacity to the great powers of Europe, and the unreservedly expressed condition to that relationship was a faithful discharge of its solemn responsibilities. It is liable to be held to account for the manner in which it has discharged them; and there is the strongest reason to believe, unhappily, that the day of reckoning has been delayed too long.

Already the Porte is preparing excuses for the outrages which there is no longer any possibility of denying. Every precaution was taken to prevent the disclosure being made, but despite the censorship of the press and the manipulation of the telegraph wires, the facts have been established beyond the possibility of further denial. Hence, another attitude has been adopted. It is now boldly stated that the Armenians were the aggressors, that they rose in rebellion and perpetrated outrages on the Mussulman tribes living near their villages, and that whatever bloodshed took place was the necessary consequence of the process of restoring order. We must not be deceived by this denial. Similar defences were set up for the atrocities in Bulgaria, and when they came to be investigated they were found to be utterly baseless. The defence put forward in the case of the Armenian outrages bears its own condemnation on its face. It is alleged that the Armenians were incited to revolt by an English consul. It surely is not the interest of the English government that the flames of war should be lit again in Asia Minor, and no British consul is likely to step outside the line of his duty or his instructions through a mere spirit of knight-errantry.

As the very existence of Islam was pronounced to be a standing *casus belli* by one of our greatest of pontiffs, so in these days the fanaticism of the Moslem is a perpetual danger to the peace of Christendom. It is a thing inflammable as gun-cotton, and whenever it bursts out it bursts out in massacre, suddenly and unexpectedly. The incident at Salonica about then or twelve years ago is a very good illustration of the sort of berserker rage which seizes upon the fanatical Moslem, like rabies on dogs in summer. It is a fury like that of the Malayan when he runs amuck—uncontrollable by the will of the homicidal maniac until its rage has spent itself in satiety. Many Europeans fell in that massacre, were murdered for no reason other than that they were of the race of the hated Giaour.[93] Although a heavy reparation was exacted from the Porte for this infamy, its lesson has been easily forgotten.

A very peculiar position is that of Turkey. Its power is spread over a territory which embraces almost every form of Christianity. It sits upon the ruins of many antique civilizations, beautiful even in their catalepsy. It is a Cyclops—immense and savage—clutching the fair form of Caucasian civilization, its only eye aflame with brutality and sensualism. A foe to progress itself, it will have no progress amongst those enslaved peoples. An enemy to letters, it discourages literature. Conscious of its enormities, it hates newspapers as thieves hate the light of day. There is no censorship so rigid as that which it has established over the press. The more permanent forms of literature are equally discouraged. This is the normal condition of things in times of tranquility. We may easily surmise the strenuousness of the efforts which are put forth in periods of disturbance to prevent the truth from leaking out. It took seven or eight months for the discovery of the real truth about the horrors of Bulgaria, and not all the diligence of the powers could prevent the escape of the principal ruffians whom Mr. Gladstone denounced in connection with that monumental horror. They were encouraged in their career of rapine until the whole horrid work of "pacification" was over, and then rewarded for their share in it. When the cry for their punishment arose from the horrified outside world, their escape was deliberately connived at.

Now this is the very course which is being repeated with regard to the desolation of Bitlis. All the avenues of intelligence from that stricken province were carefully guarded until the work of butchery and violation was finished and the victims hidden away under the earth or devoured by the vultures and the jackals. Then the story was stoutly denied; now it is partially admitted and defended; and at last the Porte is reluctantly coerced to issue an irade [decree] for a commission to inquire into it. Meantime it is openly asserted that the Porte has sent honors and rewards to the leaders of the troops engaged in the massacre. This is quite in keeping with the reputation which the Ottoman Porte has enjoyed from its earliest days. Duplicity has been its best defined characteristic. It lies like truth—at the beginning, and when it is detected in the lie it endeavors to palliate and defend.

In one respect there is an essential difference between the horrors of Bulgaria and those in Armenia, and that point makes the case infinitely worse against the rulers of Islam. The regular troops of Turkey were the chief perpetrators of the massacres, there is no doubt. In Bulgaria the ruffians concerned were altogether Bashibazouks, or irregular soldiers, not directly under the command of the Turkish war office, but in its pay. This fact was accepted as a sort of apology for the ruling power at the time, but the case stands on a different footing now. This point is too important to be overlooked in holding the Porte to account for its crime.

It is a grim satire upon the civilizations of Europe that this barbarous power should have no better claim to continue its oppressions than the necessity of its existence as a make-weight and an obstacle to the ambition of one of the rival states. In this sense the European powers are no better than their protégé. Turkey is a Bashi-bazouk, known to be a lawless ruffian, but retained in their service solely because of his fighting powers.

The general instincts of humanity compel our sympathy with the suffering Christian population of Armenia; there are special reasons which give them a strong claim upon the active moral support of their fellow-Christians more happily circumstanced. They are an ancient people—perhaps the oldest race in the whole world. The land which they inhabit is regarded as lying close to the very cradle of the human species. From the earliest times this region has been connected with the most sacred tradition. Through its midst flow the Euphrates and the Tigris, the rivers by some supposed to have watered the soil of Eden. Its skies are pierced by the heaven-climbing peak of Ararat, where rested the Ark on the subsidence of the Deluge. It was holy ground, in a certain sense, under the old dispensation.

From the dawn of Christianity it has played a very important part. It has formed an insuperable bulwark against the Zoroastrianism of Iran, as against the encroachments of Islam later on. Though the Moslem power crushed the princes of Mingrelia, it could not stamp out the religion of the people. To that and to their national language, national dress, and national customs the Armenians clung through every vicissitude of fortune. Their tenacity in adhering to these heirlooms of ancient autonomy extorts our warmest admiration. When it is remembered that the strongest inducements, in the shape of honors and rewards, were held out to these oppressed Christians if they would only embrace the faith of Islam, it will be confessed that they deserve to take rank with the Irish people and the Poles in love of religion and nationality.

We may estimate approximately how a free Armenia must have progressed, in this age of universal progress, by looking at the condition of Bulgaria now and comparing it with its sorry plight a generation back whilst it lay powerless under the plantigrade hoof of the Ottoman. Bulgaria, the downtrodden pashalik, has sprung into potency as the powerful principality, of high international rank, able to hold her own in the field of war, as she proved in the campaign against Servia, and making giant strides forward in every avenue of human progress. The Armenian race is confessedly one of the brightest of the Oriental nationalities. With a fair field for its energies, it must become a power for civilization in those eastern regions which, despite the forward movement of the world, remain practically still in the same state of barbarism and brigandage as the soldiers of Xenophon found their people when they hung upon his flank and harassed his march all through that retreat which his pen has made immortal.

A multitude of reasons compel our sympathies for the people of Armenia, but the immediate and irresistible one is the demand of nature and humanity. The day has gone by, if it ever existed, when civilized people could look on with *sangfroid* upon the flaying alive of Christian victims by their Mohammedan oppressors. This was the favorite punishment for the Greek rebel officers after the massacres at Scio and Crete. There are people still living who remember it. And there are plenty of men in the Russian army who have seen their dead comrades mutilated and their bodies impaled in the Balkan passes no later than the last war. The power stained with such abominations as these must be regarded as outside the pale of civilization, and if it be proved guilty once more, after its solemn undertakings to the combined European powers, it ought to be for ever removed from the control of Christian races and rigidly confined in its own barbarian limits like a dangerous beast in its den.

The Armenian Trouble

E. L. Godkin[95]

There is imminent danger that the attempt of the European powers to interfere on behalf of the Armenians will come to nothing. England is the only one which is pushing vigorously for an inquiry today, and the Sultan is resisting her fiercely. He has long borne her a grudge as the most persistent of his persecutors, and this has been aggravated by the occupation of Egypt, concerning which the French lose no opportunity of inflaming his mind. Against this, however, England could contend if she had the hearty support of Russia, for Russia is the only power capable of coercing the Porte without much trouble or outlay. She could occupy Armenia at any moment, and the Sultan could do nothing either to prevent or avenge it. But Russia gives only a half-hearted support to the English remonstrances, and is quite ostentatious in her display of friendliness to the Turks. It is not impossible that, were the facts all known in Russia, there would be an outbreak of sympathy with the Armenian Christians not unlike that which followed the Bulgarian massacres in 1876, and led to the war of 1877. But pains are taken, as is credibly reported, either to prevent the news from reaching the Russian people or to minimize its importance. Germany turns a cold shoulder to the whole affair, following her policy of non-interference established by Bismarck in 1877, when he announced that he would not sacrifice one Pomeranian grenadier for the whole Bulgarian population. Italy's help, in the present condition of her morals and finances, is, of course, hardly worth considering. To crown all, the snow at the scene of the massacres is so deep, and the cold so intense, that it is doubtful whether commissioners and witnesses could get at each other, without great difficulty and hardship, for at least two months if not more.

All this brings out in a striking manner the value of the stern policy of Lord Beaconsfield, who was for twenty years one of the great Tory idols, and to whose memory they still burn incense. He stipulated, indeed, with the Turks at Berlin that the Armenians were to be well treated, but, as plainly appears, without the smallest expectation of enforcing the stipulation or of providing any means of doing so. In truth, he concluded a sort of defensive alliance with the Turks, for which the island of Cyprus was to be the consideration. But Cyprus has turned out not only a worthless possession but a great burden. The defensive alliance, moreover, is something with which the Turks would be glad to dispense, and the existence of which is offensive to Russia, for it provides that if Russia seeks to occupy any more Turkish territory, besides what she had already seized in the war, "England engages to join his imperial Majesty the Sultan in defending it by force of arms." It is now quite certain that England would do nothing of the kind, and would gladly be rid of the island of Cyprus.

Moreover, there is every likelihood that, during the coming summer, home affairs will withdraw English attention from most foreign topics. It is generally acknowledged by the Liberals that the dissolution of Parliament and a general election are near at hand, and the prospects of a Liberal victory are not good. Not only have the Home-Rulers "soured on" Lord Rosebery,[96] as our politicians say, but the Independent Labor party is attacking the Liberals in the rear, and in many localities making a return of the Liberal members hopeless. It is quite possible that if the Tories come in, Lord Salisbury[97] might seek to divert attention from home troubles by an active foreign policy: but one of the things in the democratic movement in England which most alarm Conservatives is the growing indifference of the masses to imperial or foreign affairs, so that the probabilities are in favor of some sort of fostering of socialistic nostrums for which the Tories have of late shown a strong taste.

What our Government can do in the Armenian matter, or whether it can do anything, is a fair subject for discussion. We have had one snub, in the attempt to take part in the inquiry, and, generally speaking, the methods of Turkish government are none of our business. But wholesale massacre is in our time the affair of the civilized world. It is not government, or a method of government. It is a crime against the human race. We can no more pass it without notice because we do not suffer from it, than pass pirates without notice on the high seas because they attack none of our ships. The whole of Christendom, including ourselves, has a right to refuse to treat a power which perpetrates such atrocities as are said to have occurred in Armenia, as within the pale of ordinary diplomatic intercourse. Diplomatic relations rest on the basis of a common civilization and common notions of humanity and justice, so that we might very well consider the refusal of the Porte to satisfy us as to the truth of the charges, as a good reason for an interruption of friendly diplomatic intercourse. The solemn warnings of Washington against foreign meddling, the wisdom of which has been proved by the experience of a century, do not touch this case. He denounces passionate attachments to, or passionate hatreds of, foreign nations. He denounces foreign influence on our domestic politics. He denounces political connections and permanent alliances with foreign states. But none of these warnings cuts us off from remonstrance with the perpetrators of gross cruelty or injustice, on a great scale, in any part of Christendom, and there is no nation which could speak with greater force for the common rights of humanity than we could, particularly just now, when every power in Europe seems to be approaching the Armenian horror with the Tammany question, "What is there in this for me?"

An Eye-Witness to the Armenian Horrors

A highly esteemed prelate in Armenia, whose diocese lies in part of the country recently given over to sack and slaughter, sends us an affecting letter, a portion of which we translate:

Over the whole province the work of destruction has been pursued, every town and every hamlet having been given over to pillage and murder. Two large Catholic mission stations have been entirely wiped out. The churches, the presbyteries, and the schools, having been first sacked, were given to the flames. The sacred vessels, the pictures and the crucifixes were carried off or destroyed. The inhabitants who have been spared have been stripped of everything of use or value. Those who fled from the doomed districts were pursued and cut down mercilessly, without regard to age or sex, by the barbarous Turks. The bodies of many children and young girls lie under the charred *débris* of the ruined homes. No such gigantic affliction has ever before fallen upon any nation. Generous help is being given the Protestant survivors by the American relief societies; the Catholic bishops and priests are incessant in their endeavors to produce aid for their unhappy flock; and the schismatic Armenians, seeing how great is their devotion in this regard, are manifesting a disposition to rejoin the church. But the priests find themselves wholly unable to meet the demands made on them by the starving people; and the markets being closed as a result of the terror, the whole population is thrown upon the resources of the charitable organizations for the relief of their daily wants. To add to the horror of the situation, these massacres and burnings went on in the depths of a most rigorous winter and spring.

AN EYE-WITNESS TO THE ARMENIAN HORRORS

What is of most immediate concern is the pitiable condition of the Catholic Armenians on whose behalf our correspondent writes. Unless the outside world come promptly to their aid very many more victims must be added to the butcher's bill of the unspeakable Turk. The most stringent precautions are being taken by the Turkish government to prevent any word of these shocking transactions getting outside the empire, and our venerable correspondent has been compelled to adopt a round-about means to get his letter forwarded to us. Twice he narrowly escaped death at the hands of the Turkish butchers, and his priests have had many hair-breadth escapes also.

Lord Salisbury and Armenia

Lord Salisbury's natural predilection is for foreign affairs, and his equally natural predilection is to conduct them with a high hand. The big majority now behind him will not have a tendency to reign him in. The chances are, therefore, that he would, in any case, adopt a peremptory tone in the negotiations with Turkey about ravaged Armenia; these chances really amount to a certainty in view of the powerful and united sentiment in England now clamorous for such a course.

A highly significant fact about Mr. Gladstone's recent speech on the Armenian horrors is that it was made practically at Lord Salisbury's request. Some of the latter's friends and supporters, notably the Duke of Westminster, chairman of the Chester meeting on August 6, arranged the demonstration and obtained Mr. Gladstone's promise to speak. He had steadily refused to say anything until the general election was over, lest a partisan twist might be given to his remarks. Then he virtually came forward to strengthen Lord Salisbury's hands. This was put beyond all doubt by the terms of resolution he introduced, which declared that the Government would have "the cordial support of the entire nation, without distinction of party," in providing effective guarantees for "the safety of life, honor, religion, and property" in Armenia.

This cooperation of two rival leaders in such a cause is an incident which might be used to point a moral to some of our small-minded politicians. To have invited the assistance of Mr. Gladstone was practically a confession by Lord Salisbury that he and his party were not the only ones concerned about the national honor, not the only ones in whose keeping that honor was safe. And for Mr. Gladstone to go forward cheerfully, even ardently, not to put his old antagonist "in a hole," but actually to help and strengthen him, betrays woful mismanagement from the standpoint of higher American politics. But the one great result of such a union of forces is to assure Lord Salisbury of support in the most vigorous measures he may see fit to adopt with the Porte. When Gladstone cries out, "Do not let us be afraid of the word coercion," it is safe to say that Salisbury will not be afraid of it.

The question is now an old one, but in its present phase it may be said to date from 1878. In that year England and Turkey made a convention, by the first article of which the Sultan agreed to introduce reforms into the government of his Christian and other subjects in Armenia, and the same year the Treaty of Berlin was signed. It provided for religious liberty in all Turkey, and the Sultan undertook "to carry out, without further delay, the improvements and reforms demanded by local requirements in the provinces inhabited by the Armenians, and to guarantee their security against Circassians and Kurds." It was further required that the Sultan should report periodically what steps were being taken to carry out this article, and that the Powers should superintend the application of them. The Porte, being responsible to all the Powers, has stood in real fear of none, and the Powers, not having decided upon the *modus operandi* to be employed in superintending the carrying out of the reforms, have stood idly by while the Turks and Kurds have played into each other's hands, and, actuated by a common hatred of the Armenians, have run riot in outrage and oppression. "Christian and civilized Europe," as M. Rolin-Jacquemyns[98] said in an article in the *Revue de Droit International* in 1887, "was more occupied with its intestine quarrels and jealousness than with its collective duties." That since the Treaty of Berlin the condition of the Armenians has not improved, and that Turkey has not introduced any real reforms in amelioration of their conditions, there is abundant evidence.

Soon after the treaty went into effect, the British Consul at Erzerum wrote to his Government that the condition of the Christians was worse than ever, that the Kurds had the upper hand, and that in some localities arson, assault, and rape were committed with impunity. The regular troops were as bad as the Kurds, and committed precisely the same offences. Bribery of officials existed almost everywhere, and the occasional pure official was powerless in the face of extended organized official corruption. In 1879 Sir A. H.

Layard, British Ambassador to Turkey, wrote as follows to Lord Salisbury: "Unless the Porte takes care, and acts with prudence and forethought, there will be an Armenian question in Asia similar to the Bulgarian question in Europe, from which the last war arose. The same intrigues are being resorted to in Asia Minor to establish an Armenian nationality, and to bring about a state of things which will cause a cry of horror among the Christian population, and a European intervention."

In 1880 the Powers addressed a collective note to the Porte on the subject of Armenia. It called attention to the fact that anarchy existed in the provinces inhabited by the Armenians, and that the existing state of affairs, if not remedied, "would, in all probability, lead to the destruction of the Christian population of vast districts." To this remonstrance the Sultan made no reply whatsoever.

But the question has now reached the stage where common humanity demands that it be settled. Whether Armenia is taken entirely away from Turkey and erected into an independency, or whether the Sultan shall be permitted to govern it only in such a way as European influence or coercion shall direct, are questions for discussion; but that existing conditions cannot be endured much longer is palpable. The extent of the massacre near Mush a year ago cannot yet be estimated accurately, and, in view of past experience in similar cases, it is probable that it will never be entirely known. That it embraced fully 10,000 people is not at all improbable. As the Armenians are not permitted to carry arms, there can have been no real contest, nor can the inspiration of the slaughter be properly attributed to a rebellion against the Turkish government. An organized uprising is an impossibility under the circumstances. Mr. Gladstone, in his speech at Chester, merely repeated what he said in his speech of December last. After touching upon the evidence of the massacre which tended "strongly to a conclusion to the general effect that the outrages and the scenes and abominations of 1876 in Bulgaria had been repeated in 1894 in Armenia," he added:

> As I have said, I hope it is not so, and I will hope to the last; but if it is so, it is time that one general shout of execration—not of men, but of deeds—one general shout of execration, directed against deeds of wickedness, should rise from outraged humanity, and should force itself into the ears of the sultan of Turkey and make him sensible, if anything can make him sensible, of the madness of such a course.

The Evil of the Turk

*By an Armenian**

The questions are often asked, "Why does Turkey wage perpetual war against her Christian subjects? what are some of the grievances to which they are subjected, and of which they complain? and why are the Turkish displays of barbarism allowed to go unchecked and unpunished at the close of the enlightened nineteenth century?"

I would answer these questions from the standpoint of one reared in that country, and under those conditions of enslavement and persecution that surround all Christians there. The answer to the first question may be found in the teachings of the dominating religion of the Government. Mohammedanism, whose watchword from the past to the present has been, "The sword is the key of heaven and hell"—meaning that those who accepted Mohammedanism, even from the terrors of the sword, should be saved, while those rejecting it should die by the same weapon and be damned. This is the only means used in propagating the religion of Islam. On either side of the pulpits of St. Sophia and the Mosque of Eyub are two flags hanging; one representing Judaism, and the other Christianity. When the imam goes up to the pulpit, he carries a wooden sword in one hand and the Koran in the other, to indicate that the conquest of the Koran over Judaism and Christianity is to be accomplished by the sword, teaching the people that their wars are holy wars, and that a Mohammedan soldier is the executor of God's will and vengeance.

No military service is required of either Jews or Christians, as

---

*The author of the article is a recent graduate of one of the leading theological seminaries.

they cannot be depended upon to defend Mohammedanism. Indeed, the Government goes so far as to prohibit Armenians from possessing arms of any kind, even a penknife being forbidden them.

This freedom from military service, which is a mark of degradation in the eyes of a Turk, has had some compensations. It has saved the Christians from the "wasting influences and destructive diseases of the camp and the battle-field, and has accustomed them to industry and thrift." But while they are free from military service, a special tax is imposed upon them for the support of the Turkish army and State. The taxes are classified as follows: (1) One-tenth of all the crops and fruits; (2) four percent of the renting value of houses and lands; (3) five percent on every transfer; (4) an animal tax of thirty-three pence on every sheep and goat. Besides these there are the road and labor taxes on the imaginary earnings of the Christians, and the military tax laid upon every male.

The tithes are sold to the highest bidder, and the competition is so keen that the successful bidder is forced to pay more than the entire just amount of the tax. Consequently the tithe farmers are forced to resort to the worst form of extortion from the poor Christians, and, instead of making a careful and honest estimate of the taxable produce, assess it without examination, often to more than double its amount. If the farmer has reaped his grain, he cannot store it in his barn until the tax-gatherer has surveyed it and taken out his lion's share. If the official is busy elsewhere or is waiting for a bribe, the grain must be left on the field for days or weeks, exposed to drenching rain and scorching sun, until the whole crop becomes spoiled or is carried away by the rapacious Kurds.

If the farmer is then unable to pay the tithe in kind, he is obliged to pay in ready cash. But as he rarely has enough to meet these exactions, his household utensils are seized and sold. The tax-gatherer, with his *zabtiehs* (policemen), is an ever-present scourge to the country. He is heartless and without honor. During the business transactions he must be entertained and provided for, with all his retinue and horses. If the farmer can by any means raise the money, he is only too glad to do so and free himself from this burden; but if he is unable, he is often maltreated and thrown into prison. False receipts, too, are often given, and the amount of the debt has thus to be twice paid. Should a Christian at any time seek redress for continued outrages on person or property, he can appeal only to the local governor or officials, and never to the Sultan, whose time is considered too valuable to be taken up in looking after the welfare of his subjects. The press also is muzzled, as the following rules governing journalism in Constantinople will show:

> Art. 5. Avoid personalities. If anybody tells you that a governor or deputy governor has been guilty of embezzlement, maladministration, or of any other blameworthy conduct, treat the charge as not proved, and say nothing about it.
> Art. 6. You are forbidden to publish petitions in which individuals or associations complain of acts of mismanagement, or call the Sultan's attention to them.

The Turkish officials, to whom the Christian is supposed to appeal in cases of grievances, are exceedingly corrupt, committing even more crimes than their inferior accomplices, whose administration is an abominable scourge. A few years ago one of the missionaries in Erzeroum told me that while he was on one of his mission tours he came across a poor Christian shepherd who had just been attacked by the Kurds and despoiled of thirty sheep from his flock. The next day, upon the missionary's return to Erzeroum, he called upon the commander of the army to complain of the outrage, and discovered fifteen of the thirty sheep in his yard!

Under the ruinous management of these mercenary officials, the country which God made so rich in resources has become poor. These men have transformed their official privileges into prerogatives of tyranny, and there is no bound to their avarice. Such is the system of political economy practiced in the internal affairs of the provinces in the name of Padishah by officials who are "lofty in adulations and calumny, perfidy, and treason." In the eyes of the Turkish Government, suspicion of her non-Mussulman subjects is equal to proof, intention to mischief, and the intention is not less criminal than the act. This was the attitude of the Government in relation to the recent Sassoun massacre. As soon as the Pasha of Bitlis sent word to Constantinople that the Armenians were in rebellion, without waiting for proof, the Turkish troops were sent to the scene with orders to suppress the revolt—orders which they knew they must interpret as meaning the extermination of whole villages if they would please the Sultan. After wholesale butchery, Zeki Pasha[100] reported that, "not finding any rebellion, we cleared the country so that none should occur in the future." This stroke of policy was afterward praised in the Court as an act of patriotism.

Canon Malcolm MacColl,[101] who was the first to draw public attention to the Bulgarian atrocities in 1877, has just published a letter in which he declares that the Sultan is responsible for almost every recent massacre in Armenia.

Why has the Sultan failed to perform his obligations as pledged in the Berlin Treaty? Because, according to Mohammedanism, "no promise can bind the faithful against the interest and duty of their religion." For nearly twenty years he has occupied the throne, but all the justice which he has shown, and the peace that he has been able to maintain, must be ascribed to the pressure brought upon him by the Treaty Powers. Take, for instance, the case of Mussa Bey. When all Europe demanded an investigation, the Sultan bestirred himself to a pretense of political reformation, but it was short-lived. Duplicity, shiftlessness, and deceit are his great characteristics.

No pledge made in the Berlin Treaty has been respected. According to that, there was to be religious toleration in Turkey. Has there been? Far from it. The Sultan has scarcely lived up to the injunction of Mohammed, who said, "Christians and Jews may have their churches or synagogues, repair or rebuild them, but no new churches or synagogues shall be built."

It is the delight of the Turks to profane and pillage Christian churches, and in this sacrilege they are upheld by the weakness of the Sultan.

Who is this man? Well may one ask,

> Upon what meat doth this our Caesar feed,
> That he has grown so great?

He is the son of a slave of obscure parentage, with no endowments of mind or heart that should fit him for the responsible position of sovereign and pontiff. He is utterly incompetent to remedy official vices, and leaves the affairs of the country to adjust themselves while he busies himself in deciding what shall be the costumes of the comedians and actresses in the French Opera, for which he has a great fondness. His palaces and kiosks exceed all former examples of royal luxury. His domestics number six thousand, and eleven million dollars is required to cover the annual expenses of his royal house and table. Nothing arouses his lethargy save the sound of pleasure or music, or the talk of his concubines, wives, and comedians, who are really his ministers. While six thousand courtiers (who are the mercenaries of many fragmental tribes) wait on his holy person daily, the Christians are supporting his tottering throne; yet the whole policy of the government of the officials of the Kurds and Circassians is the extermination of the Armenians. This is all in accordance with Said Pasha's policy, who said: "The solution of the Armenian question consists in the annihilation of the Armenian race." Will the following well-authenticated instance, which is but one of hundreds, be a surprise to you? During the spring of 1889, in the Armenian town of Zeitune, consisting of about twenty thousand inhabitants, six hundred boys alone were poisoned by the doctors, who were bribed by the Government to use impure vaccine matter; while individual cases of murder of noted Armenians are of daily occurrence all around the empire.

Although the Kurds and Circassians are by no means the only agents in satisfying Said Pasha's[102] craving for Armenian blood, they are very powerful factors in carrying on the work of destruction. When Sultan Medjid was talking of driving them out of the country, the cunning advice of his counsel was: "Let them alone to exterminate the non-Mussulmans, or to keep them subject to your throne."

Ever since they have been the favorites of the Sultan and Government, who have equipped them with modern rifles in defiance of Article LXI of the Berlin Treaty, to assist them in their work of rapine, confiscation, and depredation. Yet, lawless and barbarous, they are not only tolerated by the Government, but upheld. A numerous swarm of these mercenaries assisted Zeki Pasha in the recent massacre, led either by bribes or by the hope of spoil or by the threats of fanatic mufti, whose cry echoed far above the groins of the dying, "Fight, fight! Paradise, paradise!"

To day Turkey presents an awful picture of death and ruin. War, pestilence, and famine press their rival claims, and we cry from a full heart, "How long, o Lord, how long?"

What, then, is left to us? The sad experience of five hundred years has shown that neither obedience nor submission can secure to us the safety of our mothers, sisters, wives, and property. These many years we have submitted our bodies to the Turk; but patience is no more a virtue. It is an evil and unjust government that forces us to raise the voice of righteous indignation. If a government is a divine appointment, then its mission should be to work for the welfare of the nation, holding its interests in trust. Since the Berlin Treaty, intoleration by ruler and officials has gone from bad to worse. While subjects to the Sultan, we are considered as strangers and treated like enemies. The Turks claim that the recent troubles came from organized revolutionary societies among the Christians. Were the Armenians organized in societies when the massacres of 1835, 1860, 1876, and 1878 took place? Nay! Yet Armenian mothers were torn from their children, wives from their husbands, daughters from their parents, and given over to a fate more horrible than death. Is it necessary, then, in order to justify our claim and secure the intervention of Europe, that the Turks should massacre twice or three times more than 15,000 Armenians? The present existing struggle resolves itself into a conflict between Christianity and Mohammedanism; between Christian civilization and the effete civilization of Islam; between aggressive Christian progress and the indolence of the fatalistic Turk. Instead of being allowed to develop the industries of the country, we have been oppressed for five centuries by the iron hand of tyranny. We have been obliged to abandon agriculture, our farms being usurped by the officials for the support of Turkish mosques. Misfortune after misfortune, however, has but intensified national love, and we would fain be prepared to support our own autonomy. Should not Christian nations feel an interest in our country and in our struggle for life and liberty, and appoint a European governor, vested with full power of governing the country?

Turkey and the Armenian Crisis

Theodore Peterson, B.D.

The old game of procrastination is being resorted to by the Sublime Porte with regard to Armenia. No longer is there any pretence at denying the barbarous outrages lately perpetrated in Sassoun. The commission has inquired into the matter on the spot, and despite the strenuous efforts of the Turkish functionaries to hide the truth, the case against the Kurds and the government troops has been fully proved. It is too horrible to be put into print. Action has been taken by the European powers concerned in the treaty of Berlin. Reforms in the administration of the country, including the appointment of a high commissioner for Armenia who shall be approved by the European powers, have been recommended to the Porte, and as the Porte shuffled as usual, orders were given for a naval demonstration in the Bosporus. Then the Porte backed down, and a little more time has been given it for consideration. Meantime events are moving rapidly outside. The tide of Moslem fanaticism is rising, and the massing of a Russian army corps on the borders of the disturbed province shows that at least one European power may be depended on to take a bold step for the protection of the Christian subjects of the Sultan, should such an extreme measure become necessary.

In speaking of the Armenian outrages Mr. James Bryce,[103] M.P., lately said: "What do you expect from a country where one-half of its population calls the other half 'dogs' and treats them as such?" It is unquestionably true that there is no security of property whatever, no redress for loss, no punishment for the guilty, no justice for the Christian, no respect for the honor of Christian women, no safety of life; but a reign of terror everywhere, and robbery—official and unofficial—plunder, pillage, outrage, violation, desolation, perpetual poverty, and an everlasting famine in a beautiful land. This is not all. There is the fear every moment of a wholesale massacre.

The empire is rapidly going down, and its inevitable fall is simply a matter of time; no effort is made to stop the corruption that has stricken it from the crown clear down to the sole. If the Turkish sovereignty would exercise the energy that is displayed to suppress the truth and influence public opinion to reform the present administration, it might perhaps become a good government; but things are otherwise, and the government is encouraging the corruption and hastening its own destruction. The high honors conferred on those connected with the late massacres, and the public thanks given to the Turkish troops, have impressed the officials everywhere with the idea that the more they persecute, plunder, and slaughter the Armenians, the more rapid will be their decoration and promotion. Yet this is not all. Add to it, if you please, the tribal hostilities dating centuries back, the religious hatred and the Moslem fanaticism, and we have the nameless atrocities and oft-repeated massacres. When the fanaticism of the Turk is excited he is as barbarous as his ancestors under Timor the Tartar, and there is no atrocity of which he is not capable. He freely massacres the defenceless women and the little ones, and the wounded; even the death of the unbelievers, or Christian dogs, does not satisfy him, and he delights to mutilate the corpse. The reports of consuls, as well as of travellers in Armenia, even before the recent horrors, show the condition of the land to be intolerable. This state of things comes to us from ages back. "The history of Christians under Moslem law," says Van Hammer, "is only an uninterrupted scene of tyranny, violation, and slaughters." It is carried on by the functionaries as the only means to strengthen and perpetuate Moslem supremacy. Nejib Pasha of Damascus said to a confidential agent of the British consul in that city: "The Turkish government can only maintain its supremacy by cutting down its Christian sects"; and we heard later on the sickening tales of the Damascus and Lebanon massacres. The grand vizier says: "To get rid of the Armenian question is to get rid of the Armenian people"; and we have a series of Armenian massacres, among which is that of Sassoun, which drew the attention of the civilized world. The following figures give but a faint idea of the desolation caused by the Turkish massacres during this century:

1822 In Scios Isles,	50,000 Greeks	(Lathem, P. 417)
1850 Mosoul,	10,000 Armenians	(Cont. Rev., P. 16, 1895)
1860 Lebanon,	11,000 Syrians	(Churchill, P. 219)
1876 Bulgaria,	14,000 Bulgarians	(Schuyler)
1877 Bazarid,	2,400 Armenians	(Norman, Armenia, P. 273)
1879 Alashgird,	1,100	(Armenian Patr. Const.)
1892 Mosoul	2,000 Yezidies	(Perry's Rep. to Brit.)
1894 Sassoun,	12,000	Armenians.

Victor Hugo has truly said: "If a man is killed in Paris, it is a murder; the throats of fifty thousand people are cut in the East, and it is a question." Unless a check is put upon the lawless band—unfortunately called the Turkish government—the atrocious procession will steadily and surely go on to its goal—the annihilation of the Christian element. A check upon the Turk means but one thing—the withdrawal of those provinces from the control of Moslem fanaticism. It is noticeable that the greatest number of these horrors have taken place in the reign of "the most merciful," "the most good-hearted," and the most polite and gentlemanly Hamid II, whose praises have poisoned the air of this land of the free. The Sultan is not to blame; he is a typical Moslem, and the most faithful ruler that ever came to the throne of the empire. He is but doing what Mohammed has commanded him to do in the forty-seventh chapter of the Koran, where he says: "When ye encounter the unbelievers, strike off their heads until you have made a great slaughter of them." Who, then, is responsible for the blood shed? We do not hesitate to answer "England," who has pledged before God and man to protect the Christians there. Now then, since England comes not forth to fulfil her pledge, and since the Christians have been voted to a wholesale slaughter by the Prophet and his followers, what comes next?

The next thing, in order to escape a wholesale massacre, is a wholesale emigration. This scheme seems to be the natural consequence of conditions in Armenia, and it is also strongly advocated by some of our papers here, which say: "Let him alone and let him come out of his dominion, if the Armenian does not like the Turk." One might think this advisable for the Armenians, as they can find security of property, and safety of life and religious freedom, elsewhere, especially in the neighboring provinces of Russia, where are millions of their brethren, as well as the Catholicos, the father of all the Armenians, of whom it is said that he is about to make an application to the principality for a large tract of land on which to settle the emigrants. Yet it would, of course, be ridiculous to plan such an undertaking. The temptation is very dangerous, both for Asiatic civilization and for the Turkish Empire itself.

Those who have travelled in Turkey, or who reside there, and those who study history and are interested in ancient civilization, will agree that the Armenians were in the past better civilized and farther advanced in art, in commerce, and in literature than the Turks of today. Their progress, in the past and present, in spite of endless obstacles, is not surpassed by that of any race in Asia. The richest and most fertile provinces in the world, once possessed by them, are today a desert, where the foxes and jackals howl and wander among ruins whose desolate columns stand as monuments of an ancient prosperity, and which are an eternal reproach to that Turkish rule of which it has been truly said that "The grass never grows where their horses have trod."

Are not the Armenians today the most intelligent, loyal, industrious, enterprising, and moral race in the empire? Are they not the better civilized people, the Yankees of the Orient, the far-advanced in art, in architecture, in science, and in all departments of life? We are told that the Armenians, numbering three millions perhaps, have more than thirty periodicals; while the Turks, numbering over fifteen millions, have about twenty papers, and that even these are managed by Armenian editors.

To expatriate such an element from a country is a vital blow to the civilization of that country. Will the lovers of civilization and the leaders of progress, while striving in the darkest parts of the earth to liberate mankind from the chains of ignorance and the degradation of slavery, allow this already civilized and elevated race to be wiped out by a diabolical machine, and stretch not out a helping hand in this critical hour? We hope not. There seems to have been a purpose in the preservation of this long-suffering people through ages of blood and fire. It is not too much to say that they, having done so much for Christianity in the past, will surely have a large share in the future in civilizing and Christianizing the neighboring races. God has chosen this enduring race as an instrument in his hand, and preserved it as a leaven in that vast land, and the future is theirs.

Their extermination were fatal to the empire from a political stand-point, though the Turks do not appreciate this fact. It is an unquestionable fact that the Armenians are superior to their masters, as were the Greeks of old to their Roman masters, in political, commercial, and governmental affairs, whenever a chance is offered to them. Not only they, but the whole Christian population, are far in advance of the Mohammedans, and if an equal footing in the administration had been granted them, the empire would be much richer and larger than it now is. Christians are excluded from the army because they are considered infidels and it would defile the Mohammedan soldiers to come in contact with them. The army is a religious band and its soldiers must stand for and serve the Moslem faith. If the sultans were wise enough to see their interest, and had courage enough to liberate themselves from the superstitions characteristic of the orientals and predominant among the Turks, they would admit the Armenian youth to the military as well as the civil services. They would then have generals like Loris Melikoff, who was about to introduce the constitutional administration in Russia had not the Nihilists killed Alexander II, and who is the conqueror of Kars, the key of the Sultan's Asiatic provinces; Lazaroff and Gugassoff[104] and many others, Armenians by birth and most distinguished in the Russian army; also capable statesmen like Nubar Pasha—another Armenian—the prime minister, and, as he has been truly called, "The Grand Old Man of the Egyptian politicians," the originator of the International Tribunal of Egypt. These are Armenians and they could give to the world others of like character had not the world declined to give them the privileges to which they are entitled.

To compel a people of such rare endowments to leave their needy country is more than foolishness; it is a crime for which there is no atonement in the world of civilization. This ancient people, whether for the love of humanity, or for that of the rocks and hills of their fatherland, affections equally noble and sublime, do not dare to commit such an inexpiable crime as the evacuation of the land. They love to sit on the banks of the sacred Euphrates and Araxes and to repeat their sweet old melodies, and to add their tears to the waters crimsoned by the blood of their children; and those who have been compelled to leave for various reasons look back with longing eyes from every part of the world, and with hopefulness and sympathy. Since, then, their patriotism is so strong, and their removal so dangerous both to civilization and to the Sultan's government, no one, except the Turks, could conscientiously think of their emigration. This being the case, the question still confronts us—what is the alternative? To change their religion. Some think this would end all the trouble; but some still believe that it would make no difference. The maltreatment and torture of Turkish and Kurdish peasants is as bad as that of the Armenians. No doubt there is some truth in this, and we sadly acknowledge that the lower class of Turks are also molested and robbed by the common enemy—the officials; but it is not just to say that the Moslems are treated with such cruelty as the Christians, for that would be placing the two sects on an equality which is utterly impossible in the Mohammedan world, and contrary to the immutable teachings of the Koran and the infallible will of the sultans. If we can lift the veil of this mystery and penetrate to the depths of the question, we shall see it in an altogether different light. It is true the Turks and Kurds are imprisoned, and they rightly deserve it as a wild, cruel, and criminal class; but the Armenians are imprisoned and tortured because they are educated and refined and have the Western civilization, and above all are Christians. Their wives and daughters are violated and made booty of by all believers of the Koran; but we have never heard and will not, so long as the Crescent reigns, of the ill-treatment of the wives and daughters of believers by a Moslem. The harem is sacred to every believer of the Koran.

We have heard much of life imprisonment and death punishment of Christian students, of teachers, of preachers, of priests, of bishops, and of archbishops; moreover we have seen dozens of Christians suffer capital punishment, lifted up to the guillotine or beheaded publicly; but we have not yet heard of a Mohammedan preacher or priest who was sent to life imprisonment or received the capital penalty. Why? Is it because the latter class is better than the former? No, by no means. It is simply because the one asks the blessing of Heaven in the name of Christ, while the other asks it in the name of Mohammed and carries out the command of his book, to make "a great slaughter among the infidels." Not only are they not punished—they are encouraged and decorated by the successor of the Prophet for their aggressive projects. It is stated by those whose names, if attached, would give weight, that the Mufty of Moosh, a theologian and commentator of the Koran, made the following address: "To violate the wives and daughters of Christians-dogs, infidels—is just; to ruin their churches is a virtue; to plunder and pillage their property is the command of God; and for every Christian whose blood is shed by a Moslem the reward is a nymph in God's paradise"; and he was decorated by the Sultan as an honest and faithful servant.

Now we reach the bottom of the mystery, and it is clear, from the Mohammedan point of view, that it is a religious fight, a "holy war," and if the Armenians were kind enough, or wise enough, as some say, to change their creed, they would be allowed to live. In this free land of ours even Christians have confidentially said that it is not worth while to die for a religion—even for Christianity it is foolish; they might embrace the Mohammedan faith in public and serve Christ in secret. To do this would be actually impossible for the people of Ararat. Centuries of cruelty, of oppression, of the most odious tyranny, have failed to shake the faith of the Armenians; and although their country has been depopulated by the most ruthless massacres, and although the infamous policy of their conquerors has driven them out like hunted animals to seek refuge in distant parts of the earth—in India, the Island of Java, Europe, and America—they have always preferred the crown of martyrdom to the white turban of Mohammed.

We are told by students of history that the Armenians were the first to embrace Christianity as their national religion, 302 A.D. [in fact, 301 A.D.—Author's Note], and the first to lead a campaign against the religion of Zoroaster, which threatened the whole of Asia Minor with its fire-worship in 451, at which time the cross was victorious. From that time on they have been marching through blood and fire for their belief and adding to the long list of their martyrs. I do not permit myself to enter into a description of the campaigns of the crusaders, when the service rendered by their co-religionists was very great, and for which it is said they lost their small independence in Cilicia; but this much can be said—that they have suffered more than their share and done more for Christianity than Christendom seems likely to do for them.

At the present time we have the statements of eye-witnesses to their faithfulness to Christianity. We hear of one woman who, after witnessing a heartrending scene and realizing that there was no hope of escape—unless to change their religion—nor any hope of mercy from the enemy, steps out on a rock and cries: "My sisters, you must choose to-day between two things, either deny your holy religion and adopt the Mohammedan faith, or follow my example." Then, lifting her eyes to heaven, she dashed herself from the rock into the abyss below, and others followed her. A proposition was made to some of the more attractive women to change their faith, in which case their lives might be spared. "Why should we deny Christ?" they answered; "we are no more than these," pointing to the mangled forms of their brothers and husbands; "kill us too"; and they were killed. Every true-hearted Christian ought to be filled with admiration for such brave answers, and moved with sympathy for that unfortunate people whose lot has been cast among thieves.

We see that the suggestion that they change their religion fails of accomplishment, for they would rather die than give up their faith. But supposing they should be driven to this, will Christian people allow it and not come to their rescue? I do not mean the statesmen of Christendom, but the Christians who sing "The world for Christ!" who spend millions and send their sons and daughters to evangelize the world—will they not raise their united shout and make it audible in the ears of him who keeps his head in the sands of the Bosporus? Indeed, if they remain silent, the angels from above, the inhabitants of hell beneath, and the Sultan with his hosts on earth will shout, "There is no more Christianity in the world."

These suggestions failing, we see before this people a perpetual struggle, endless bloodshed, and now and then extended uprisings which will not deserve the approval of any who might consider themselves friends of the Armenians, and which means for them but to beard the lion in his den. I doubt if the Armenians would entertain such a reprehensible idea. We have heard of occasional outbursts, but they indicate the despairing struggles of those whose burdens have become intolerable. It is safe to say that they ask but security of life, of property, and the right to worship God according to the dictates of conscience, and to educate their children in the Christian faith, to which every person is entitled by the law of God, of humanity, and of civilization. Yet the Turks are not inclined, and obviously never will be, to grant these fundamental rights of humanity, until a pressure is brought upon them from without, or a general uprising combining the different elements from within. Should there be no outburst of general indignation from an outraged humanity, we shall be unfortunate enough to see still further tragedies.

The Armenian question is certainly the burning question of the hour, and its sparks must sooner or later inflame the so-called "peace of Europe," that has thus far been maintained by shutting ears and eyes to the horrors endured by the Asiatic Christians. It is the question for all, and must be solved once for all. We have to consider whether the Turk shall be compelled by the powers, especially England—for unless forced by England he will never do it—to grant without delay the graciously promised but shamefully ignored privileges of equality for all subjects in the administration of the empire without discrimination as to creed or race, and to keep the agreement made by the Sultan in the Berlin Treaty and at the Cyprus Convention for the protection of Christian subjects; or whether certain provinces, inhabited by Christians, shall be annexed to Russia; or shall the Turks be allowed to exterminate these Christian people? This question should be kept before the world in its simplicity until it is solved in one way or the other.

Who is responsible for the shedding of this innocent blood? It is England. Why? Because if England had not opposed the treaty of San Stephano, agreed upon between the Sultan of Turkey and Alexander II of Russia, the reformation in Armenia would long since have been introduced. The world is about to record in its history some such item as the following: "There was a small but goodly civilized and Christian people in Asia who became victims of the selfishness of England and were exterminated in this most enlightened age." Would the English people like to have such a blot upon their history? I think not. The prompt action of Great Britain, or of any other power, depends on the support of public opinion. Since this is so, there is a power that can overcome any obstacle that stands in its way, namely, the people—the ministers of justice and the guardians of humanity. The indignation and sympathy of the civilized world is almighty, and the Armenians ask nothing to-day but the aid of that power. They do not cease to hope for it.

Let the Powers understand that outraged humanity cannot endure any more, or permit such carnages to be repeated over and over again. If it be true that of one blood God made all the nations of the earth, to dwell on the face of the earth, then when our brothers and sisters are outraged and slaughtered and despoiled of all that makes life worth living, we cannot help but wake to sympathy with them. It is enough that the cursed demon of might has lived for centuries on the blood of the innocent children of our God. "A government which can countenance and cover the perpetration of such outrages is a disgrace to civilization and a curse to mankind," is the belief of the Grand Old Man. It is time that a universal shout of indignation be directed against the Monster of the Bosporus, the author of nameless fiendish deeds. Our liberty is indeed but nominal if it does not make us the missionaries of liberty. The English-speaking people have been accustomed, in the time of crises like this, to say to the oppressed: "Be of good cheer; we are not dead; the spirit of our fathers is alive within us." If feelings of humanity and pity still exist on the earth, there is no need of argument to be persuaded that the Armenians are subjected to a diabolical treatment and condemned to annihilation for their religion. If we could realize the extent and intensity of their suffering, we should be stirred to action if we have not lost our chivalrous impulses and the sense of justice and freedom.

The Armenian crisis is an established fact. There was no need to wait for the commissioners' report. Eight months have already passed and nothing is yet done.

Why We Catholics Sympathize with Armenia

Rev. R. M. Ryan

The Armenian question has ceased to be national or even merely international. It has become universal. It is one in which a common humanity prompts all men who retain living and activate instincts of humanity to become interested. These the "unspeakable" Turk seems to have abdicated. The writer has seen a dog—a good faithful one—turn on its own master, who savagely beat its fellow-dog. This much feeling no portion of the Turkish people has had the common animal instinct to show in behalf of their unfortunate fellow-mortals and fellow-subjects of Armenia. The blood in *human* veins runs cold at the bare recital of the atrocities this heroic nation has had to suffer. Daily recurring accounts make so overwhelming the evidence that "All the horrors of war before known or heard of were mercy to this new havoc"—as was said of Warren Hastings' exploits in India—that no one now, not even the sublime Porte, that has so long been notorious for its sublime duplicity, dares deny them.

These cold-blooded savageries have been inflicted, not on barbarians—like the inflicters—but on a refined, religious, renowned race—one than whom there is no nobler on the face of the earth. The Armenians are the oldest and most pure-blooded, they are the longest Christianized, and the most devoted to their region, of any other nation in the world. With only a tithe of a chance that all the European nations have had they would, centuries ago, have civilized and Christianized the effete pagan nations surrounding them. Unfortunately the odds have always been over a hundredfold against them, and all on account of their religion.

Great as have been the sufferings of Ireland and Poland in the same cause, they do not compare with those of devoted Armenia. Poland's persecution is of comparatively recent date; and prolonged as have been poor Ireland's (*poor*, although nature's paradise!) "for justice' sake," Armenia was in the midst of the conflict ere Erin won her proud title of "Island of Saints and Scholars."

As early as A.D. 480, whilst St. Patrick was still preaching in Ireland, Perozes, King of Persia, was engaged, as the Turkish Sultan now is, in endeavoring to exterminate the Christian Armenians, or make them apostatize to Zoroastrianism. Becoming thoroughly convinced of the impossibility of doing either, he, by the advice of a self-constituted Nestorian bishop named Barsumas of Nisibis, directed all his efforts to make them give up their adhesion to the Catholic Church; and, whilst remaining Christians, turn Nestorians; feeling assured that the step from heresy to Parseeism was much shorter and easier than from Catholicism. The king put unlimited power into the hands of Barsumas for this purpose. The latter commenced in the way that has been followed ever since by insidious persecutors. A decree was published *allowing* the clergy to marry. The French Masonic trick of a few years ago is the latest instance of this silly and sinister mode of undermining the true faith. The English statute books still contain similar modes of attack on the same lines.

It is needless to state that Barsumas, like the sixteenth century heresiarchs, led off the hymenial performance, that he hoped would be a procession of many other semi-sacerdotal couples, by taking unto himself a fair partner to help him govern the Armenian clergy, who, however, to a man, objected to petticoat rule, and appealed to their metropolitan of Selucia against him. He was at once excommunicated. The renegade sent the decree to Perozes, who ordered the archbishop to be suspended to a beam by the annular finger and there scourged to death.

Christopher, patriarch of Armenia, after seventy-seven hundred faithful Catholics had been immolated to the fury of the persecutor, feeling that one of three courses alone was open to the remainder, apostasy, extermination, or the defeat of the Persians in open war, decided on risking the latter. He issued a circular to all those subject to his jurisdiction advising them of his determination, and calling on them to be ready to die gloriously if necessary, like so many of their fathers of the two preceding centuries. They rose up as one man and defeated the Persians in a pitched battle A.D. 481. In the spring of the following year Perozes renewed the attack, and, although with vastly interior numbers, the Armenians were completely triumphant.

With only half a chance they would do the same thing today. What a pity the half-hearted Christian nations of Russia and England would not afford these brave warriors a similar opportunity! No one doubts the result. Asia and Europe would gain immensely thereby. With civilized Armenia on the West, and civilizing Japan on the East, Asia's redemption would be soon brought about, and the Turk's long-deserved day of retribution would not be long deferred afterwards.

The "Judas Machabeus" of the Armenians was Vahan, a descendant of the Chinese imperial family, who had found refuge in the country. He followed up his successes with untiring energy. Until the death of Perozes, A.D. 484, he held out against all the forces of Persia. The successors of the persecutor became terrified at the gigantic strength evoked by the determination of a whole people, sworn to die rather than deny their faith, and accordingly honorable terms of peace were offered to Vahan. Thus ended one persecution; thus, and more easily even, might the present one be made to end.

On the hero's entry into Dovin [Dvin], the capital of Armenia, he was met by the patriarch and clergy in solemn procession, and conducted to the cathedral, where the whole city joined in solemn thanksgiving to the God of Victories, through whom liberty was achieved. Not less remarkable was the modesty than the heroism of Vahan. To the divine aid and the bravery of his followers he attributed all the success; in testimony of which, he deposited on the altar the sword that had won him so much renown.

Accustomed as we have been to look upon the eastern nations as semi-barbarians—as indeed they now are, almost all of them—it was not always so; nor is so at present with the few that have remained Christian, in spite of the brutal and blighting Mohammedan yoke that keeps them under. Conspicuous amongst these is Armenia, surrounded though she be on all sides by the followers of the impostor. But great as is the glory of Armenia for remaining thus faithful and for maintaining a civilization superior to that of all her neighbors; equally great is the fame of her exploits not only on the field but in literature, science, and the arts; in fact, in everything that makes a people renowned. Had not the cursed shadow of the crescent blighted all her energies and eaten up all her resources, she would be second to no country in the world to-day. Hence civilized nations owe it to themselves and to humanity, to once for all break the fetters enthralling a people whose onward strides would otherwise keep up with themselves, and set the pace for the miserable laggards encompassing them. He who wishes for the civilization of Asia must sympathize with downtrodden Armenia.

When the rest of Europe was contending against hordes of barbarians—Goths, Vandals, Heruli, Tartars—as Armenia now struggles with her oppressors—she was cultivating, during the short intervals from persecution which she enjoyed, all the arts of peace with most singular success. Literary treasures little dreamed of now by Europeans lie hid in Syriac and ancient Armenian. The roman Martyrology alone—not to speak of the Greek or Syriac—contains references to hosts of saints, martyrs, and scholars of Armenia. There was St. Gregory the *Illuminator*, than whom no nation can boast a scholar more erudite. St. James, called the *Doctor*, Bishop of Batnoe or Sarup, devoted a life of seventy-two years to the defense of the Catholic faith, against the Nestorians and Eutychians. He died 522, leaving numerous works in Syriac which are as remarkable for their flowing elegance of style and richness of imagery as for soundness of Catholic doctrine. Another great saint, and his contemporary, was, St. Isaac, Bishop of Nineveh, who on the very day of his consecration became so terrified with the awful responsibilities it entailed that he resigned all the dignities and emoluments it brought him, and betook himself to a hermit's life in the desert of Scete in Egypt. Here he wrote four works on the *Monastic State*, and was looked up to as the model and teacher of all the other cenobites. Another elegant writer of the same century was John Sabbas, who has left several learned treatises on mysticism. Ecclesiastical history furnishes the names of many more. The works of the writers on profane subjects had a poorer chance of preservation outside the monasteries, although enough remain to assure us of the high attainments of their authors, and of the advanced civilization of their nation.

There is a species of madness peculiar to Turkey when it is

seemingly in *extremis*. The moribund body becomes suddenly galvanized into horrible activity, the resuscitating power being the ineradicable passion of religious fanaticism. While this frenzy lasts the Turks behave exactly like Malayans running amuck. Kill, kill, kill, is the watchword everywhere, though the sating of this bloodthirst mean instant ruin to the Turkish power. This fit is now upon the Ottoman. Horrible butcheries of Armenians have taken place, even in Constantinople itself. Large numbers of the unhappy people went there lately for the purpose of demanding justice of the Porte, but instead of justice they met the edge of the scimitar. They were slaughtered in the streets and in the houses in which they took refuge, their murderers being the class of fanatic Mussulman students known as Softas. The pretence alleged for the massacre was that the deputations to the Porte were in reality revolutionary Armenians intents of mischief. But this excuse does not cover the subsequent massacres of Armenians in the provinces of Bitlis and Van, reports of which are now beginning to arrive. All this horror has been going on while the war-ships of the European powers threaten the Turkish capital and hold the Bosphorus and the Dardanelles in iron grip. With their guns trained upon his palace, the Sultan still hesitates to concede the reforms the European powers demand for Armenia; and the reason of his hesitation cannot be other than the dread of his own subjects. The tiger-blood of the Turk is up, what may happen now, with this danger in prospect, may be decisive not only of the late of Armenia but of the accursed Turkish Empire.

It is full time to end the sufferings of this highly-gifted and cultured race. All Christians should join in the effort, and conspicuously Catholics; for, although the Armenians are now mostly Nestorians, it is more their misfortune than their fault. In common with Russian and Greek Catholics, they want but the permission of their rulers to enter the one true fold. Give them freedom first; the little separating them from the true church will quickly disappear.

The Armenian Question

James Bryce

My friend the editor of The Century asks me to say a few words regarding the sufferings of the Eastern Christians whose misfortune it is to live under the sway of the Turks. Those sufferings have evoked so much sympathy from the American people, and the moral influence of America may be so helpful to them, that no one who has followed the history of the Armenians during the last twenty years of oppression and misery can refuse the opportunity of addressing American readers on the subject. Nor is it merely that the recent demonstrations of feeling in the United States upon this subject have been so deep and wide-spread: nearly everything which has been done for these ancient seats of Christianity by modern Christian nations has been done by American missionaries, whose schools and colleges, planted in various parts of western Asia, have rekindled the flame of knowledge, and stimulated the native Eastern churches to resume the intellectual activity which once distinguished them. Americans have therefore a special reason, over and above their quick responsiveness to sentiments of humanity, for feeling a warm interest in the condition of the Armenian Christians.

The Armenians are a civilized people, a people of great natural gifts, and a people who have played a considerable part in history. Since their ancient monarchy, which has suffered severely in the long and desolating wars between the Roman and Persian empires from the third to the seventh century of our era, was finally destroyed by the Seljukian Turks, a large part of the race has been forced to migrate from its ancient seats at the head waters of the Euphrates, Tigris, and Aras. Some of them went southwest to the mountain fastnesses of Cilicia, where another Armenian kingdom grew up in the twelfth century. Others drifted into Persia. Others moved northeastward, and now form a large, industrious, and prosperous population in Russian Transcaucasia, where many have entered the military or civil service of the Czar, and risen, as the Armenians used to rise long ago in the Byzantine empire, to posts of distinction and power. Russia's three best generals in her last Asiatic campaigns against the Turks were Armenians. Others again have scattered themselves over the cities of Asia Minor and southeastern Europe, where much of the local trade is in their hands. But a large number, roughly estimated at from 1,300,000 to 1,700,000, remain in the old fatherland round the great lake of Van, and on the plateaus and elevated valleys which stretch westward from Mount Ararat to Erzerum and Erzinghian. Here they are an agricultural and (to a less extent) a pastoral population, leading a simple, primitive life, and desiring nothing more than to be permitted to lead it in peace and in fidelity to that ancient church which has been to them the symbol of nationality, as well as the guide of life for sixteen centuries.

Unfortunately, peace is just what they are forbidden to enjoy. The tribes of robber Kurds who roam over the mountains in summer with their flocks and herds descend in winter to quarter themselves upon the Armenian peasantry in the valleys and plains, and at all times carry on marauding raids, which the peasantry, whom the Turkish government deprives of all weapons, are seldom able to resist. Thus the country is the scene of continual disorders. Sheep and cattle are driven off, villages are plundered, men are murdered, women are carried away to the mountains, and when attempts are made to recover them it is alleged that they have become Mussulmans, and the Turkish officials refuse to interfere. Sometimes a whole village will be burned, and the horses of the Kurdish bands turned into the standing corn in sheer wantonness. These grievances are of long standing. They might have been expected not only to destroy the prosperity of the Armenian peasantry, but also to reduce their numbers. Yet such is the power of patient industry that, in spite of these constant attacks, the Christian population has maintained itself, and would, indeed, have increased faster than the Mussulman, sapped by the practice of polygamy, has shown itself able to do, were it not for the ravages of these robbers, and the unremitting oppression of the Turkish government. For in Turkey the government is a praise to evil-doers and a terror to them that do well. So far from trying to keep the Kurds in order, as the Russian government does the nomad Kurdish tribes, who live within Russian territory, the Turkish Valis and Kaimakams, usually encourage, and scarcely ever check their depredations, while at the same time themselves fleecing the Christian population by all the arts which corruption and avarice can suggest.

Things were so bad seventeen years ago that when Russia compelled the vanquished Turks to sign the treaty of San Stefano, in 1878, a special promise was made in it that the government of the Armenian provinces should be reformed and the Christians protected against the Kurds. When at the Congress of Berlin the treaty of Berlin was substituted for that of San Stefano, this provision was carried over to the new instrument, and the Armenians were thus placed virtually under the protection of the six great European powers. But their condition, so far from growing better, has since that time grown steadily worse. The British government has incessantly remonstrated with the Turks on their maladministration, and has tried, through its embassy at Constantinople and its consuls in the interior, to impose some sort of check upon the excesses of tyranny, and to procure the dismissal of the most cruel or corrupt officials. But it has received, until quite recently, very little support from the other five powers; and the Turks have opposed to its demands that dogged, sluggish resistance, and those endless evasions and vague promises of amendment, which are the usual resource of Oriental diplomacy.

Meanwhile two new factors have entered into the situation which have made it more acute. One is the growing fanaticism of the Mussulman population, stimulated by the Sultan himself. Claiming to be calif,—that is to say, supreme spiritual as well as temporal head of the Mohammedan world,—he has conceived a higher conceit of his ecclesiastical position than has any of his predecessors for centuries past, and has been striving to strengthen his religious authority all the more because he feels that his material power is fast slipping away. Thus, in appealing to the Mussulman feelings of his Turkish subjects, he has revived their antichristian feelings, and has, indeed, followed during the last ten years a distinctly antichristian policy, which has had the most pernicious results on the relations of the two creeds. The old spirit of hatred to the giaour has become strong in the East, and might (in many places) lead at any moment to conflicts in which the Christians, fewer in numbers and almost always without arms, would be the sufferers.

The other factor is the growing sentiment of nationality among the Armenians themselves. They have become proud of their history; they have developed a keen interest in education, and while continuing to use and value the American schools and colleges, have now also founded others of their own. They have conceived hopes of a brighter future for their nation when the decaying fabric of the Turkish empire shall have finally crumbled away, and they have been encouraged by the sympathy shown them in Britain and in the United States to take a somewhat bolder line than formerly, and to raise their voices in complaint against the tyranny they have to endure. It is said that some among them have formed secret societies, and that the representatives of Armenian patriotic committees in two or three cities of continental Europe have been moving about Asiatic Turkey trying to rouse their fellow-countrymen. This is probable enough, though little or nothing is authentically known; nor can anyone be surprised that some among the victims of Turkish misrule should combine against it, however hopeless the prospect of a rising by an unarmed minority against a government which not only possesses a large army furnished with modern weapons, but has on its side the bulk of the Mohammedan population, which is generally armed. The result of this growth of national Armenian sentiment has been to alarm the Turks, to stimulate their hatred of the Christians, to make the officials more cruel and the courts even more unjust than they were previously, and to dispose the Turkish ministers more and more toward the policy which one of them is said to have expressed thus: "The way to get rid of the Armenian question is to get rid of the Armenians."

Under the influence of these causes there has been of late years added to the old disorders in Armenia proper a general reign of terror over Asiatic Turkey. The industrious Armenian population in the cities of Asia Minor, which had previously suffered from misgovernment not much more than its Mussulman neighbors, and which had lived on friendly terms with them, has been subjected to more outrageous oppressions and more horrible cruelties than probably it has had to endure since the fifteenth century, and that under a monarch who holds his throne only by the permission, and owing to the jealousies, of the Christian powers of Europe.

Every one has heard of the massacre of Sassoun. It was an absolutely unprovoked massacre, and has all the appearance of having been deliberately planned in order to exterminate the Christian population of a district almost entirely inhabited by Armenians, and in which they had retained in an unusual degree the primitive simplicity of their life and habits, as well as their physical strength and courage. Taken by surprise, and surrounded by vastly superior forces, the unhappy people fought as well as they could for their wives and their children, whose lot, if captured alive, was far worse than death. Of the slaughter and the revolting cruelties which accompanied it no more need be said than this: that the accounts which have appeared in the newspapers are not in excess of the truth as it has been ascertained by careful official inquiries not yet made public. The details sometimes vary, but the main features admit of no doubt. Nor were the Kurds the guiltiest parties. All they did was surpassed by the ferocious cruelties of the regular troops, directed by Turkish officers. But these terrible events are hardly more shocking, except in their scale, than the things which have been monthly and weekly happening in many other towns and villages, and of which no report ever reaches the European press—the defilement of churches, the abduction of women and children, the imprisonment of innocent men in loathsome dungeons where they are often subjected to frightful tortures under which many perish, the acts of brutal and revolting lust perpetrated without fear of punishment upon helpless victims. Much of what is contained in the British consular reports is too horrible for print; and if the American missionaries were able, without endangering their own position in the country and the lives of their informants, to make public what they know, they could supply a not less ghastly record.

American readers will ask what, in these circumstances, the European powers propose to do. They are morally responsible for the sufferings of the subjects of Turkey to this extent: that they have kept in being a monarchy which has long since deserved to perish, and which would long since either have fallen to pieces by its own weakness, or have been conquered and annexed by one of its neighbors. They perceive, moreover, that the state of things which now exists in Turkey cannot go on indefinitely, and may produce some explosion which would cause a grave European crisis, perhaps a European war. Something, therefore, must be done. At the moment when these lines are being written the British government, pursuing under Lord Salisbury the line of action which his predecessor initiated, is in conjunction with Russia and France pressing the Sultan to accept a scheme of reforms. Long before these lines can be read in America it will be known whether they have extorted the consent of the Sultan to these reforms, or to some others, which may hold out a hope of better days for the Armenian Christians. There would be no use, therefore, in discussing the situation as it stands at this moment. But there are some permanent aspects of the question, not likely to vary for years to come, which may properly be adverted to, because they are not fully realized in western Europe, and are probably even less familiar to Americans.

Although the other nations of Europe now treat the Turks as if they were a civilized state, hold diplomatic intercourse with them in the usual way, and even talk of "respecting their susceptibilities," they have no title to be so treated, and ought never to have been admitted to a place among civilized communities. Even if we do not, as Mr. Freeman did, describe them as "merely a band of robbers encamped in a country whose inhabitants they despoil," still the words of Edmund Burke, who more than a century ago denounced the idea of deeming them to form a part of the European states system, remain true, and have received from events the strongest confirmation:

> I have never before heard that the Turkish has ever been considered as any part of the balance of power in Europe. They despise and contemn all Christian princes as infidels, and only wish to subdue and exterminate them and their people. What have these worse than savages to do with the powers of Europe but to spread war, destruction, and pestilence among them? The ministers and the policy which shall give these people any weight in Europe will deserve all the bans and curses of posterity.

Having no idea of responsibility to its subjects, and not recognizing any duty to promote their welfare, the so-called government of Turkey has been at all times inaccessible to the considerations by which civilized governments are moved, or to which they must at any rate—even the worst of them—profess to defer. Hence the difficulty of making any impression on the Turks by remonstrance or persuasion. Nothing moves them but fear. They are, moreover, most of them, so purblind, so incapable of looking forward or around and foreseeing the action of the causes now in motion, that they cannot be made to learn by experience, or to realize that the course they are pursuing must at no distant date involve the ruin of their power. These faults have been aggravated during the last few years by the policy of the present Sultan, who leaves very little to his ministers, is jealous of any talent that shows itself among them, tries to direct everything himself, and is, in fact, largely swayed by a camarilla of ignorant personal attendants and hangers-on at the palace. There are some able Mohammedans in Constantinople who detest the present regime and see its perils. Now and then a good governor is found in the provinces, who tries to improve the local administration. But the able men are never listened to, and the good governor is speedily recalled. In every government more depends upon them who administer than upon the system; but in a despotic government men are everything. In Turkey the men and the system are equally corrupt; and to try to reform the Turkish monarchy is like trying to repair a ship with rotten timbers.

Why does not such a government go to pieces, according to the law of nature which happily provides that corruption and weakness bring dissolution in their train? There are three reasons. One is the jealousy of three great European powers, which has had the effect of preventing two of them from annexing what remains of Turkish territory. Another is the fact that the Mussulman population, being in the majority, is so fanatically ill disposed to the Christians (who are the greatest sufferers) that it is not only willing to help the government to hold the Christians down, but even disposed to tolerate evils which would produce Mussulman insurrections, were there no Christians in the country. There is, however, a great deal of latent discontent among the Mohammedans, and but for the fatalism which Islam engenders, and which has made the masses listless and resigned, one may doubt whether even jealousy of the Christians would suffice to prevent outbreaks. The third reason is the enormous advantage which modern weapons give to a government which can raise money to purchase them. Two centuries ago insurrections were far easier and more likely to succeed than now, because the insurgents were more on a level with regular troops than they are in these days of swift-firing guns and rifles of long range. There is therefore little ground for hoping for any speedy extinction of the Turkish power by natural causes.

If, then, it is going to last some time longer, can nothing at all be done, if not to reform it, yet to abate its evils? Experience has shown that there is only one way of reforming an Oriental government, and that is by putting it into leading-strings, by either superseding the chief officials and putting Europeans in their place, or else by giving them European adjutants who shall virtually direct them. This might be done in Turkey if the European powers were willing. But it would be necessary practically to supersede the Sultan—that is to say, to prevent him from interfering either with administrative policy or with appointments. And it is a method which, though capable of being efficiently worked by a directing and protecting power, as England works it in the minor protected states of India, cannot be well applied, at least on a large scale, by three or four powers conjointly, because each would suspect the other of obtaining some advantage for itself.

Another expedient would be to detach from the rest of the empire those parts of the country where disorders were most frequent, placing them under a specially constituted administration. This was done in the case of Lebanon, and with very good results. It has been proposed for Armenia, and would probably succeed there. If the powers chiefly concerned were to compel the Sultan to erect Armenia into a distinct province, with a European governor who should be irremovable except with the consent of those powers, who should control the revenues of the province and maintain out of them a strong police, and who should be free to introduce administrative and judicial reforms, the country might in ten years' time be brought into the same perfect order, and obtain a measure of the same prosperity, as has attended the rule of Count Kallay in Bosnia, which was delivered from the Turks in 1878. There are, no doubt, as many Mussulmans as Christians in Armenia, but the former have also much to gain by the establishment of good administration, and would welcome it. Russia, however, is unwilling to set up on her borders what she fears might become an Armenian principality toward which her own Armenian population would gravitate; so it is to be feared that this course, however promising, will not be taken.

We are brought back, then, to the question of what the European powers can or will do to deal with a situation which every one admits must not continue. Their present plan is to introduce small changes in local government—changes too numerous to be stated here—which may give the Christians a better chance of preserving their lives and property, and to institute a commission of supervision at Constantinople, with which the European ambassadors may be in communication, conveying to it the reports of their consuls, and pressing it to see that justice is done in the provinces. This scheme, though somewhat complicated, may, in the opinion of several judicious British and American residents, be made to work. But it will require the closest attention by the European consuls and ambassadors, and the most unremitting pressure must be brought to bear on the Sultan if its provisions are not to be neglected or evaded in practice. Nothing but fear and threats will move a government which has up till now never expressed the slightest penitence, nor shown the slightest remorse, for the Sassoun massacre, nor taken any serious step to put an end to the hideous prison tortures which the British Embassy has so often brought to its notice.

One closing word as to the influence which America may exert in these questions. She has very wisely, and very fortunately for herself, abstained from joining in any of the treaties which determine the relations of European powers to one another; and she has neither obtained any such legal right to interfere for the protection of the native Eastern Christians, nor incurred any such responsibility toward them, as is the case with six great powers. But she has missionaries in many parts of Turkey, whom, and whose churches and schools, constantly threatened by the local Turkish governors, she is entitled to protect; and she has the enormous advantage of being obviously disinterested in all Mediterranean questions, having nothing to gain for herself in that region of the world. Hence any action taken by her, either on behalf of her missionaries or from sentiments of humanity and sympathy for the oppressed and persecuted, cannot be misunderstood by the Turks or misrepresented by the press of continental Europe, as that press constantly misrepresents the action of England, though in interfering on behalf of the Armenians England has not, and cannot have, any selfish motive. The position of America is therefore a very strong one. The appearance of her gunboats off Turkish ports has before now had a wholesome effect upon the Turkish mind; and these gunboats would do well to appear promptly whenever the rights of her citizens and the safety of their educational establishments are threatened. At Constantinople much depends also upon the capacity and the firmness of the envoy who embodies and speaks the will of a foreign power.

Dark as the prospect before those unhappy people may at present seem, no one who remembers the calamities they have already endured and survived will despair of their future. During ten centuries of humiliation and suffering they have clung to their faith, when at any moment by renouncing it they might have obtained complete equality with their oppressors. Alone of all the races that once inhabited the inland regions of western Asia, the Armenians have retained their language, their national feeling, and their hold upon the soil. A race with so much natural vigor, so much tenacity of life, and so much capacity for assimilating and using modern ideas, cannot be destined to extinction, and may some day, when countries that were among the earliest homes of civilization have been delivered from the tyranny of the Turk, help to repeople those now desolate and poverty-stricken lands, and restore to them some measure of their ancient prosperity.

Rational Sympathy

The more rational sympathy is, the more effective it is. The sympathy of hysterical persons is seldom welcome and never useful to anybody. Therefore, in all our talk about the Armenian horrors, we should take pains to show that it emanates from sober-minded and well-informed people. Rationality, even in sorrow, is what distinguishes man from the animals, and one of the marks of rationality is a just estimate of the possible. Children never know what is possible, and one of the first signs of insanity is an ignoring of the limits of human powers. Some of our Jingo friends forgot all this some weeks ago when they wailed over the want of a navy to protect the Asiatic Christians against the Kurds and Turks, and there is still a loud call on our government to do something or other in that direction. What this thing should be, no one seems exactly to know. The *Tribune* comes as near telling us as anybody, when it says that the President should show "genuine American feeling" and "should have something to say about the perils of our American missionaries in Turkey," and "give forth an American voice from the White House."

What would be the effect of any of these processes on the Turks, it is impossible to say without knowing more about their exact nature. As described here they simply mean more noise, whereas what we want is plans and specifications. If the Turk were frightened by infidel denunciations of him, he would long ago have taken refuge in the inner recesses of Tartary from which he issued a thousand years ago. The documents which the Armenians circulate among us here are so highly colored, vague, and extravagant in their diction that they fail of their purpose. We have always felt reluctant to quote them lest they should prejudice sober-minded people against a good cause. The horrors in Armenia have been so great that they will not bear rhetorical embellishment. Plain narrative, fortified if possible with proof, is all they call for. Senator Hoar, in a despatch to the President which the *Tribune* printed on Monday, offered to stand by the President in the Senate if he should go so far as "to determine to treat the persons who massacre the Armenians as pirates and common enemies of the human race." The Senator would relieve the anxiety of many persons about his mental condition if he would explain how the President is to "treat" persons in the interior of Asia Minor as ruffians of this description. To "treat" anybody as a "pirate" I must have some means, or a fair prospect, of getting at him. As long as he knows I cannot reach him, my epithets are wasted on him, and we fear all that the Kurds know of President Cleveland is that he is a noted Western robber, who is dissatisfied because he cannot "take a hand in the racket." The Senator's remedy is therefore clearly inadequate. The measure he suggests to the President is only seemingly desperate. In reality it would be quite harmless.

There are only two things which we can do with effect. One is what Mr. Terrell is doing, to address vigorous remonstrances to the Porte about the safety of our own citizens. These have apparently been effective thus far, but more by good luck than anything else. Threatening the Porte with our navy would be bad policy, because he knows that our navy cannot do anything more to him than the combined navies of Europe which are threatening him already. The Armenian trouble is hundreds of miles from the sea, in a roadless region, and his difficulty is that he has neither the money nor the men to restore permanent order—a fact which the Powers have probably already found out and are much puzzled by. The only one which can reach the scene of disorder with a land force is Russia, and she has apparently reasons of her own for refraining from interference at present. It would be far more rational for our Government and people to urge on Russia to march an army corps or even a division into Armenia, than to threaten the Porte or call the Kurds names. That would be the use of means adapted to the end in view, and, therefore, a human and rational process. Austria might intervene also by marching an army into Macedonia, but this would simply exert pressure on the wretched Sultan, who, as we have shown, is in Armenia powerless for all practical purposes. No one has yet suggested the despatch of our little army or of the Seventh Regiment to occupy Armenia and fight the Turks in the snow. When that proposal is made, we shall discuss it with the gravity which it merits.

The other thing we might do, and ought to do, is to send money, provisions, and clothing for the thousands of unhappy people, mainly, in all probability, women and children, who will have to face the terrible winter of Asia Minor without any protection against weather and hunger. If there were more of this going on, we could do with very much less "voicing" of indignation and less vituperation of the Turk. It is a feasible work and ought to be actively prosecuted. A fighting rôle on the Turkish question is not open to us. The humane rôle is. Jingoes ought to reconcile themselves to the fact that Providence has clearly not intended that we should have a hand in *all* fights, or it would have made all parts of the globe accessible to our navy. The ruffians and the oppressors who carry on their atrocities in the interior of large continents are clearly meant to be chastised by other hands than ours.

The Armenian Massacres

Rev. Cyrus Hamlin, D.D.[106]

The administration of government in the Turkish Empire is more evidently affected by the personal character of the Sultan than is true of any other government of this era. The writer has lived under three Sultans—Mahmoud II, Abdul Medjid, and Abdul Aziz. The personal character and policy of each one was felt throughout the Empire. It is not so with the Russian despotism. That goes on the same from age to age. Its policy never changes. For four hundred years it has had Constantinople constantly in view. It has made vast additions of territory and population. It has the greatest army in the world. It is building a great navy, and it is gradually approaching the glittering prize that inspires its toil.

Turkey has no invariable policy which controls successive Sultans. Mahmoud II was a great reformer. He destroyed the Janizaries, reorganized the army, relieved the "rayahs" (Christians and Jews) of many burdens and humiliations, and aimed to establish friendly relations with European States, and to have a regular cabinet of ministers. The rayahs regarded him as their friend. The fanatical Moslems called him a giaour. He employed many Armenians in the under offices of state. One was his chief architect, one collector of the customs, another the head of the mint; and he made an American, Mr. Eckford, the chief of the naval arsenal. Under his reign the Turks had to respect the rights of Christians.

He had a reign of just thirty-one years, full of incidents, and weakened by a disastrous war with Russia and the rebellion of Mehmet Ali, the Pasha of Egypt.

His son, Abdul Medjid, came to the throne in 1839—a boy

of sixteen. He endeavored to push forward his father's design to Europeanize the government. He issued the celebrated constitution called the "Hatti-Scheriff of Gulhane." He introduced many Armenians into government employ. The old Turkish party, the unchangeable Moslem, was disgusted with his reforms, as was Russia. A reaction became dominant in 1843, and the old party again ruled, to the terror of the rayahs. But the great English Ambassador, Sir Stratford Canning, took the Sultan under his protection, and many important improvements were made in the administration, and generally in favor of equal rights to the Christian subjects.

The Crimean War saved Constantinople from the grasp of Russia, but the peace of Paris, through the treason and ambition of Louis Napoleon, rejected the policy of England and gave Turkey over entirely to herself, forbidding all interference from any one of the signatory powers. From that time onward the condition of the rayahs can hardly be said to have improved. Abdul Medjid died after a reign of twenty-two years—'39 to '61. Abdul Aziz, the successor, was stupid and brutal. He got the finances into hopeless entanglements by excessive loans at ruinous interest, and by palace squanderings. Russia made him her tool for the ruin of the Empire. June 4, 1876, he was found dead in his chamber, having been assassinated or having committed suicide. There were two parties to that question, but all agree that he died, and his memory may as well perish.

We now come to the present reigning Sultan, Abdul Hamid. He has always been regarded as a fanatical Mussulman. He came to the throne with the inborn resolution to exercise all the power of the successor of the Prophet. He is a skillful diplomat. He believes in the supreme power of lying. He covers up all that he does by falsehood or false testimony. He can always bring any number of witnesses to prove that there has been no violence where hundreds have been slaughtered.

He secludes himself in his palace, is seen by very few; but those who are called to an interview pronounce him a most fascinating man.

He very early took upon himself the entire care of his Empire. He resolved to govern it alone. He went into every department—army, navy, naval construction, public works, education, finance—in order to have everything exactly right. Finding a great many Armenians in these departments, he cleaned them all out and put in Turks—often an incompetent man for a competent. If his ministers did not please him, he changed them, and then changed them again. A still worse habit is his sending commands direct, superseding the orders of any of his cabinet ministers, without their knowledge. The favorites of the palace are able thus to upset the best plans of the Grand Vizier without notice. More than one has been dismissed and degraded for remonstrating. If things did not work smoothly under this new regime, his indignation was excited, and another overturn of officers would follow. This personal administration of every department has caused general confusion and dissatisfaction, and poverty and ruin.

The department of education early attracted his attention. He saw that his rayahs were better educated, more intelligent, and more thrifty than his Moslem subjects. He resolved to change all that. He began to impose laws upon school-houses, text-books, and teachers. No school-house could be repaired without Government permission, which was never given; no new school-house could be built. School-books once approved and bearing the imperial seal were subjected to a new censorship and utterly defaced, and thousands of dollars' worth destroyed. Many schools were shut up under frivolous pretenses. At the same time convenient school-houses were built for Mussulman schools and a great impulse was given to Moslem education. The rayahs, if they complained, were exhorted to profess the true faith, and these benefits would be theirs. Abdul Hamid has all along had an eye to the conversion of his rayahs.

But more stringent means must be used. He could operate, for the present, only upon the Armenians—the Gregorians and the Protestants. They have no defender. The Greeks are protected by Russia and the Catholic Armenians by France. Not one of them is to be touched. England's protection of the Armenians amounts to nothing. Complaints are made, immediate reforms are promised, England is satisfied—and the persecution continues. He has played this game with England for many years.

Sultan Hamid very early saw that the Armenians must be dealt with after another fashion. He made little progress in his efforts to unify his Empire by gathering the wandering sheep into the one fold. On the eastern borders of his Empire lie the Kurdish Mountains, and along their base, or foot-hills, are many Armenian villages, often ravaged by the Kurdish robbers—and they are all robbers, more or less. He thought it would be well to have only one people, or at least one faith, on all his eastern border. The Armenians should have their choice, Islam or Gehenna! For this purpose the Kurds would serve him well. He called to Constantinople the chiefs of the principal tribes, treated them with flattering distinction, and gave them uniforms and arms for an imperial cavalry to bear his name—the Hamidieh cavalry. Their work was gradually to efface all the Armenian villages, saving all who would profess Islam. This work has been going on for some years in those distant regions. The survivors made their appeals to England, and the consuls faithfully reported them. Doubtless England tried to persuade the Sultan to do better; and he has always been ready with stout denials that any wrong has been done, and with lavish promises that nothing more of the kind should happen. For four years or more the outrages upon the Armenians have been growing in frequency and cruelty, and have unquestionably been patronized by Hamid.

A very regrettable element comes in here to intensify the evil. A revolutionary party, formed in Russia, and having branches in England and America, have formed, or claim to have formed, secret societies for promoting a revolution and securing "Armenia for Armenians." The Turkish Government might smile at the folly of this infantile organization. But for Russia, it never could have come into existence, and her power behind it supports it.

But this revolutionary movement is just what Abdul Hamid desires. He hails it as a justification of his plan to destroy the Armenians, except they repent and turn to Islam. He now extends his operations all over the Empire, which has become a slaughterhouse. And these two and a half million of Armenian peasants and traders have been his most useful and faithful subjects! According to the Koran, and the great codified law called the "Multeka," he is under sacred obligations to protect them in person and property, and in the enjoyment of their religion.

The Sultan does not fear in the least the "Great Powers." He knows that they cannot agree to do anything. They can present schemes of reform, and he promises to execute them, but goes on with his schemes of outrage and assassination. The six Great Powers, in the persons of their Ambassadors, stand and look on, and can do nothing; and the Sultan has his own way. Russia and England oppose each other, and neither can move a step.

The Ambassadors at Constantinople are apprehensive of a general rising of the Mohammedans to slaughter all the Christians of the capital indiscriminately, and have demanded each an additional gunboat for safety. The Sultan, being made by treaty the guardian of the Dardanelles, will not allow them to come up, and the six "Great Powers," thus far, obey the Sultan!

Russia will act only when there is an outcry of the civilized world calling her in. Should there be a general slaughter of all Christians, she would march in and take possession, and England would not dare to resist her. She is waiting for such a result, and secretly preparing it. Perhaps "he that sitteth in the heavens laughs, and has them in derision."

The Sultan has awakened all the slumbering fanaticism of his Empire, and it is doubtful if he can now control it.

There is one power the Sultan would fear, had it any power visible to him; and that is the United States of America. That is a country that can act for itself. It can send an ironclad to any Mediterranean port with a demand that can be enforced, and no other country will say a word. The Sultan has destroyed American property very freely, and has no thought of paying a piaster for it all. Americans have been insulted and maltreated, but in these recent assassinations the Turks have taken no American lives. Our Government is acting vigorously, and Mr. Terrell is full of energy and pluck. Hamid will probably receive some useful lessons from Mr. Olney.

We wait to hear that the work of extermination has ceased. But what shall follow? Famine and pestilence. Not less than 250,000 will die of cold and starvation this winter unless relief comes to them from abroad. Why should not our great and rich country send them a million of dollars, with agents clothed with power to see to the distribution, so that it should not be perverted?

Armenia, Past and Present

Rev. Henry Hyvernat,[107] D.D. (Catholic University)

It is a huge mountain island, bounded on the north by the Caspian and the Black Seas, on the south by the Mediterranean Sea and the low plains of Mesopotamia and Assyria. Its altitude averages to five and six thousand feet above the level of the sea; it is crossed in every direction by deep valleys and high mountain ranges, and contains innumerable lakes, some of which are amongst the largest sheets of water on the old continent. From its many high, snow-capped peaks flow some of the most famous historical rivers, like the Araxes, the Tigris, and the Euphrates. Of these three rivers the Araxes is the most important in the eyes of an Armenian; as from the mountain of the Thousand Lakes, where it rises, to the Caspian Sea, it flows in Armenian soil. It is in its valley that Echmiazin, the Rome of Armenia, lies; also the ruins of Ani, the capital of the Bagratide dynasty, the greatest and most beautiful city ever built by Christian Armenia; and it is there again that, according to the ethnographists, we must look for the cradle of the old Armenian race.

The Supposed Site of Paradise

Not less interest attaches to the large basin of Lake Van. This wonderful lake is situated five thousand feet above the Mediterranean's level. The high, steep, and often snow-capped mountains which closely gird it make its scenery amongst the most striking in the world. The deep blue of its waters, combined with the clear atmosphere of Armenia, gives to the eye the illusion of a portion of the Mediterranean Sea transported by the magic wand of a wizard into the highest regions of Switzerland. Like a genuine sea, it has no outlet; its depth is such that it could be crossed in all direction by our heaviest iron-clad vessels. It is a small sea rather than a large lake, and is therefore called the Armenian Sea. The climate of the basin of Lake Van is pleasant; its fertility is renowned far and wide. From the remotest antiquity its shores were bordered by important cities, and it seemed quite natural to the Armenians to suppose that their beautiful country must have been the site of the terrestrial Paradise as we find it mentioned in the second chapter of Genesis.

Sacred Ararat

Between the low valley of the Araxes and the high plateau where lies Lake Van rises the famous mountain, Ararat, the king of the volcanic cones of Armenia, and doubtless the most celebrated of mountains in the history of the human race, it being supposed to have been the spot whence the children of Noe dispersed through the world; a scriptural fact which, say the Armenians, is confirmed by the remains of the Ark still visible on the summit of the gigantic volcano. Though Ararat is only seventeen thousand feet high, and consequently considerably lower than several of the Himalayan peaks, yet I can say, speaking from observation, that none of the latter presents such an impressive appearance as the Armenian giant viewed from the low valley of the Araxes, as it rises perfectly isolated, so regular and symmetrical in its shape that the eye follows without any obstacle its bold ascending slope from its sunny and warm base to its snow-capped summit. The farther one stands from it the more he is impressed by its size, as all the other mountains around it look like insignificant mounds, whilst Ararat towers alone and grand above them; an impression very much like that which the tourist receives when, standing on the Alban hills, thirty or forty miles from Rome, and looking towards the Eternal City, he sees clearly with the naked eye the gigantic cupola of St. Peter's, though he has to use a fieldglass to discern the other monuments of the city.

Armenia was inhabited, within the historical period, by two different races, the ancient and what we may call the modern Armenians. The ancient Armenians, whilst they had all the anthropological characteristics of the white race, belonged to the Mongolian family by their language.[108] They were a strong, robust, energetic people, the most dangerous enemy of their powerful neighbors, the Assyrians. Eight centuries before our era they had reached a high degree of civilization, and the monuments their kings left to posterity are still the admiration of all.

Armenian Ethnology

The modern Armenians belong entirely to the Aryan white race. They are designated in the Holy Scripture by the ethnic name of Thogormah, third son of Gomer. Formerly established in the plains north of Caucasus and the Black Sea, they migrated, after centuries of wandering B.C., into Armenia, where later on, by a slow infiltration of new ethnic elements, under the Persian dominion, they grew into a new people, presenting all the chief characteristics of the Armenians of to-day. Unfortunately for this active and intelligent race, they took possession of their new home under most unfavorable circumstances. They passed immediately under the sway of the Assyrians, whose boundless resources and skilful strategy had finally got the better of the old settlers of Armenia. When, half a century later, Nineveh fell under the combined blows of the Medes and the Persians, they were still too young as a nation to resist the new masters of the world. They were only freed from this dependence by passing under the dominion of Alexander the Great and the Seleucides, his successors. Armenia was then administered by native governors appointed by the Seleucides. The last of these governors, Ardavatz, was driven away by the Parthian, Arsace the Great, or Mithridates, who established his brother Valarce as King of Armenia, a century and a half B.C. Thus commenced the Armenian dynasty of the Arsacide, which kept itself, as well as it possibly could, upon the throne until the middle of the fifth century A.D., when it perished under the attacks of the Sassanians.

Early Introduction of Christianity

It was under this dynasty that Armenia first became Christian. The country was evangelized, according to the traditions, by four Apostles, Sts. Bartholomew, Thaddeus, Jude, and Thomas. They wrought there many conversions, founded churches and consecrated bishops, and so on. Sts. Bartholomew and Jude died in Armenia. It was not, however, until the dawn of the fourth century that Armenia became as a whole officially a Christian country, when King Tiridates, the reigning monarch, was baptized by St. Gregory the Illuminator, who may well be considered as the true Apostle of Armenia; the country was covered in a few years with churches and monasteries, and a powerful hierarchy, depending upon the patriarchal see of Echmiazin, was established. It was towards the end of the same dynasty that a learned monk, by name Mesrob, invented the Armenian alphabet, thus enabling his countrymen to obtain a liturgy in their own language instead of the Greek or Syriac which up to that period they had used owing to the lack of their own letters. It was then that the Bible was translated into Armenian, and Mesrob became the founder of numerous schools of literature, to which we are indebted for translations of important Greek and Syriac works, some of which cannot be found either in original or any other language but Armenian. Unfortunately, in the year 428 the dynasty of the Arsacidae fell under the assaults of the Sassanians of Persia, who ruled the country for the two next centuries, and endeavored to uproot Christianity. While we rejoice that many of the literary treasures escaped their devastating fury, we have to deplore the loss of all the architectural monuments of that early and interesting period. After the Sassanians came the Arabs of Bagdad, who were the rulers of the country during the seventh century, and did not prove more partial to Christianity than their predecessors; whatever the latter might have overlooked was destroyed by these fanatical followers of Mohammed. After this long period of persecution the Armenians remained unmolested, though still dependent on the caliphs, and were permitted the free and public practice of their religion. It was the dawn of an era of independence. In the ninth century they finally succeeded in getting a dynasty of their own, under whose government they developed into a robust nation, and reached rapidly a high standing in the culture of arts and letters as well as in the civil and military institutions. This dynasty, called Bagratide, after Bagrat its founder, lasted nearly three hundred years, and must have lasted much longer but for the political mistakes of the Armenians. Instead of remaining united under one government, they quarrelled among themselves and divided into numerous small kingdoms, each of which pretended to control exclusively the politics of the nation, just when they most needed to be united against their many enemies. The Greek emperors of Byzantium, who since the end of the fourth century had been masters of the Armenian provinces of Asia Minor, were always on the lookout for a pretext for interfering in the politics of Armenia. Naturally they profited by the dissensions of the petty kingdoms to annex them to their already too extensive empire. Both by main force and by treachery they relentlessly labored to attain their end. Repeatedly did the Armenians defeat them; but each victory left the nation weaker before an enemy of superior resources, until it finally succumbed. The last Bagratide king, kidnapped by his cunning adversaries, was compelled to exchange a crown too heavy for him for a castle on the Bosphorus. This took place in the year 1045. Armenia then became a province of the Greek Empire, and was treated in the most cruel way by her new masters. The headmen of the army and all the influential citizens of the nation were banished to distant provinces, and whatever of the population had escaped destruction or exile were taxed far above their means. It seemed, indeed, that nothing worse could befall the Armenians; but these atrocities were but little in comparison with misfortunes still awaiting them.

Mohammedan Invaders

The Seljukide sultans, not less bigoted and far more cruel than the Arabs, had just snatched the military power from the weak hands of the caliphs, whom they pretended to protect. Their ferocious hordes soon invaded Armenia. A number of flourishing cities were burned to the ground, after the population had been put to death with the exception of such as could adorn the harems of the conquerors. Many Armenians took refuge in Cilicia, which from the remotest antiquity had been one of their colonies—the kingdom generally known as Lesser Armenia. Whilst the Greeks were making desperate but useless efforts to defend Greater Armenia against the Seljuks, the new kingdom developed rapidly under the wise administration of the Roopenian dynasty, and when, in 1097, the crusaders came to Cilicia they found the Armenians strongly established in their new home and most willing to help them in every way in their war against Islam. For two centuries Armenians and Franks fought side by side against the ever-reappearing heads of the Mohammedan hydra, and there is no doubt that their joint efforts would have had more enduring results but for the short-sighted policy of the Greek emperors, who could never understand that the existence of a strong and flourishing Christian kingdom on the east of their dominions was the best protection against the invading Asiatic hordes. Instead of helping them in their struggle for independence against the Mohammedans, as Christian spirit and even mere worldly prudence suggested, they attacked them themselves repeatedly when they could not excite the sultans of Konjieh to do so. If the Greeks had received the crusaders with the same cordiality as the Armenians, there is no doubt but the crescent would have been driven back to its sandy deserts. It is true that the unexpected start taken by Egypt under the famous Saladin, and after him by the still more famous dynasties of the Mamelukes, had brought new resources to the enemies of our faith; but the flood of the Mongols was advancing rapidly from the steppes of Northern Asia.

Unlike the Arabs and the Turks, the new-comers brought no creed with them. Christianity and Islam were novelties to them, which did not correspond to anything in their traditions; they would have embraced the one as well as the other; nay they seemed at first to have a decided inclination towards Christianity. The Armenians of Cilicia, like the pontiffs of Rome, understood this, and received with every mark of friendship the new conquerors, who soon became the protectors of the Christian faith. It is not improbable that if the Greeks had followed the same policy the Mongols would never have adopted the tenets of the Koran. But the narrowness of their views made them miss this last opportunity of saving their own empire and Christianity. In 1300 the Mongols became Mohammedans, and as such the enemies of the Christians. This was practically the end of Armenia; her independence was lost for ever. She became a province of the empire of the sultans of Egypt, and her last king, Leon de Lusignan, died in Paris, where he had taken refuge towards the close of the fourteenth century.

During that time a little Turkish tribe, fleeing before the Mongols from its original home in Central Asia, settled in the western portion of Asia Minor on the Byzantine frontier. They took the name of Othmanlis from Othman, their leader. Early in the fourteenth century they inherited their provinces from the Seljuks of Asia Minor, on whom they depended and who had been swept away by the Mongols. They soon developed into an irresistible conquering nation, to whose prowess the Greek Empire finally succumbed in 1453.

Since that time Armenia has been the great battle-field between Turkey, Persia, and Russia, and it is hard to tell which of the three is most unfavorable to her claims.

No doubt the political misfortunes of that country may, to some extent, be accounted for by its geographical position. For this reason an absolutely independent kingdom of Armenia neither has been nor will be ever possible. Besides it was not, nor will it ever be profitable to any European power to annex Armenia as an ordinary province, since its remoteness from the centre of such a power will always make it impossible to defend it for any length of time against a powerful invader. But between these two extremes a middle course could be pursued, namely, to establish Armenia as an independent state, governed by local princes, under the protection of one or other of the civilized nations of Christendom. The Roman emperors understood the situation very well, and therefore always favored the political independence of Armenia, which policy proved most profitable both to the latter and to the Roman Empire. I have already indicated how the Greek emperors, taking another course, lost both Armenia and their own dominions. But independently of that great political mistake, the Greek emperors committed another, religious in character, and which proved far more fatal to Armenia, no matter how considered.

Religious Troubles of Armenia

So much for the historical and political aspects of the question. The more important consideration of the spiritual interests involved in it remains to be dealt with briefly.

The conversion of Armenia under king Tiridates was so complete that centuries of cruel persecutions could never uproot the tenets of the Gospel from the hearts of its inhabitants. The whole of their religious history shows that they wanted to keep their faith in all its purity, as they boasted to have received it from Rome. They consequently rejected with horror the error of Nestorius, admitting two persons in Christ. When the Council of Chalcedon condemned Eutyches, who sustained the contrary error, maintaining one person, but only one nature in Christ, the Armenians were absorbed in a desperate struggle for their religious and political independence against Persia; and were easily deceived by the cunning partisans of the heretic, who made them believe that the council had approved of the error of Nestorius, and strange to say, whilst they anathematized Eutyches, they anathematized also the Council of Chalcedon. The Armenian bishops in the course of time understood the question and willingly accepted the decrees of Chalcedon. But the Greeks, who wished, in the interest of their political ends, to separate Armenia from the rest of Christian world, were not satisfied with this acceptation. They objected to the Armenian ritual, which they represented to the Roman authorities as teeming with heretical practices.

Being surrounded by enemies of a different faith, the Armenians, like other nations in similar circumstances, had soon identified their own religious rites with their nationality. The Greeks, who desired the annihilation of the latter, attacked the former *per fas aut nefas*. They claimed besides for the See of Constantinople the right of appointing the patriarch of Armenia, who had the political as well as the religious control of the nation. From one point of view their efforts failed completely; the Armenians clung always more tenaciously to their ritual and privileges. Yet the Greeks succeeded in their ultimate end, the isolation of Armenia from the other Christian churches, to the great injury of Christianity, and especially to the injury of both the spiritual and political interests of Armenia.

The spiritual and intellectual benefit that Armenia could derive from her union with the old Roman See, the corner-stone of the Holy Church, as it is still styled in the Armenian liturgy, is but too clearly demonstrated by the flourishing condition of the United Armenian Church, and by the unceasing and successful efforts of the Papacy to ameliorate the temporal condition of her subjects. Unfortunately, the prejudice against Rome is still so deeply rooted in the mind of the Armenians that very few can think they can join the Catholic Church without losing their nationality. The Greek Empire has been extinct for many centuries, but its works have outlived it as far as Armenia is concerned. And strange to say, the latter looks now towards its successors, the Russians, for protection. Under Russian government they might, perhaps, find temporal advantage, but they would lose the control of their religious affairs.

All their bishops must be what their patriarch, the Catholicos of Echmiazin, has been for some time, the humble servants of the Czar, who would see that no religious denomination excepting the orthodox, so called, shall come in contact with them. The mode in which Russia would administer Armenia may be surmised from this instance of my own personal experience. Journeying through Asia lately, I was permitted to travel freely through Russian Armenia as long as I had nothing to do with the Armenian hierarchy, but when I manifested my desire of visiting the monastery of Echmiazin, whither I was attracted by a number of cuneiform inscriptions, the aim of my scientific mission, I was prevented from doing so by an order which emanated from St. Petersburg, and was seen safely off to the Persian frontier.

No wonder that Armenians, persecuted and oppressed by the masters of their native land, seek elsewhere freedom and justice. Closely resembling the Hebrews, they display an extraordinary vitality as well as a great aptitude in settling among other nations, adopting their mode of living without losing their own nationality. Like the sons of Abraham, again, they show wonderful business tact, and in the Orient they may be called their superiors. Hence the Oriental saying: "Where the Armenians have settled, the Hebrews need not come; it takes three Hebrews to outdo a Greek, and three Greeks to outdo an Armenian."

Kindly Character of the Kurds

A few remarks on the probable cause of the recent troubles which have so engaged our interest and sympathy may fitly close this paper. Some lay the blame on the Kurds, whom they represent as a blood-thirsty people who revel in taking the lives of Christians just because they are Christians; others place the blame on the Sultan himself, and say the slaughter of the Christians was not perpetrated by the Kurds, but by the regular military force of Turkey. On the other hand, the Sublime Porte pleads that the facts have been considerably exaggerated and entirely misrepresented; that it is not true that thousands of Armenians have been murdered in hatred of their faith, but it is true that some of them were put to death for having tried to excite their co-religionists to rebellion against the lawful government of the country. But what amount of truth may be contained in these various contradictory reports no one can tell, nor will ever be able to tell—not even the Sublime Porte itself; so inaccessible is the scene of the troubles, so unreliable are the different rumors on account of the many interests at stake. Because of the lack of evidence, we cannot see where, of what kind, and on what side was the first wrong; nor how an incident, in itself insignificant, such as the theft of a horse or a gun, could develop into a political imbroglio that stirs the governments of Europe and America. I can tell you, however, from similar events which have taken place in the past, whom the chief actors in this sad tragedy must have been—not only the actors, but, what is more important and more desirable to know, the authors. First of all, what share of responsibility rests on the Kurds? I do not hesitate to say very little, in spite of the very serious charges brought against them by misinformed lecturers. Of course the Kurds are not exactly types of Christian meekness; they do not deny that they are thieves—they are even proud of that title. Amongst them a thief is equivalent to an independent man, a gentleman. They justly consider themselves as the only true masters of the mountains where they live, having the right to levy a tribute on the caravans that go through their territory. Occasionally they will plunder a village, Armenian or other; but very rarely will they kill those whom they rob, unless resistance be offered; which is very seldom the case, inasmuch as the Kurds do not deem it wise to attack a caravan or village that can offer them resistance. Besides, by killing people they would destroy a precious and durable source of revenue—a dead sheep cannot be fleeced twice. Occasionally they have murdered people, but in almost every case they seemed to have been the instrument of some other party. I lived five months amongst them, not in one place only, but in the Russian as well as in the Persian and Turkish portions of Armenia—nay, in the environs of Lake Van and Mount Ararat, where they are most dreaded on account of the facility with which they can flee from one country into the other, and in that manner escape official punishment. I always found the Kurds kind and hospitable. I can say that my life was never in real danger amongst them. I wonder, indeed, whether I could go through the mining camps and ranches, of our Western States with as much safety and comfort.

Helplessness of the Porte

As far as the Sublime Porte is concerned, I do not think it deserves more to be blamed than the Kurds. Neither the Sultan personally, nor his advisers, have anything to gain by the shedding of Christian blood in those remote portions of the Empire. The walis, or governors, although appointed by the Sultan, are independent as to their administration. They are never molested, provided they pay to the Sultan the yearly sum of money which is supposed to be equivalent to the taxes levied in the country, minus a competent salary for the governor himself. You can, therefore, easily understand how widely the doors are open to corruption and injustice. From the lowest up to the highest, the officers of the local administration impose on the helpless population in the most outrageous way. The victims, when tired of that play, will, of course, try to appeal to the Sultan. Maybe, also, some dissatisfied inferior officer will bring accusations against the governor in Constantinople, where the accusers will find the support of some intriguer who aspires to the governorship of the province. The governor is then in danger of losing his situation, and even his life. His usual device then is to represent himself as the discoverer of some conspiracy against the government. To find witnesses among his favorites is easy for him, but he wants more than this; he must have the testimony of the Armenians themselves. Innocent men will be seized, thrown into jail, and tortured until they reveal an imaginary conspiracy. As soon as the conspiracy is discovered, the governor wires to the Sultan the good news announcing that he is at work repressing the rebels. Then begins a series of persecutions of every description on the Armenian people. Sometimes the victims will resist; who will blame them for that? The governor finds in resistance a pretext for additional vexations and cruelties. What he does not do himself he will pay the Kurds to do; and of course, in spite of their good qualities, the Kurds when well paid can easily be coaxed to plunder and kill. The whole province is then in insurrection. The governor sends to Constantinople for more troops; and when, after long delays, they come he starts to put out the fire he kindled himself.

Russian Intrigues

The governor is not always the only one to play that game. There is another party who generally takes a hand in it, and plays it well too; this other player is Russia. You all know that Russia owns a large portion of Armenia—very nearly half of it. It is no secret in political circles that she wants more, and watches very anxiously every opportunity of interfering in the political affairs of Turkish Armenia. The fact that Echmiazin, the Armenian Rome, is in their hands gives the Russians a great prestige in the eyes of the ignorant Armenians of Turkey, who have no one to guide them but their priests, who in turn are guided by the patriarch, who is himself the humble servant of the Czar. The Russian consul of Van has, therefore, considerable influence, which he uses in the interest of his government. Either he or his chancellor are constantly travelling from one end of the country to the other. He is everywhere. Every Armenian knows him and welcomes him as the representative of a powerful and friendly Christian neighbor, of a protector, maybe a liberator. Of course the governor hates him, but he fears him too much to act directly against him. He will take his revenge out of the Armenians, some of whom will be arrested and made confess a conspiracy. Officially both the governor and the consul complain of and throw the blame on one another. Secretly both rejoice and expect a reward from their respective governments. I need hardly add that one of them only has a right to it. The governor plays the game for himself, to the detriment of the Sublime Porte, whilst the consul plays faithfully for the Czar, whose ever-growing empire will soon extend down to the plains of Mesopotamia, and that, I am afraid, to the great injury of Christianity.

The Eastern Question

W. J. Stillman[109]

The sudden halt in the English action in the Armenian redemption has surprised every one, and irritated some of the political agencies which had hoped, for various and different reasons, to see England plunge into the solution of the interminable and insoluble Eastern question, and are correspondingly either dismayed or disappointed by the sudden and hitherto unaccountable recoil from the advanced position Lord Salisbury had taken. It is well known that Russia had at all times opposed the English plans, because they promised a solution of the problem of what to do with the Sick Man, by eliminating the cause of the malady, viz., the gangrene of Mussulman misrule—deposing the Sultan and imposing a ruler who would have to admit the right of Europe to dictate the conditions of government where it had the duty and the charge of protection; or of finally dividing the country according to the general interests of the protecting Powers and of the populations. I suppose that it may be taken as indisputable that there were those among the powerful, if not among the Powers, who desired that England should precipitate the eternally impending conflict in Europe, to give them a chance to settle some outstanding accounts of their own; and others who really desired the final regulation of the Eastern question in the real interests of European tranquillity. Others there were who fully expected, without any especial interest, that England, having put her hand to the plough, would go through the furrow. All were alike surprised at the sudden halt. Writing to an esteemed correspondent in London, one of the oldest and best informed journalists of England, I had expressed some of these feelings as entertained here and by myself, as warmly interested, through past experiences, in the Turkish problem, and was surprised to receive from him the following reply:

> It is never of much use to prophesy in politics, but I venture to differ with you about Turkey. It is the old story. England is always defeated, as she was about Egypt, until suddenly she strikes some tremendous stroke, and then the world says, Who would have thought it? Of course if Mr. Cleveland is seeking war with us, all calculations are vain; but if not, I venture to say that nothing but the removal of this Sultan can save Turkey from partition. Very slowly and very silently the English are getting to their white heat. However, it is useless arguing about the future. At present the only thing certain is that we are going to add two millions a year to the grant for the navy.

Not having been looking westward for some time, absorbed in Eastern questions, I had no knowledge of the controversy, rather than negotiations, going on between the United States of America and England with regard to Venezuela, and I replied, supposing I knew something of public opinion in America, that there could be no danger of such a fire in the rear, and that nothing in the Venezuelan question justified a fear that the United States would provoke a quarrel when this so important question was pending of the existence of millions of Christians in Turkey, whose only hope was in the efficacy of English intervention. I could not believe that Cleveland could so far melt into the Jingo as to join in the hullabaloo of the shallow-pated crowd whose highest ambition seems to be "twist the lions tail."

It seems that I was mistaken, and now I recur to an earlier letter of the same respected correspondent, written in November, in which occurs the following passage:

> If you will read attentively the latter part of the speech of Lord Salisbury at the Mansion House, you will see that in his own mind he has doomed the Ottoman Empire, and he has a majority of 152. I dare say you know, better than I do, that the confidential reports to this Government represent the massacres in a much worse light than the papers do.* The Sultan has

---

*This I did know. The confidential reports received in Rome far exceed all that the governments have allowed to appear in print.

> *resolved on the extermination of the Armenian people. I expect some "incident" hourly which will bring matters to a head—perhaps a great massacre of American missionaries, in which case we should act instantaneously, even if all Europe opposed and threatened us. Inferior Turks know nothing of America, and are furious with the missionaries.*

The writer of the above is eminent Liberal, not a partisan of Salisbury, a consistent and devoted Christian, and, like the greater part of the English people, interested in the work of our missionaries and in the pure humanity of the Turkish problem. The position of the English nation was greatly controlled by this sentiment, and perhaps, of all the late great movements of English public opinion, this was the least selfish and profoundest in its appeal to the best part of the English nature. Adequately supported, it must have settled the question of how long Christian Europe would let the slaughter of unoffending Christians be carried on by a fanatic Sultan, served by a bloodthirsty mob and an equally bloodthirsty and fanatical soldiery, under the protection of Christian Powers. From Russia nothing was to be hoped for, as the Russian (people or Government) detests the Armenian only less than does the Turk; and as the Armenian is the most civilized and teachable of the many races in Asia Minor, he is that one who will most easily be brought to the work of putting in order the reformed Empire—which does not suit the schemes of Russia.

Thanks to President Cleveland and his fire in the rear, England has been stopped in her benefaction, and it is Christianity, not English interests, which must pay the bill; for, with this nefarious attack at such a critical moment, it is out of the question that England could allow herself to be engaged in any difficulty on the other side of the Atlantic. England had only to do her best that the attempted solution shall not lose ground and human interests go backward, and hope in the spring to be able to resume the action where it was left off, with the tide perhaps at the ebb, while it was before at the flood, with Russia thoroughly prepared and her ascendancy over the Sultan assured beyond any contest. The missionaries are not murdered because the Power that could have protected the Armenians, and would not, would have the missionaries protected for fear of the intervention becoming more prompt and effectual; but the murdering and outrage go on as steadily if not as multitudinously as before, and the extermination of a Christian people goes on from day to day systematically and deliberately, though in such a way as to permit the great Powers not to be driven, despite themselves, to recognize the fact that nothing has been done to redeem the situation, and that when the spring comes with the Russian intervention ready, there will be the new pretext that the remnant of the Armenian population is not large enough to justify the chance of war on their behalf.

This is the triumph of Mr. Cleveland. It is hardly necessary to say that throughout Italy, where there are no enemies of the United States, but mostly warm friends, the voice of condemnation for this unprovoked and unnecessary crisis, which disturbs the best intentions of Italy as well as England, is universal. Not a single journal or public man speaks otherwise than in condemnation of the course of our Government; and in a land where constitutional law has a special study, not a constitutional lawyer can frame an excuse for the same.

Rome, December 22, 1895

Aid for Armenia: An Appeal for Immediate Help

The situation of the Armenian Christians is pitiable almost beyond expression. Leaving the political and international phases of the Eastern question out of view altogether, the entire world of humane people is urgently called upon for sympathy and assistance. This aid must be prompt to be of avail. Letters from the ravaged districts show that famine is following massacre. One letter just received from Van says: "All business and work of all kinds have been stopped for two months—which means starvation to hundreds. And, worst of all, there is no light ahead!" The misery in Harpoot, Bitlis, Erzeroum, and scores of the villages is intense, and increases as winter approaches. In this terrible need the Red Cross Society, the Armenian Relief Fund, the Evangelical Alliance, and the American Board are combining their efforts to direct the contributions of Americans into their most useful channels. So far the response has been in no way adequate to the pressing demand. As our readers know, the actual work of relief is to be undertaken by the National Red Cross Society. Miss Clara Barton,[110] at a great meeting held last Saturday night in the First Congregational Church of Washington, announced her intention to wait no longer for the accumulation of funds, but to sail within two weeks to the scene of work. She will be accompanied, it is understood, by the financial secretary of the National Red Cross Society, Mr. George E. Pullman, by Dr. Hubbell, the general field agent, probably by Mr. Stephen E. Barton, the second Vice President, by Miss Bettina Hofker, Sister Superintendent of the New York Red Cross Hospital, and by several other assistants of trained ability and executive force. The collection of funds is in charge of the National Armenian Relief Fund, of which

Justice Brewer, of the United States Supreme Court, is President. Branches of the Committee have been formed in many large cities, and the work of organization is being pushed rapidly forward. Information may be had from the headquarters of 45 William Street, New York. The Relief Fund Committee has already sent large sums of money and much clothing to Armenia, and reports of the distribution show that the facilities for the work are greater than many suppose. The Committee say: "If for any reason the National Red Cross should be prevented from accomplishing the work of relief through its own agency by the opposition of the Turkish Government, responsible existing agencies will be utilized, or new ones organized, so that all contributors may be assured that their gifts will as speedily as possible reach the sufferers for whom they were intended." Next week the Outlook will print an illustrated article on Miss Barton's personality and her connection with the Red Cross Society, and will present fully the claims of the cause upon the sympathy of the American people. Meanwhile we shall be glad to send forward any subscriptions which our readers may mail to the Outlook. The need is for instant financial aid. All sums sent by check payable to the Outlook Company will be forwarded with all possible dispatch. To begin the movement, the Outlook itself now subscribes the sum of $250.

The Turkish Legation gave out on Monday afternoon at Washington the following official communication:

> The Imperial Government will not permit any distribution among its subjects, in its own territory, by any foreign society or individuals, however respectable the same may be (as for instance the Red Cross Society) of money collected abroad. Such interference no independent Government has ever allowed, especially when the collections are made on the strength of speeches delivered in public meetings by irreconcilable enemies of the Turkish race and religion, and on the basis of false accusation that Turkey repudiates. Besides, the Sublime Porte is mindful of the true interests of its subjects, and, distinguishing between the real state of things and the calumnies and wild exaggerations of interested or fanatical parties, will, as it had done heretofore, under its own legitimate control, alleviate the wants of all Turkish subjects, living in certain provinces, irrespective of creed or race.

The reason for this extraordinary declaration is patent; if the Red Cross Society goes, with its agents, into the desolated region, the news about the desolation will assuredly come back to stir still further the already profoundly stirred hearts of Christians. But it is not true that the Porte either can or will adequately alleviate the suffering of the Armenians. A letter from Aintab, printed below, gives one illustration of the employment of American means to alleviate Armenian distress. This was both right and necessary. If in one case, why not in many? Nor is it true that such a distribution of benevolence is an interference such as no independent government could ever allow. No such case has ever before arisen, but benevolence by one nation to the citizens of another, suffering from whatever cause, is happily no longer uncommon. China did not resent such benevolence when her subjects were dying of famine. We are glad to see that the Red Cross Society is not discouraged, but proposes to go on with its work, and we trust that the pressure from Christian Powers for the admission of its ministering messengers will prove to be too strong to be resisted even by the Sultan.

The Aintab Atrocities

The following personal letter has been received from a medical missionary at Aintab, Turkey, on the border of the devastated districts. The writer, Dr. Caroline F. Hamilton, was a graduate of Smith College in the class of 1885, and was a worker at the College Settlement in this city before her departure for Turkey. Her calm statement of the scenes about her reforms as an effective appeal for aid in the general relief work which we speak above.

Aintab, December 4-10, 1895
For weeks before the outbreak here, there had been much alarm felt in the city. Troops were passing through constantly on their way to the north, and in the markets and streets insults were offered to Christians, goods were taken without payment, etc., till the people kept indoors as much as possible, and the schools were closed for a few days, but afterward were opened. Had we known of events outside we should have felt far more uneasy. Our first news came from Oorfa and Marash, both sacked, and then our turn came. The morning of November 16, on going to the hospital, the cook told me that there was trouble in the city, and the horror-stricken faces of the servants confirmed the word. One glance from the windows—for the hospital stands on a hill which overlooks nearly the whole city—was sufficient to show that there was cause for alarm. A great mob was

surging through the streets, to a quarter so near that we could look down on the houses being plundered and torn to pieces—could watch the mob as it filled the streets and courtyards, and could hear the yells of the Kurds and the shrieks of terror from the poor defenseless people—while all the time the constant firing of the Kurds (for they are permitted to carry arms), with, underneath all, a hoarse roar like that of wild beasts, made up a frightful combination of sounds. The poor servants who had come a few hours before from their homes in that very section were entirely demoralized, and could do nothing but cry and wring their hands, for all had left little children.

Our gates were instantly closed and barred; no one admitted except a good Moslem neighbor whom we shall always regard as our guardian angel. He begged us to take refuge in his house, but there were patients too ill to be moved, and we, of course, could not leave. The servants could not work, so terrified were they; and we two women, the only Americans on the premises, settled down to dressing patients and waiting on them, giving comfort as we could to the frightened, sorrowful people about us. It was not till night that we learned how our neighbor had held a mob at bay till the soldiers arrived, thus saving us from being sacked, if not from worse things. All day long our chief work was to comfort patients and servants, and try to keep them away from the windows. No one could go home, and we found what accommodations were possible for them all. However, nobody could sleep, the least sound startling us all.

Sunday morning (November 17) a sight met our eyes that was far from reassuring. From all directions villagers were seen flocking in toward the city, and soon they had massed down near the old castle. At every spare moment I looked to see what was forthcoming—hearing again and again a great noise as this new mob were repulsed in their attempts to gain an entrance into the city. As we were at dinner, they made a move toward our end of the city, and after a half-hour they had passed the guards—who were forbidden to fire—and were rushing toward the houses close at hand. Never can I forget that sight. They were not men, but beasts, wild to get at their prey. The feeling of utter helplessness and the knowledge of what we were handed over to were awful. We called together all the people who were in our house and quietly told them to go with us to the hospital, thinking it would be easier to die together. To understand how we were shut off from other people, I might here explain that every house, or group of houses, is walled in, with one large door opening out into the street. Thus our house and the hospital are in one inclosure, the girls' seminary in another, while the boys'

Aid for Armenia: An Appeal

college and professors' house are some ten minutes distant from here.

We could not see what was taking place, and only wondered that we remained safe. After a couple of hours the good old Moslem neighbor came in with the first detachment of wounded. It was a sight to sicken the bravest heart, for most of the wounds were made with axes and large knives, and little children, women, and old men as well as the young and strong had been attacked as they fled.

Dr. S—— could not get over from the college, and our native physician was shut up in his house, so we two women went to work with our touring missionary, Mr. Sanders, and the nurses and even our house servants for assistants. It was a question where to begin, with a shattered leg, hands and arms nearly hewn off, heads fairly laid open, and a terrible abdominal wound all lying before us, besides over a dozen with minor injuries. By dark we had them all in beds, or in a room over our stables, cold and dreary, but comparatively safe.

It was another hard night. Our nurses, etc., had no news of the fate of their families, and could not go to inquire. We knew not whether the dreaded villagers were preparing for other attacks. All night long the northern sky was brilliant, and we knew some dreadful fate must have befallen our neighboring city, where we had dear friends. Not a sound could be heard from without, and the very silence seemed to forebode evil. If we had not had our work in those two days and nights, it would be well-nigh intolerable.

No outbreak has occurred since November 17, save for an uprising a week from that date, which was promptly put down by the soldiers. Strong guards are all about us, and four soldiers are in the hospital—quiet men, who are very friendly.

The neighbor mentioned above has been as good as a father to us all. He and his brother, whose life was saved by a former American physician, were up night after night, afraid of some sudden raid. They secured provisions for the hospital and for us, even sitting in the bakery while the bread was being baked, for fear it would be carried away. They went for news for our people, protected the poor refugees as they went to recover what was left in their houses, and if any disturbance alarmed them when in other parts of the city, home they hurried to see that all was right here. Both the 16th and 17th they saved our premises and the Seminary.

November 19 those wounded three days before were brought in in squads by the soldiers, who had received orders to hunt them up in the stables and holes whither they crawled. In two days over seventy were registered.

I never saw such a sight in my life. Covered with blood which had dried on head, hands, clothing—weak from lack of food, from the loss of blood, and the pitiless cold—frightened so that several were wildly insane, one could not endure the sight except to go to work and try to make them more comfortable. Beds were soon full; others were glad to lie on mattresses on the floor; those half well camped down on any old cushions we could give them—some finding a lodging in our operating-room even—while some poor creatures lay on the floor in the clinic-room. The hospital has been feeding fifty-five people without one penny of income, while giving shelter, fuel, and occasional food to thirty more, who were driven from their homes. We are besieged every day by those who would gladly find shelter here, but we are so crowded now that we can scarcely turn. One poor woman saw her husband killed before her eyes by the villagers, and her house plundered of everything except two beds and two blankets. With four little children, no home, and no food, she is utterly heartbroken. Another woman, whose husband was so badly injured that his arm had to be amputated, said that this was the first winter since their marriage that they had been able to put in their wheat, charcoal, etc. She used to "pat the box" where these were stored, so glad was she at their prosperity. Now all is gone, and the wage-earner crippled for life. She, her old mother, and her sister have but one pair of old slippers between them.

These are only instances.

The churches and school buildings are filled with women and children, cold and hungry, the husbands and fathers in prison or dead. Efforts are being made to provide food and clothing, but industry is paralyzed, and only a few have means to help, and there are multitudes to be cared for. Scarcely a Christian shop but has been plundered, and there is no capital to begin with if confidence is restored. Houses are not only sacked, but even doors and window-sashes are carried away. With winter before us, it almost seems better had the utter annihilation of some other regions been the lot of these poor people, and not the hopeless poverty into which they are plunged—and yet that is a cruel thing to say. Except for the few wealthy ones, and the few who have assured salaries in our schools and families, all are plunged into destitution.

The Armenian Resolutions

E. L. Godkin

There has been more debating in the House and Senate over the Armenian resolutions than there was over the Venezuelan correspondence, but no more real taking of counsel. The discussion in the House on Monday had the aerial character which usually marks the fiery utterances of young men's debating clubs. Where else but in the proceedings of such a body would one find it solemnly resolved that "it was an imperative duty, in the interests of humanity, to express an earnest hope" that somebody else would behave properly? What other body would order the Secretary to send this resolution to six first-class Powers as an encouragement to execute one of their own treaties to which we are no more a party than the Y.M.C.A.? We may imagine the hilarity with which it will be received in the various European chancelleries, and the mock solemnity with which its receipt will be acknowledged. We doubt whether it is worth while to notice that the resolutions abandon that part of the Monroe Doctrine which denies our right "to take part in the wars of European Powers in matters relating to themselves"; also Secretary Olney's recent interpretation of the Doctrine, which shuts us out from "wars or preparations of wars with whose causes or results we have no direct concern," and which closes with the remark: "If all Europe were to suddenly fly to arms over the fate of Turkey, would it not be preposterous that any American state should find itself inextricably involved in the miseries and the burdens of the contest? If it were, it would prove to be a partnership in the cost and losses of the struggle, but not in any ensuing benefits."

In fact it would not be easy to make up, by inference, a more complete repudiation of our doctrine of non-interference in European matters, as the complement of the non-interference of Europe in ours.

The new revised Doctrine now is, that we may interfere in European affairs when we see the European Powers plainly neglecting their duty to each other, or when in any part of Europe "the hand of fanaticism and lawless violence" seems to us too strong, or when "men and Christians" in any part of Europe seem to us to be deprived of due legal protection. But surely we ought not to refuse this sympathy to "men and Jews", and yet we have never threatened Russia for expelling her Jewish population under circumstances of great cruelty. Lastly, how are we to assert this right to look after the manner to which European Powers discharge their domestic duties, without granting them the right to pass resolutions and address exhortations to us about our negligences and failure—about our mob law, for instance, as expressed in the unpunished murder of the Italians in the jail in New Orleans a few year ago; in the massacre of the Chinamen in Wyoming; in the numerous, continued, and horrible lynchings all over the country? Are we prepared to accept meekly resolutions of reprobation on these topics from the British Parliament, and the Reichstag, and the Russian Chancellery, and the retort courteous from the Sultan? We doubt it greatly, and yet the probability that we shall have to put up with it, on principles of reciprocity, was never mentioned in the debate.

This vain talk was followed, as usual, by a stern resolve to "stand behind" the President in "the most vigorous action he may take for the protection and security of Armenian citizens" in Turkey. What would or could "our most vigorous action" be? The whole of our fleet put together would not be more than sufficient to force its way up to Constantinople, if all the Powers agreed to stand aside and let it be done. Some of our ships would be sunk in the process. The others would arrive in a dilapidated condition. Both banks of the Bosphorus would be in possession of the enemy, and that enemy a hostile and fanatical population, which fights Christians with great fierceness. Without the land force, where would our coal and supplies come from, and how would the ships get back again after the Turks had time to prepare for their return? Suppose the Sultan, under treat of bombardment, were to agree to restore order in Armenia, how would this benefit the Armenians?

They are hundreds of miles away from Constantinople, and they are being massacred by local Mussulmans who pay no attention to the Sultan's orders. *The Sultan has already made to the Powers all the promises which we could possibly extract from him by any action, however vigorous*, without helping Armenians in the smallest degree. Moreover, there is no proof that we have received any injury from the Sultan, except the destruction of property, and for this, according to all accounts, he is willing to pay.

If we were talking to practical men of business, or serious diplomatists, and not mere Jingoes, we should point out that there are only two ways in which we can do anything for the Armenians. One is to threaten Russia with war if she, the only Power which can act promptly and effectively in the matter, does not occupy Armenia and restore order. The other is to offer to support Great Britain in any measures she may take to carry out the Treaty of Berlin. She has undoubtedly been checked in her recent attempt to coerce the Sultan by the fear that she might find herself acting alone or in the face of a powerful opposition, for she is not a general favorite, and France wants Egypt, and Russia Constantinople. But such support, to be really effective, would involve the despatch to the Mediterranean of a powerful naval squadron and say 50,000 men of a land force. We have little doubt, speaking under naval and military correction, that this, with the troops which England could assemble from England and India, would carry everything before it in Asia Minor, and that the spectacle of the two great Anglo-Saxon Powers acting together, not for aggrandizement but for order and civilization, would be one of the finest the modern world has ever seen. But, Jingo brethren, it would involve the abandonment of the sacred Doctrine of "the immortal Monroe," and it would commit you to the cares and responsibilities and dangers of European politics, and—harder than all—it would compel you to be civil to the odious "Britishers." If you are not ready for something of this sort, the less you vapor and threaten, the more the civilized world will respect you.

The Turks and the Armenians

Elbert Francis Baldwin

One of the three most remarkable epochs in the world's history was the Gothic age. With it we irresistibly associate the barons of Runnymede, and the great names of Saint Louis and Saint Ferdinand, the greater name of Dante. We rarely remember to put with them another name representing, it is true, no Christian advance; instead, one in Islam. The name is Othmân or Osmân, and from that name is derived Ottoman or Osmanli. Othmân's father was the leader of a wild heathen band from Central Asia. Until recently the subjects of the Ottoman Empire have recognized only the names Ottomans or Osmanlis, not that of Turk, which applies to a wider race. The Uighurs, or Turks, were pushed forth from Central Asia by the Mongols. The Turks gradually came west, and were probably, like the Kurds of to-day, a wild race supplying neighboring rulers with mercenary troops. They settled in Khorasân (the northeastern province of Persia). They began their career first as slaves and then as mercenary soldiers. Being of great beauty and vigor, they were favorites with all the princes with whom they came in contact, and whom they well served. They developed before long into a military aristocracy, and ended in becoming Seljuk Sultans, governing most of the Khalifs' dominions in Asia. They even controlled the power of the Persians and Arabs. Out of the many tribes of Turks, one came into Asia Minor, and it was the good fortune of its leader to help the Seljuk Sultan in battle against the Mongols at Angora (1250). Gaining the victory through his help, the Sultan gave to his supporters a few square miles of land under Bithynian Olympus; the name of the place was Sugat, and these few square miles became the nucleus of the Ottoman Empire.

The leader of the Turks had managed affairs so well as to obtain for his son Othmân the succession of the Seljuk Sultan. Othmân–a prince of much physical prowess, bravery, and patience, qualities which he transmitted to his descendants—continually advanced his small domain (making Brûsa his capital), until it absorbed northwestern Asia Minor. One of the cleverest methods of conquest was in the formation of the Janissaries (new troops), composed of children taken when young from conquered races, generally Christians. The new soldiers were compelled to become Muslims and to undergo a life of severe discipline. Separated from family and country, given great pay, and opportunity for the gratification of ambition and pleasure, this military organization became a redoubtable instrument. Seventy years ago the Janissaries were suppressed: they had grown too arrogant. The Ottoman civil and military government was regarded in such a friendly way that the Greek Emperor did not even object when the Turks crossed the Hellespont, and for the first time took possession of European soil. About this time a convenient earthquake happened and the walls of Gallipoli fell down. The Turks immediately marched in, declaring that Providence had opened the city to them and they could not think of disregarding so clear an instance of divine interposition. From Gallipoli in a few years the Turks had all over what is now known as Turkey in Europe, and then began to conquer the outlying provinces—Servia, Bulgaria, Rumania.

This development of Turkish aggrandizement had been a wonderful one, and it occupied only a century and a half. We shall look far and wide to find a parallel. The reason for this growth was not in the circumstances which surrounded the Turks, but in the great abilities which each of their rulers represented. Cruel they were, and rudely ruled a rude race; yet there is no question as to their pre-eminent power in militarism and statecraft. Now, however, there came an event which not only delayed fifty years the capture of Constantinople, but seemed to blot out the Ottoman Empire. It was the descent of Tamerlane. This great warrior was himself of Mongol-Turkish race, and had established his dominion throughout lower Russia, Central Asia, India, Persia, and Syria, but he had been resisted by the Mamluk Sultans of Egypt, and by the Ottoman Sultan of Turkey. The latter was crushed by Tamerlane on that same plain of Angora where the Ottoman Empire had taken its start. The Muslims, believers in fate, regarded the Empire doomed where it had begun.

Yet, by the energy of a great man—the Sultan Mohammed—the start was made all over again, and only half a century sufficed to rebuild the Empire, to overwhelm the Christians with just retribution for their perfidy, and to capture Constantinople. How could all this be done, and so soon? First, because of the superiority in physical and moral worth of the Ottoman Turks; because they represented a better government than those about them; because the disintegrated peoples of Asia Minor in the south and the conquered Christians in the north had become so impressed with these things that they were ready to fuse with the Turks, even to accepting the religion of the latter; and because the clever Ottomans made no difference between born and converted Muslims in preferment; indeed, most of the Grand Vezirs have been of Christian or of Jewish birth.

After Constantinople, the Crimea, Greece, Armenia, and Kurdistân were taken, while a foothold was gained on the Italian coast, at Ottranto. More important conquests now followed—those of Mesopotamia, Syria, Arabia, and Egypt; this was not only a vast addition, but, what was of infinitely greater moment, gave to the Ottoman Sultan the title of Khalif, for by the conquest of the Mamlûks he succeeded to their supremacy over the sacred cities of Mecca and Medina, while the last of the Baghdad Khalifs made over to the Ottoman Sultan the symbols of his high office—namely, the cloak and the standard of the Prophet himself. Then came the conquest of Hungary; but when Suleïmân the Magnificent would take Vienna, his siege came to naught, and the Ottoman Empire met its rebuff. Still, its conquests increased, as a rule, in spite of a second check—this time at Lepanto; Cyprus, Tunis, and Georgia were added to the Empire, and the first conflict experienced with Russia. The year 1600 marked the point of greatest territorial extent.

Then followed a decline; Turkey itself receded, then it was dismembered. Hungary was first lopped off, then Transylvania, then Wallachia, and so on; and the Empire had to acknowledge the independence of peoples once subject to it. We have noted the causes of growth; those of decline are no less evident. In the first place, Turkey has ever been a consumer, not a producer; a military power, she has fattened on what conquered lands could give her;

she gave them nothing. Often she gave them worse than nothing—cruelty, brutal lust, slavery. After Suleïmân–a prince who held his own in that Renaissance age which saw a Charles V, an Elizabeth, a Francis I, a Leo X,—there was, in place of barbaric but direct government, indirection and the growing seclusion of the Sultan, induced largely by the pernicious harim influence. The first ten Sultans had been robust, able, cruel; the last twenty-five (save Mahmûd II) have been no less cruel, but no longer robust, no longer able. There were now, however, external causes to accentuate the internal, the chief of which was Russia's rise. By 1700 the Turkish dominions in Europe had shrunk to half their former extent. The next century saw Russian aggrandizement come to such a point that not only did the Crimean Khanate become independent of Turkey, but gates at Moscow and Kherson were inscribed "The Way to Constantinople," and Constantine became henceforth an honored name in the Russian Imperial family. Later events—Navarino, the disaffection of Egypt, the treaty of Unkiar-Skelessi (last week rumored to have been readopted), the Crimean war reaction, quickly followed by the Lebanon affair, the independence of Rumania, the successive revolts of the Herzegovina, of Bulgaria, Servia, and Montenegro, resulting in the Russo-Turkish war, and the further dismemberment of Turkey in both Europe and Asia—are not these summed up in Lord Beaconsfield's phrase, "Peace with honor"?—a phrase which has meant so much peace to some of the European states, little and big, so little honor to Great Britain and Turkey. The latter's hold in Europe, both in area and population, is now reduced to less than one-fourth of what it once was. It still has much of its vast area and population in Asia; but in Africa the loss of Algiers, Tunis, and Egypt takes away two-thirds of its area and twelve times the present population in Tripoli.

  Fifty years ago the Emperor Nicholas said to Sir Hamilton Seymour[111]: "We have on our hands a sick man, a very sick man." The present invalid is the Sultan Abdul-Hamid II. He succeeded to the throne in 1876, on the desposition of his older brother, Murad V, who was declared to be suffering from idiocy, and has since been kept in strict seclusion. Abdul-Hamid is the thirty-fifth sovereign in uninterrupted male descent of the House of Othmân, the founder of the Empire. No family in European history can show such an example of continuous authority. The crown is inherited by the eldest male descendant in the Imperial line, no matter whether he be the Sultan's son, uncle, cousin, or nephew.

The Government of Turkey is often called the "Sublime Porte." This name is taken from the only gate in general use along the quay which runs outside the whole length of the sea wall of Constantinople. It is called Bab-i-Humayûm (the great gate of the Seraglio), or the Sublime Porte. In the old days, just without this gate pyramids of heads used to piled up, trophies of war. The Sublime Porte really means the Sultan. He is absolute in matters both temporal and spiritual. He delegates his authority in temporal things to his Grand Vezir, and in religious affairs to the Sheik-ul-Islam. In connection with the Sultan and Grand Vezir is the Privy Council, the Ministers of which, however, are little more than secretaries. Connected with the Sheïk-ul-Islâm is the Ulema, a body comprising priests and lawyers, and also the Mufti, the interpreters of the Koran. The Government is thus before everything a theocracy, and is irreformable to any permanent degree. True, a constitution was proclaimed in 1876, but it lasted only a few months. There can be no equality of Muslim and Christian before the law. Yet the Sultan has repeatedly promised "perfect equality of civil rights" to all his subjects. What he really has had to do, however, is to exercise his Khalifate. By its votaries the Mohammedan religion is believed to be God's last expression of his will. Therefore, the Sultan, the Muslim counterpart of papal viceregency and infallibility, is not only a sovereign, but he is also an Inquisitor. He must needs compel all to embrace Islam; if the "heathen" will not, then death to them; if Christians and Jews will not, then servitude to them. The Turkish dominion in Europe is about equally divided between Mohammedans and Christians, but in Asia the former form a vast majority. The Christians number those who use the Roman Catholic liturgy, the Greeks, Armenians, Bulgarians, Syrians, Maronites, and Protestants.

The Empire is partitioned into thirty-one departments called Vilayets. These are subdivided into provinces (Sanjaks), and these in turn into districts (Kazaks), and these again into sub-districts and communities. The Governor of a Vilayet is called a Vali, and is assisted by a Provincial Council. The provinces, districts, etc., are governed by authorities, and the names of the Governors of the sub-districts and of communes—Mudir and Muktar—have lately become familiar. The making and carrying out of Turkish law have not yet come to such a state of perfection that foreigners feel like giving up their own consular courts, which they retain, and by means of which are under the same laws as in their respective countries. Cases between foreign and Turkish subjects, however, are tried in the Ottoman courts. Through the prevailing dishonesty, foreign governments are also compelled to maintain their own post-offices in Turkey. Yet, by England at least, Turkish government is apparently thought good enough for unarmed Christians, since, in spite of solemn obligations incurred eighteen years ago, not one thing has the British government done to succor those Christians.

The Turks today are still nomadic. Their agriculture is backward, not so much from soil-sterility in Albania or Asia Minor as from the apathy of the inhabitants to settled vocations. In Macedonia and in Thrace, the soil is fertile, but the same poverty is seen. The people have ruthlessly destroyed their forests. Their mines are unworked despite the gold, silver, copper, and salt known to exist abundantly. With an empire possessing every kind of soil and climate, vegetable, animal, and mineral product, the Ottomans are bankrupt; they seem as alien, as when, six hundred years ago, they emerged from obscurity.

Armenia is a country lying about Mount Ararat as a central point. The country is now partly in Russia, partly in Persia, partly in Asia Minor. Turkish Armenia is about the size of New England; it is a mountain land, some of the Taurus peaks, rising over 10,000 feet. There are a few valleys in which scant rice and cotton may be grown, but the high plateau is mostly a grazing-place. As in the rest of the Ottoman Empire, agriculture is in a pitifully primitive state, and, though there are abundant deposits, mining does not exist. The climate is one of extremes of cold and heat. The sources of the Euphrates and Tigris are in Armenia, and there is also Lake Van, a salt lake. The roads are nothing but bridle-paths; they are infested with brigands, and there are no inns. Geographical isolation is not the least of the hardships in the present crisis.

The Armenians represent an ancient civilization, and have kept their individuality through all ages. Their name comes from an early king, Haik, a descendant of Japhet. Armenia is mentioned several times in the Old Testament; for instance (2 Kings xix., 37), when the sons of Sennacherib are said to have escaped thither. The best-known Armenian king, Tigranes I, was an ally of Cyrus the Great, and in Xenophon's Retreat of the Ten Thousand we have a description of Armenia as it might be today. Then came Alexander's conquest, followed by those of the Parthians, Romans, Byzantines, Saracens, and Turks. The latter overran the country in the eleventh century.

The Armenian language is, like Greek, an independent branch of the Indo-Germanic. The Gothic Bishop Ulfilas was the first to give form to the early German, by his translation of the Bible, and so did the Armenian Bishop Mesrob to Armenian; he invented the Armenian alphabet, and then translated the Bible into that tongue. The language is distinguished by two characteristics; there is no gender, and all words are accented on the last syllable.

There are now about four million Armenians, of whom only 600,000 are in Armenia—a fourth of the entire number in all Turkey. There are 1,250,000 in Russian Armenia, and they are fairly prosperous there; 150,000 in Persian Armenia; 100,000 in Europe; and about 5,000 in this country. The saying runs that if it takes ten Christians to cheat a Jew, it takes ten Jews to cheat an Armenian, and the cleverness of the latter in trade is well known. They go to Constantinople and the great cities whenever possible, and often become affluent. The stay-at-homers attend to their flocks, till their soil, make their honey, and weave their carpets and rugs.

Half the population of Armenia is Muslim, and it is made of Kurds and Turks. The former are by nature brave and hospitable, but are still unsubjugated, and have become brutal from contact with the degenerate Turk. Contrary to the customs of other Mohammedans, they go about unveiled and enjoy much liberty. The Kurds are now organized into guerilla regiments of the Turkish army.

According to legend, the Apostle Thaddeus founded the Armenian Church; according to history, St. Gregory the Illuminator, in 289, when the king was baptized and Christianity became the national religion. The Armenian is supposed to be the oldest of any national Church. As they were at war during the Council of Chalcedon, the Armenians did not attend it and did not approve its decrees. This led to a separation, and about five hundred years ago, a division in the Armenian Church itself occurred when a branch of it acknowledged the Pope's supremacy. The highest Armenian ecclesiastical dignitary is called Katholikos. He resides near Erevan, the capital of Russian Armenia, and at least once in their lives, all Armenians must journey thither. There is a belief in the worship of saints in the Armenian Church, but none in purgatory; there are ignorance and superstition, but the work of foreign missionaries is doing much to break through the dry ecclesiastical crust. In Armenia and Asiatic Turkey, there are about 250 Americans, who hold over $2,000,000 worth of property for religious, medical, and educational uses. These figures do not cover our large commercial interests there.

Until the Crimean War, Russia had exercised for a hundred years a kind of protectorate over the Ottoman Christians, but in 1856 she was deprived of that protectorate, and the Great Powers of Europe, in a collective protectorate, took her place. Russia had always accomplished something with the Sultan; he never forgot that, with one exception, for two centuries Russia had defeated him in every war. Therefore he was delighted at the chance of escaping from dealing with one Power to dealing with a number, for what was everybody's business was nobody's business. Furthermore, he was convinced that the integrity of his Empire was essential to the balance of power in Europe. The best proof of this was that Turkey had been admitted to the comity of nations. British preponderance was meanwhile growing, and in 1880 England bound herself to defend the Armenian frontier against Russia, and to see that reforms were carried out in Armenia. The curious situation is that, should Russia decide to interfere with the awful iniquities which have been going on in Armenia, the Sultan could, under this convention, call upon England to protect him. An added responsibility of England's is found in the Treaty of Berlin. The sixty-first clause of that Treaty declares that the Porte shall carry out the reforms demanded by local requirements in Armenia. As a part of that agreement the Sultan guarantees the security of Armenia against the Circassians and the Kurds, and agrees that he "will periodically make known the steps taken to this end to the Powers, who will superintend their application." Not once has Turkey announced any reforms; there have been none. In the Russo-Turkish Treaty of San Stefano the Sultan had bound himself to introduce reforms in Armenia, and the Russian troops were to remain in that province until such reforms were established. To her shame be it said, England was the only Power insisting upon the submission of the Treaty of San Stefano to the revision of the Congress at Berlin.

Thus eighteen years ago, England and Turkey made their compact. Neither the Christian nor the Muslim Power has since done anything to relieve the situation. For England there is no excuse; for Turkey, the only apology has been that, the population of Armenia being mixed, reforms cannot be instituted applicable to Christians and Mussulmans alike; but, as Canon MacColl points out, precisely the same objections were made to the constitution which Lord Dufferin drew up for Lebanon after the Syrian massacres in 1860. That, however, did not prevent Great Britain insisting that the constitution should be accepted by the Porte, and events since then have abundantly justified such firmness. During these eighteen years, despite the Berlin Treaty, the Armenians have suffered as much as ever—latterly, far more. Their testimony is rarely taken in the courts; it is never acted on (while the uncorroborated evidence of a Mussulman is enough to send a Christian to jail). They may not bear arms. They are harassed by intolerable taxes. In addition to ordinary taxation (the assessing and collecting of which are outrageously performed), for all Christians who refuse to embrace Islam there is either death or ransom from death, a capitation tax. Christians are excluded from the Ottoman army; in place of that service a tax is put on all males from three months old. There are extraordinary taxes for temporary purposes, which are never removed—we learn that the extraordinary tax levied in 1867 to pay the cost of the Sultan's visit to England is still being imposed, though the promise was that it should be levied only for that year. Taxes are often demanded a year in advance, a promise being made that the interval shall be exempted—a promise never kept. Then there is the dreaded hospitality tax. Every Christian subject of the Sultan is legally bound to provide three days' gratuitous hospitality for any Muslim traveler who may chance to demand it. These Mohammedan guests are as unwelcome as they are omnipresent. They require not only the best the house affords in food, drink, and shelter, but they regard no sanctity of person as inviolable; indeed, Canon MacColl sees nothing improbable in the allegation that there is scarcely a Christian woman in Armenia who has not been outraged. While this is probably an exaggeration, we know that failure to pay a tax is regarded by Turkish law as rebellion. The penalty is forfeiture of property or of life. The Armenians have long been compelled to pay blackmail to the tax-gatherers, so that property and life, and that which is dearer than life—the dignity of their women—might be preserved. The Christians have now become so impoverished that they cannot meet all these extortions, for, after paying ordinary taxes, the peasant's share of his crop is but one-third.

This impoverishment was the cause of the Sassun massacre a year and a half ago. The Christians had no money. The Kurds stole flocks from the villages. The Armenians tried to recover the flocks, and a fight took place in which some Kurds were killed. Then it transpired that the latter were enrolled as soldiers. This was exactly what was wanted. The Christians had doubly forfeited their right to life, and an Imperial order went forth to diminish the population. The population was diminished by just so much; it would not do to exterminate the Armenians—the milch-cow business is too good to be destroyed—but the Armenians must be cut down to a certain level. Killing goes on, say from ten to four, when the level is supposed to be reached, but woe to a Turk who kills after four; he himself is summarily shot.

The Turks allege that the Armenians were preparing for a general uprising, and that their minds had been inflamed by paid agitators. The first charge was that the Armenians wished to set up an autonomous government, eventually comprising their co-religionists in Russia and Persia. The next was that the agitators were trying to sow the seed of discontent and anarchy in order to prepare the way for a strong power (Russia) to step in and keep order. A third charge was that the agitators were Nihilists. It is true, as we are told, that the real aim of the Armenians, as a whole, is somewhat obscured by the utterances and acts of a few irresponsible Armenian hotheads.

Whatever may be said as a choice of evils as between Russia and Turkey, in the case of the Armenians there is no longer any question. In his recent book, Mr. Frederick Greene[112] well says:

> Russia is crude, stupid, and, in certain respects, brutal, but she is not decrepit, debauched, and doting like official Turkey. . . . Christians and Mohammedans cannot live together on equal terms under a Mohammedan government, because the Mohammedan religion forbids

that they should; but Mohammedans and Christians may perfectly well live together under a Christian government. They do so under the governments both of England and of Russia.

While there are undoubtedly some honest Turks, no reliance may be placed on any promise of the Sultan, for no Sultan could every carry them out. Religious principle and temporal policy alike forbid. Reform in the Ottoman dominions cannot come from within; it must come from without.

Why the Sultan Is Responsible for the Armenian Massacres

*By an Armenian**

According to the Koran, the Sultan is the absolute and only representative of both State and Church, embodying in his own potentiality the duties and responsibilities pertaining to the government of both. Under the two preceding reigns of Abdul Medjid and Abdul Aziz, the responsibility of the government of the State was delegated, in large measure, to the Porte, and as there were many enlightened statesmen then in office, the more rigid demands of Mohammedan law received a liberal interpretation, and were held in corresponding abeyance. But when Hamid II ascended the throne, being a Pharisee of the Pharisees, a Mohammedan of the Mohammedans, he resolved to do away with anything like interference, and take the whole responsibility upon himself. Therefore he dissolved the so-called parliament created by Midhat Pasha, and proceeded to govern by his own theocratic, autocratic will. Henceforward the Sultan alone was to be Sultan, and the officials were to be but puppets pulled about by the will of their own imperious master. As, in the eyes of Allah, there is nothing great and nothing small, but all the things are of equal importance, so it is with the chosen of Allah who reigns at Stamboul. From the appointment of a policeman in Erzeroum, or the regulation of a theater in Stamboul, to the greatest affair of state, the Sultan is

---

*Author of "The Evil of the Turk," in *The Outlook* for August 24, 1895.

supreme. He alone orders everything, sanctions everything, superintends everything, to the minutest detail. Nothing is so common or trivial but that is must be brought before him for his signature and approval.

As an instance of this, Mr. Stead relates that the British Ambassador told him that he was unable to get his steamlaunch repaired in the Turkish dock-yard, at his own expense, without the matter going before the Sultan for approval. Another ex-Ambassador said that, in an interview with the Sultan, the latter complained of overwork, and pointed to a great pile of papers on the table awaiting his examination and decision as to their disposal. The Ambassador, glancing his eye at these important documents of state that were taking so much of the Sultan's precious time, found that the top one consisted of proposed regulations for a café chantant in Pera. If such trifling affairs cannot be settled without the Sultan's personal supervision, surely no state affairs, no wholesale massacres, could occur without his approval and consent, as his personal government is absolutism.

This is recognized and openly asserted, not only by the soldiery and Kurds who took part in the massacres, but even by the highest court officials, those who were holding the closest relations to the Sultan. Take Nazim Pasha's testimony, for instance—the Minister of Police. When the Patriarch Izmirlian sent his secretary to Nazim Pasha to reclaim the circular note which he had been obliged to issue against his will by the pressure of the Porte, exhorting all Armenians in Asia Minor "to keep quiet and lend themselves to no promoting of disturbances," accompanying his request for the return of the note with the explanation, "It would be an insult to my people to send such a note to them, when they are dying by thousands on the roadsides," Nazim Pasha replied, "You are quite right," adding, "Even the Hamidieh Cavalry are turning against him." "Against whom?" asked the secretary. "Against the one who ordered all this," was the suggestive answer of the Minister.

This is but one instance of many in which even the high officials refer to the Sultan as the instigator and promoter of all the massacres which have drenched Armenian soil with Christian blood. The object of the Sultan's instigation of the massacres has been primarily to diminish the number of the Armenians in those sections where the scheme of reform was to be applied; secondly, to scare the missionaries away from the country (as shown by the suggestion to the United States Minister by the Sultan that the missionaries be urged to leave their posts on account of the danger); lastly, to prove to the European Powers that he was correct in his statement to them that "if the foreign fleet forced the Dardanelles or enforced the scheme of reform, the Moslem population would become infuriated, there would be bloodshed, and he could not answer for the consequences."

That the latter statement was but another of the Sultan's many picturesque fictions is easy to prove to anyone at all familiar with the history of a genuine Mohammedan uprising. In that case no quarter is ever shown to any Christian. Greeks, Jews, missionaries, friends or neighbors, all alike become the object of the sword. In the recent massacres, neither Greeks nor missionaries were killed, though in many cases they were left without protection, and many instances are on record where Armenians fled for protection to their Turkish neighbors, and were accorded it. In one instance a Kurdish chief near Palu notified an Armenian neighbor that a massacre was going to take place at such an hour of such a day, and he had better be on guard. Wisely, the Armenian took his advice, and appealing to the Kurdish chief himself for protection, was taken by him to his home and kept until the massacre was over. These instances, a few of many, go to prove that the massacres were not the result of religious fanaticism only, but that they were in response to orders direct from the palace. The Sultan's denial proves nothing. Even allowing that the massacres are not prompted by his choice, but by his officials, he is still to be blamed, for the choosing of the officials is of his own option. In order to vindicate the rôle he has assumed of the "upright judge," he ought to punish his officials instead of rewarding them. It is a well-known fact that in Ak-Shair, near Nicomedia (Ismid), when the massacre took place, he not only rewarded the faithful executors of his absolute will, but one Turkish official, more humane than the rest, declining to comply with the Sultan's brutal orders, fell from the Sultan's grace, and was recalled to Constantinople, there to "eat the bread of repentance." Hamid II cannot escape the verdict of civilization and history that places him on the calendar with Nero, Caligula, Alva, and Bloody Mary, those other promoters of butcheries.

> This truth comes to us more and more the longer that we live, that on what field or in what uniform or with what aims we do our duty matters very little, or even what our duty is, great or small, splendid or obscure. Only to find our duty certainly and somewhere, somehow do it faithfully, makes us good, strong, happy, and useful men, and tunes our lives into some feeble echo of the life of God.
> Philip Brooks

The Massacres in Turkey from October 1, 1895, to January 1, 1896

Certain persons in Europe and America, misled by statements of the Turkish Government, have ascribed the dreadful massacres which have taken place in Asia Minor to sudden and spontaneous outbreaks of Moslem fanaticism caused by a revolutionary attitude among the Armenians themselves. The truth is that these massacres, while sudden, have taken place according to a deliberate and preconcerted plan. According to the statement of many persons, French, English, Canadian, American, Turk, Kurd, and Armenian—persons trustworthy and intelligent, who were in the places where the massacres occurred, and who were eye-witnesses of the horrible scenes—the outbreaks were under careful direction in regard to the place, time, nationality of the victims and of the perpetrators, who were prompted by a common motive and their true character has been systematically concealed by Turkish official reports. The following paper is based upon full accounts of the massacres, written on the ground by the parties above referred to. Their names for obvious reasons cannot be made public.

I. In Regard to Place

With only four exceptions of consequence, the massacres have been confined to the territory of the six provinces where reforms were to be instituted. When a band of two thousand Kurdish and Circassian raiders approached the boundary between the provinces of Sivas and Angora, they were turned back by the officials, who told them that they had no authority to pass beyond the province of Sivas. The only large places where outrages occurred outside of the six provinces are Trebizond, Marash, Aintab, and Cesarea, in all of which the Moslems were excited by the nearness of the scenes of massacre, and by the reports of the plunder which other Moslems were securing.

II. In Regard to Time

The massacre in Trebizond occurred just as the Sultan, after six months of refusal, was about to consent the scheme of reforms, as if to warn the powers that, in case they persisted, the mine was already laid for the destruction of the Armenians. In fact, the massacre of the Armenians is Turkey's real reply to the demands of Europe that she reform. From Trebizond the wave of murder and robbery swept on through almost every city and town and village in the six provinces where relief was promised to the Armenians. When the news of the first massacre reached Constantinople a high Turkish official remarked to one of the ambassadors that massacre was like the smallpox; they must all have it, but they wouldn't need it the second time.

III. The Nationality of the Victims

They were exclusively Armenians. In Trebizond there is a large Greek population, but neither there nor elsewhere have the Greeks been molested. Special care has also been taken to avoid injury to the subjects of foreign nations, with the idea of escaping foreign complications and the payment of indemnities. The only marked exceptions were in Marash, where three school buildings belonging to the American Mission were looted and one building was burned, and in Harpoot, where the school building and houses belonging to the American Mission were plundered and eight buildings were burned, the total losses exceeding $100,000, for which no indemnity has yet been paid.

IV. The Method of Killing and Pillaging

The method in the cities has been to kill within a limited period the largest number of Armenians—especially men of business, capacity, and intelligence—and to beggar their families by robbing them as far as possible of their property. Hence in almost every place the massacres have been perpetrated during the business hours, when the Armenians could be caught in their shops. In almost every place the Moslems made a sudden and simultaneous attack just after their noonday prayer. The surprised and unarmed Armenians made little or no resistance, and where, as at Diarbekir and Gurun, they undertook to defend themselves, they suffered the more. The killing was done with guns, revolvers, swords, clubs, pickaxes, and every conceivable weapon, and many of the dead were horribly mangled. The shops and houses were absolutely gutted.

Upon hundreds of villages the Turks and Kurds came down like the hordes of Tamerlane, robbed the helpless peasants of their flocks and herds, stripped them of their very clothing, and carried away their bedding, cooking utensils, and even the little stores of provisions which they had with infinite care and toil laid up for the severities of rigorous winter. Worst of all is the bitter cry that comes off hundreds of Christian women and children.

The number killed in the massacres thus far is estimated at fifty thousand, which includes the majority of the well-to-do, capable, intelligent Armenians in the six provinces that were to have been reformed. The property plundered or destroyed is estimated at $40,000,000. Not less than three hundred and fifty thousand wretched survivors, most of whom are women and children, are in danger of perishing by starvation and exposure unless foreign aid is promptly sent and allowed to reach them.

V. The Perpetrators

They were the resident Moslem population, reinforced by Kurds, Circassians, and in several cases by the Sultan's soldiers and officers, who began the dreadful work at the sound of a bugle, and desisted when the bugle signaled them to stop. This was notoriously true in Erzeroum. In Harpoot, also, the soldiers took a prominent part, firing on the buildings of the American Mission with Martini Henry rifles and Krupp cannon. A shell from one of the cannon burst in the house of the American Missionary, Dr. Barnum. In most places the killing was by the Turks, while the Kurds and Circassians were intent on plunder, and generally killed only to strike terror or when they met with resistance.

It is an utter mistake to suppose, as some have, that the local authorities could not have suppressed the "fanatical" Moslem mobs and restrained the Kurds. The fact is that the authorities, after looking on while the massacres were in progress, did generally intervene and stop the slaughter as soon as the limited period during which the Moslems were allowed to kill and rob had expired. At Marsovan the limit of time was four hours. In several places the slaughter and pillage continued from noon till sundown or later. At Sivas they continued for a whole day. In every place the carnage stopped as soon as the authorities made an earnest effort, and had it not been for their intervention after the set time of one, two or three days, the entire Armenian population might have been exterminated.

VI. The Motive of the Turks

This is apparent to the superficial observer. The scheme of reforms devolved civil offices, judgeships, and police participation on Mohammedans and non-Mohammedans in the six provinces proportionately. This, while simple justice, was a bitter pill to the Mohammedans, who had ruled the Christians with a rod of iron for five hundred years. All that was needed to make the scheme of reforms inoperative was to alter the proportion of Christians to Mohammedans. This policy was at once relentlessly and thoroughly executed. The number of the Armenians has been diminished, first, by killing at a single blow the most capable of taking part in any scheme of reconstruction, and secondly, by compelling the survivors to die of starvation, exposure, and sickness or to become Moslem.

It is the very essence of Mohammedanism that the *ghiaour* has no right to live save in subjection. The abortive schemes of Europe insisting on the rights of Armenians as men has enraged the Moslems against them. The arrogant and non-progressive Turks know that in a fair and equal race the Christians will outstrip them in every department of business and industry, and they see in any fair scheme of reforms the handwriting on the wall for themselves. If the scheme of reforms had applied to regions where Greeks predominate, the latter would have been killed and robbed as readily as the Armenians have been. Are the Greek massacres of 1822 forgotten, when 50,000 were killed, or the slaughter of 12,000 Maronites and Syrians in 1860, and of 15,000 Bulgarians in 1876?

VII. The Turkish Official Reports

The refinement of cruelty appears in this, that the Turkish Government has attempted to cover up its hideous policy by the most colossal lying and hypocrisy. It is true that on September 30, 1895, some hot-headed young Armenians, contrary to the entreaties of the Armenian patriarch and the orders of the police, attempted to take a well-worded petition to the Grand Vizier, according to a time honored custom. It is also true that the oppressed mountaineers of Zeitoun drove out a small garrison of Turkish soldiers, whom, however, they treated with humanity; it is likewise true that in various places individual Armenians, in despair, have advocated violent methods. But the universal testimony of impartial foreign eye-witnesses is that, with the above exceptions, the Armenians have given no provocation, and that almost, if not quite, all the telegrams purporting to come from the provincial authorities accusing the Armenians of provoking the massacres are sheer fabrications of names and dates. If the Armenians made attacks, where are the Turkish dead?

And the dreadful alternative of Islam or death was offered by those who have dazzled and deceived Europe with Hatti Shereefs and Hatti Humayouns, promulgating civil equality and religious liberty for their Christian subjects.

Strangest of all, he who is the head of all authority in Turkey, and responsible above any and all others for the cold-blooded massacres and plundering of the past two months, wrote a letter to Lord Salisbury, and pledged his word of honor that the scheme of reforms should be carried out to the letter, at the very moment when he was directing the massacres. And the six great Christian powers of Europe, as well as the United States, still treat this man with infinite courtesy and deference; their representatives still dine at his table, and some of them still receive his decorations.

VIII. The Solution

If the Armenians are to be left as they are, it is a pity that Europe ever mentioned them in the treaty of Berlin or subsequently; and to intrust reforms in behalf of the Armenians to those who have devoted two months' time to killing and robbing them is simply to abandon the Armenians to destruction and to put the seal of Europe to the bloody work. The only way to reform Eastern Turkey is by forcible foreign intervention, not the threat of it, but the intervention itself.

The position and power of Russia give her a unique call to this work. Should she enter on it at once the whole civilized world would approve her course. Russia should have as free a hand in Kurdistan as England has insisted on having in Egypt. By frankly admitting this, England would gain in the respect and sympathy of the world and strengthen her own position.

Who Is Responsible?
A Question from Armenia

The stories of massacre, outrage, torture which came in dismal monotony all last year, imply that someone is running up a very big bill for the Nemesis to settle. The responsibility for this bill, although primarily due from the Turk, lies at the doors of many other people.

According to Mr. Dillon,[114] who for months past has been acting as the special correspondent of the *Daily Telegraph* in the desolated region, Great Britain comes in for a large share of the responsibility. In the *Contemporary Review* he says:

> The time has come for every reasoning inhabitant of these islands deliberately to accept or repudiate his share of the joint indirect responsibility of the British nation for a series of the hugest and foulest crimes that have ever stained the pages of human history. The Armenian people in Anatolia are being exterminated, root and branch, by Turks and Kurds—systematically and painfully exterminated by such abominable methods and with such fiendish accompaniments as may well cause the most sluggish blood to boil and seethe with shame and indignation. Yet we, and we more than any other people, are responsible for the misery of the Armenians.

How It Arises

There is no necessity for arguing this point here. The facts are beyond dispute. England's jealousy of Russia led her under Lord Beaconsfield's Government to insist upon re-establishing the authority of the Turk in districts from which it had been driven by the Russian Czar. She publicly and solemnly declared that she would not sanction misgovernment in those regions. From that time to this she has done nothing practically to prevent it, and at this moment her jealousy of Russia stands in the way of the adoption of the only method by which any redress may be gained—namely, the occupation of the troubled district of the Russian army, acting in the name and with the authority of Europe.

What Is Going On

The reports which reached us from Armenia, many of which were contained in Dr. Dillon's paper, render it by no means difficult to understand how it was that "a wretched, heartbroken mother, wrung to frenzy by her soul-searing anguish, accounted to her neighbors for the horrors that were spread over her people and her country by the startling theory that God Himself had gone mad, and that maniacs and demons incarnate were stalking about the world!"

What people would not think the same if they were to be treated as the Armenians have been for the last twenty years:

Kurdish brigands lifted the last cows and goats of the peasants, carried away their carpets and their valuables, raped their daughters, and dishonored their wives. Turkish taxgatherers followed these, gleaning what the brigands had left, and, lest anything should escape their avarice, bound the men, flogged them till their bodies were a bloody, mangled mass, cicatrized the wounds with red hot ramrods, plucked out their beards hair by hair, tore the flesh from their limbs with pincers, and often, even then, dissatisfied with the financial results of their exertions, hung the men whom they had thus beggared and maltreated from the rafters of the room and kept them there to witness with burning shame, impotent rage, and incipient madness, the dishonoring of their wives and the deflowering of their daughters, some of whom died miserably during the hellish outrage.

A Policy of Extermination

Bad as these things may appear to us to be, they were but the normal unpleasantness of Turkish rule in the Christian district. Of late things have become much worse, for the result of European intervention, when it is not effectual, aggravates instead of alleviates the mischief:

> Yet while the Commission of Inquiry was still sitting at Moush the deeds of atrocious cruelty which it was assembled to investigate were

outdone under the eyes of the delegates. Threats were openly uttered that on their withdrawal massacres would be organized all over the country—massacres, it was said, in comparison with which the Sassoun butchery would compare but as dust in the balance. And elaborate preparations were made—ay, openly made, in the presence of consuls and delegates—for the perpetration of these wholesale murders; and in spite of the warnings and appeals published in England nothing was done to prevent them.

In due time they began. Over 60,000 Armenians have been butchered, and the massacres are not quite ended yet. In Trebizond, Erzeroum, Erzinghan, Hassankaleh, and numberless other places the Christians were crushed like grapes during the vintage. The frantic mob, seething and surging in the streets of the cities, swept down upon the defenseless Armenians, plundered their shops, gutted their houses, then joked and jested with the terrified victims, as cats play with mice.

A Despairing Appeal

The Armenians, as Dr. Dillon, reminds us, have a right to expect sympathy from the Christian world: "Identity of ideals, aspirations, and religious faith give this unfortunate but heroic people strong claims on the sympathy of the English people, whose ancestors, whatever their religious creed, never hesitated to die for it, and when the breath of God swept over them, breasted the hurricane of persecution."

Dr. Dillon thus concludes this appeal to the conscience of Christendom: "If there still be a spark of divinity in our souls, or a trace of healthy human sentiments in our hearts, we shall not hesitate to record our vehement protest against these hell-born crimes, that pollute one of the fairest portions of God's earth, and our strong condemnation of any and every line of policy that may tend directly or indirectly to perpetuate or condone them."

The Sultan of Turkey by One Who Knows Him

The most noteworthy contribution to the first December number of the *Revue de Paris* is an anonymous article dealing with the Eastern, or, more properly speaking, the Armenian question. The writer, who is evidently well acquainted with Turkey, and, what is more important, with the Sultan, devotes a great deal of space to the "Sick Man." He seems to believe Abdul Hamid is by no means as weak and incapable a personage as he is often supposed to be:

> Most people will admit that the profession of being Sultan of Turkey is not—at any rate, at the present time—an agreeable one. The man who has now occupied the Turkish throne for nearly twenty years has certainly owed the length of his reign to the very real qualities displayed by him in the government of his peoples.
>
> The Sultan is a small dark man, with a sallow skin, roving and uneasy eyes, and a slight, feminine hand. Yet in this same frail hand he holds all the threads binding together the Mussulman world, the keys of the Holy Sepulchre and of the Dardanelles, the Koran and the Bible, the sabre and the lance—a good handful truly.

In No Sense a European

The present Sultan is in no senses a European, and when dealing with any of the questions affecting him this fact should not be shirked. Europe is not dealing with a Mehemet Ali; the Sultan is a true Turk—an "old" Turk, and a pious Mohammedan. You have only to enter his palace at Yildiz to see that this is so. In the antechambers, leaning up against the walls, sitting cross-legged on the sofas, is an endless procession which might have come out of Arabian Nights. Men with gray beards and white, their turbaned heads bent over their beads, all waiting for an audience, which, if slow in coming, is always sure to be granted. A glance at all these people, hailing from every corner of the Eastern world, is a proof of how truly the Sultan can boast of being religious head and chief of his race.

By inclination, or because he thinks it wiser to do so, the Sultan has always followed Aristotle's advice, namely, "Enfeebled governments in order to regain vigor should return to the principles upon which they were originally founded"; and the Sultan, Commander of the Faithful, has never slackened in his attempt carry out this maxim.

Apart from this principle the Sultan has shown to his other subjects gentleness, impartiality, and generosity. Foreigners have always been welcomed by him and treated with every courtesy. As a ruler and chief of state he has shown himself laborious, intelligent, and dowered with a truly extraordinary instinct for avoiding and scenting out coming danger.

Taking one thing with another, he has succeeded during the last eighteen years in prolonging, not only his own, but the existence of his dynasty, and of his Empire; and when the circumstances of his succession to the throne are considered, it must be admitted that in these matters he has done well. Whatever be the value of the councilors and advisers with whom he is surrounded, his past has been owing to himself, and it is he, and he alone, who can resolve the problem brought about by the excesses which have lately occurred in Armenia.

The writer discusses the subject with moderation and considerable impartiality. He regrets European intervention, and especially deplores the naval demonstration, which is likely, he considers, to lead either to too small or too great a result.

What Must Be Done in Armenia?

Mr. H. F. B. Lynch,[115] writing in the *Contemporary Review* for February on "The Armenian Question: Europe or Russia," expresses the strong preference for European as opposed to Russian intervention in the American provinces.

He says:

> In the first place, the use of force becomes a most remote contingency if the voice of Russia and the voices of other European powers sound in concert upon this question. Secondly, the plain object of European intervention is not territorial aggrandizement, but the maintenance of the territorial *status quo*. Nor again would it be necessary for any one power to intervene singly, and by so doing perhaps to raise the suspicions of the rest. In Armenia itself, if the Turkish authorities are by themselves incompetent to deal with the present aggravated situation, the difficulty might be met by the enrollment of a police force recruited from all European nations alike.

What Russian Intervention Means

Failing European intervention by force, Russian intervention is inevitable, and Russian intervention has its consequences. Mr. Lynch says: "As a natural corollary Persia falls to Russia, and a Russian fleet rides in the Persian Gulf. Nor is the position less commanding if we turn our eyes toward the west. Erzeroum, the gate of Asia Minor, is situated at the head of that great natural passage which, branching off into numerous smaller bifurcations, lead westward to the Mediterranean Sea."

Sepoys for Armenia!

Of all the proposals that have been made in the serious magazines for the settlement of the Armenian question the most daring is that in *Blackwood*, which proposes that England should garrison Asia Minor with Sepoys drawn from her Indian army. The writer says: "The question whether Indian troops might not well take the place for a time of the savage hordes whose barbarities are disgracing Europe and the age, in reducing the disturbed Asiatic provinces to order, is a more delicate question, and yet it is one that well deserves to be considered, if the powers would only give Britain that credit for singleness of purpose which she is laboring so hard to deserve."

The Sultan's Greatest Danger

Major Conder contributes to the *Scottish Review* for January a well-informed and rather discursive description of the state of Turkey. He points out that not Armenia alone, but all the Christian provinces of the Porte, hope to be liberated by European aid, while the disaffection of the Moslems of Syria, and still more of Arabia, forms a most serious danger to Turkish rule. Pending the European resolve to settle the Eastern question, the Turk sticks to his old policy of government by repression and extortion.

Will the Turkish Army Revolt?

"The danger of a revolt of the army is the greatest that lies before the Turk. As Moslems they can be relied on against Christians, but as human beings there must be a limit to their powers of enduring a condition in which they are not only deprived of pay, and unable to earn money for themselves, but even deprived of food and sometimes on the verge of starvation. A ruler who is unable to feed or to pay for the transport of his troops stands in great danger of a military revolt, especially among Syrian, Albanian, and other regiments of non-Turks. The Turkish army has proved its fighting powers not long since, in spite of treachery and incompetence among some of its leaders, but while the greater part of the force must be kept locked in Europe, on the northwest frontier of the empire, the presence of troops is urgently needed in Armenia and in Arabia, and the most pressing question is how they can be spared and how they can be sent to such remote districts.

WHAT MUST BE DONE IN ARMENIA?

Imminent Insurrection of Christians

"Among the subject Christians the Armenians alone have so far found courage in despair, in their attempt to win freedom from an intolerable double tyranny—of Kurdish chiefs and Turkish pashas; but if success were in the end to crown their efforts the Armenians would not stand alone. The Christians of North Syria—Greek or Syrian in creed—have many grievances of their own. The more fortunate Maronites of the Lebanon province, who have a Christian police, and who are keen politicians, might become inoculated with the idea of independence. The flame of fanaticism once lit would not distinguish Greek and Armenian Christians. Any success against the Turks in Armenia would lead to insurrection in other provinces.

"The Real Rulers of Turkey"

"Amid so many dangers the danger of Moslem disaffection must seem greatest to a Moslem ruler, convinced that the European powers are most unwilling to proceed to extremities. The attention of Russia is turned to the far East, and no power but England is really earnest in the Armenian cause, this earnestness being confined perhaps mainly to religious circles and to Liberal politicians. The real rulers of Turkey are not those ministers who are moved as pawns in the game, but the secret Dervish orders on whom the Sultan relies. They form powerful organizations bitterly opposed to all Western ideas, and perfectly informed through their lower initiates of all that goes on in the various provinces of the Empire. The realities of government in Turkey are very different from its diplomatic exterior appearances; and the Khalif dominates the Sultan.

"The Happiest Outcome"

"It may be that the Turks will once more assert their old predominances over their subjects, since their successor has not yet appeared. The Armenians are destined either to work out their own future or to perish in the attempt. It is practically impossible for Europe to interfere, unless Europe is ready to undertake the administration of new provinces in Asia. The subject populations are so much split up, and have so long been unaccustomed to rule themselves, that nothing but anarchy can be expected if the Turkish administration is overthrown. The happiest outcome that could be expected would be the creation of a new Christian province in North Syria or in Armenia, where the oppressed might find refuge, and learn by degrees to rule themselves, until fit for independent existence as a Christian state.

An American Heroine in the Heart of Armenia: Dr. Grace Kimball[116] and Her Relief Work at Van

Elizabeth B. Thelberg, M.D.

On the twenty-fourth of last June Dr. Kimball wrote in a letter to me:

> We've got to go into relief work forthwith, and I suppose I've got to engineer it. As I have only twenty dollars cash capital I am beginning mildly. Sent to town to buy some wool to-day. My idea is to buy wool and cotton, and give it to the famine-stricken people to card and spin at so much the pound. Also give out the spun thread to be made into socks, coarse woven material, sacking, etc., at regular prices; then use most of the product for clothing the people as winter comes on. Let us see how it will work!

That it did "work" the accompanying report shows. The more recent reports by cable tell of 16,000 people fed daily by the wages paid in the cotton, wool, and garment factories, and of the successful operation of six bakeries.

The pressing need now, however, is, as Dr. Kimball so wisely indicates, money for seed, wheat, and implements to enable the villagers to return to their homes. The courage, the energy, and the persistency which has carried this work through the past winter in face of well-nigh insurmountable difficulties exemplifies again the old adage: "Blood will tell." Dr. Kimball is, on the mother's side, a direct descendant of that first Pilgrim baby, Peregrine White. She is a native of New Hampshire, and was educated in Bangor, Maine.

In 1882 Miss Kimball went to Van to take charge of the Girl's Boarding and Day School belonging to that station of the American Board. After six years of very successful teaching she returned to America for the usual vacation of a year.

Having, however, been greatly impressed with the extreme need in Turkey of properly qualified woman physicians, Miss Kimball remained in this country, studied medicine, and was graduated from the Woman's Medical College of the New York Infirmary in 1892.

In July of that year she returned to Van, meeting cholera on the way, and undergoing quarantine of ten days in a stable at a small Armenian village beyond Erzeroum. Three years of active and varied practice followed—years made doubly hard, first by cholera, and then by a most serious epidemic of scarlet fever and diphtheria which, during the year 1894, swept from quarter to quarter of the city.

In those years Dr. Kimball was brought into close personal relations with the people of Van from the Governor-General to the peasants of the villages. She thus obtained not only a complete knowledge of the situation, but so general an esteem and confidence that she has been able to execute, almost unaided, the great relief work of the last eight months. Her wonderful spirit and cheer have never flagged. In November she wrote: "My one horror is lest crowds overwhelm me, but I have now two strong men to pass me in and out of the factory doors regularly."

And in December:

> But the crowds, the trials and the tribulations of this work! You would laugh if you could see how *inwardly* wild I get several times in the course of each day! What with a waiting crowd of "poors" never absent from before the time I am out of my bed until after dark; what with priests and Vortaluds, rich men and neighbors and acquaintances, committees and representatives of committees, letters and formal appeals, wounded men and sick men—what with all these and as many more demands for attention, my days pass in a whirl! *In all the dust we raise it is hard to keep the road.*

Constant anxiety about funds, and inability to get ready money except by carrier from Constantinople, added no small burden. Thus, later in December: "I am £700 (pounds) in debt, and to put down brakes and stop the machinery means taking the daily bread from 7,000 people, not to speak of clothing for hundreds of naked refugees. I am going to keep on a few days longer in the faith that some good news will come, and meanwhile I am writing and telegraphing hither and you."

Good news—financially—did come. The report speaks for that, but the need, though changed in character, has not lessened.

In addition to the industrial work Dr. Kimball has been doing from two to four hours' surgical work a day. "Mostly frozen feet and gunshot wounds—sword cuts don't count."

Vassar College

A Report by Dr. Grace Kimball on the Van Industrial Bureau and Village Relief Work

In order to understand this work in hand and the need for the future, it is necessary to have a clear idea of the conditions of the Armenians in Van City and province. Van stands almost alone of all the large cities of Armenia in having escaped the horrors of a massacre. But the most extreme fear has prevailed ever since October 26, when the news of the Bitlis massacre has reached us. On this day the bazaars were closed, goods were conveyed to private houses to a great extent, and all business was at a standstill. Thus for at least six weeks both the large central bazaar and all the smaller bazaars were absolutely closed—a perpetual Sunday. The conviction of the Armenians was doubtless correct that a massacre was imminent, and that the scene of it would inevitably be the bazaars, where, as in other places, the Armenians could be shut in and cut down without hope and escape, and with the great added advantage of rich loot. The prompt closing of the markets, together with the commendably earnest efforts of our Governor-General, and the commandant, Mustapha Pasha, undoubtedly prevented a repetition here of the terrible scenes enacted in other cities. But in view of the swift succession of disasters that swept over the length and breadth of the country, it is little wonder that in spite of earnest efforts and solemn assurances of protection from the local government, the merchants and mechanics have not, even to the present writing, felt sufficient confidence to allow of more than a very limited resumption of business. It will be remembered that the economic condition of the city was so bad even during the summer that the industrial relief work was begun early in July to relieve the situation. Add to this already existing poverty and depression the cessation of trade and all industries during the busiest and most lucrative season of the year, and it will be dimly understood in what terrible suffering are the people of the city. Practically, all the small traders and shopkeepers, all the mechanic and artisan class, are in want of daily bread. Add to these a large class of highly respectable families whose living comes from their interest in the villages. They own fields and flocks, and in the fall go to their villages, gather in their winter wheat, butter, meat, and other supplies, and bring them home as their winter support. By the sale of a part of this they are provided with ready money, and the remainder supplies their tables. Now ninety-nine per cent of these families lost every ounce of their winter provision in the general sacking of the villages. Hence, they also are applicants for aid to a large extent.

About the middle of November a campaign of systematic destruction was set on foot. Among the villages lying between Van and the Persian frontier fifty were pillaged in the space of two weeks and their inhabitants driven out helpless and naked. Already the famous Kurdish Pashas, Hussein and Emin, had devastated thirty-eight or forty villages on the north side of the lake, and a thousand of their inhabitants came to Van and its near villages for help. So a vast army of wretched men, women and children bore down on the city, filling every inch of available space. A more helpless, hopeless, wretched set of people surely never were gotten together. Just at the beginning of winter, robbed of all their winter provision, stripped of all their property even to the clothing on their backs, driven out from their homes, many of their men killed or severely wounded, wanderers on the face of the earth, with not a crust to eat, not a rag to put on, and neither house, bed nor fuel wherewith to withstand the cruel cold. And for what? Who can answer these innocent victims of a political situation of which they are as innocent as the cattle in their stables?

In addition to this the large region of Khizan (mostly in Bitlis Vilayet), comprising some thirty-five villages, has been reduced to a still more deplorable condition. It is practically under the sway of a Kurdish chief of great influence and "holiness." This man and his retainers have converted the entire population of the district to

Islam. Some two hundred refugees have found their way here, and are entirely helpless wards of whomsoever is able to take care of them.

The regions of Kavash and Moks are in great distress, though the heavy snows prevent even appeals for help. From Shadagn a delegation has come in, reporting some five hundred families as on the verge of starvation, while, in a word, all the villages in the province—some five hundred and fifty—have suffered each in its own degree from total annihilation to the milder forms of robbery, and all look to Van as the only source of help and hope. Hence, it will be seen that in the relief work we have a double problem to deal with—to relieve the peculiarly distressing and helpless condition of the city proper, and to bear the burden which the already impoverished city people cannot bear, of this immense influx of village refugees. The added task of helping the villagers in their villages must wait until safety is secured, both for those carrying help and those receiving it. Any assistance given to these poor starving wretches now would only invite further depredations by the Kurds.

The Industrial Bureau has proved itself a double blessing to the community by furnishing honest labor to hundreds of families—a happy exchange for either free bread or starvation—and at the same time it has provided us with a rich supply of the very kinds of materials needed to clothe the hordes of village refugees. As the generosity of the people of England and America permitted us, we gradually increased the number of workers from four hundred and seventy-six, reported in October, to over one thousand at the present time. Of these seventy per cent are women occupied in spinning cotton and wool; twenty per cent are weavers—men and women—of cotton and woolen materials, and the remaining ten per cent are employed as overseers, sizers, carders, spindle-fillers, knitters, and sewers of clothing and bedding, while some twenty men are employed as doorkeepers, examiners and clerks. With the exception of three men, who act as accountants and head clerks, every person in the employ of the Industrial Bureau is thereby relieved of actual hunger and suffering. These three men are well-known and respected merchants, who, in the total cessation of business, have been able to take up the work. A salary of $7 a month (1½ Turkish pounds) is given, not in compensation of service, but as a retainer on the part of management—they being to serve their own people in this capacity. The daily pay-roll averaged over two hundred last week, while one hundred and forty-six employed as carders, sizers, spindle-fillers, doorkeepers, etc., were paid their weekly wages last Saturday, as against twenty-seven shown in the October report.

As the cold weather has come on, we have been obliged in many cases to supplement the scant wages by gifts of money to buy fuel, or of clothing and bedding. A little goes a great way here, and eighty cents (a Turkish Hegidia, or about four shillings), will buy fuel for a family for two to three months. In some cases we have doubled the rate of wages to enable the family to live as by their own labor, and in some other cases we have helped them by giving an allowance of bread in addition to their wages. Thus, taking every case on its own merits, we endeavor to insure the bare necessities of life to each of our workers. The danger of imposition necessitates keeping a corps of workers busy examining into cases, since we believe no one's story until our own agents have verified it. No one can tell what a boon this work is to these poor people, and they do not fail to give frequent and enthusiastic acknowledgement of it.

The new department of sewing has been a great addition to our means of helpfulness, as it gives support to some sixty families, who could not live by any of the other kinds of work offered. This branch takes in the poor but respectable class who in consequence of the misfortunes spoken of above have been reduced from comfort to lack of daily bread. In addition to this, we keep a certain number of men and women busy making mattresses and coverlets for free distribution. Thus, in the complete cessation of the regular industrial life of the city, our work stands out as a beacon of hope and light to the poor wretches who would otherwise die of slow starvation. And the advantages of this form of help over gratuitous charity will be evident to everybody.

The cost of the Industrial Bureau at its present running capacity is some twenty-five Turkish pounds ($110) a day, including the cost of the raw material used. Hence, we are giving work to one thousand persons who support about five thousand souls at an expense to us of two and one-fifth cents per capita; while the product of their labor (already paid for in the 25 pounds daily expenditure) furnishes us with abundant supplies of clothing for distribution. We frequently supply from one hundred to one hundred and fifty families with clothing in a single day, and if we were to push our division of average cost still further it would bring us to small fractions.

November was a month long to be remembered by the Christians of this vicinity for the unprecedented devastations of the Kurds. The villagers were taken in regular order, and dealt with according to the unbridled cruelty and cupidity of their Moslem neighbors. As I have said, immense numbers of these homeless wretches crowded into the city to be housed, fed and clothed. The local Armenian authorities looked to us as the only source of material aid, while they formed committees of examination and co-operation, all applications for aid came to them in the first instance, and examined by them and sent to us with specifications as to the aid desired and as to the urgency of the case. Just at the time that this crowd of villagers bore down upon us came, most opportunely, a cablegram from the *Christian Herald*, bringing us the news that ten thousand dollars was forthcoming from the fund in process of being raised by that philanthropic journal. It was with joy like that of a drowning man at the approach of his rescuers that we and our Armenian fellow-workers received this news. Within forty-eight hours we had a bakery in operation, and the stress of the situation was relieved. After a fortnight the capacity of this first bakery was exceeded, and we opened a second. This, too, had to be supplemented by help from a third oven to the extent of eighteen hundred pounds a day. So that at the present time we are running two bakeries—"*Christian Herald* Bakeries" we call them—and hiring the extra amount needed from another oven. Three thousand seven hundred and fifty pounds of bread is given to about five hundred families or some twenty-five hundred persons daily—most of them village refugees obliged to spend the winter here. Hundreds of refugees have been supplied with bread for a longer or shorter time while waiting to return to their villages. Wherever their wheat has not been entirely stolen—in some cases it was not, thanks to a custom the people have of burying it in pits—we strongly urged them to take all risks and return to their villages, though in some cases there is great danger in so doing. Many now in the city and receiving help will little by little be returned to their homes in this way. There is a great economic danger involved in their staying and getting weaned from their ruder and less secure village life, thus deserting their lands and becoming a permanent burden on the city population. The daily cost of the bakeries is 15 pounds, or $66. The problem of housing these refugees has been entirely assumed by the

Armenian Committee, and they have also attempted to supply them with beds and shoes. These latter burdens have now exceeded their financial ability, and we have begun to supplement their efforts. The winter's severe cold is upon us. Most of these villages have little or no fuel, and the quarters allotted to them are cold, damp rooms—if rooms they could be called—the floor, the earth itself, with no mats or carpets to keep them warm. Their exposure is bound to bring about a large per cent of mortality unless relieved. Hence, we are giving special attention to bed manufacture, in the hope of speedily relieving the most needy cases.

The clothing department, inaugurated in earnest late in November, has been an untold blessing to the people. In the beginning we simply distributed the goods produced by the looms of our Industrial Bureau by the piece. But two days' experience showed that this was a mistake, as the goods being salable put a premium upon imposition and brought crowds of frauds down upon us. So we immediately called a half dozen tailors and set them to cutting out garments and took on from thirty to forty women applicants for work to whom are given out the garments to be sewed. In three days' time our new sewing department, spoken of above, was in full operation, and was giving us a supply of from two hundred to two hundred and fifty sewed garments daily. This department, up to January 1, distributed three thousand and thirty-one pieces of cotton and woolen cloth; three thousand two hundred and forty-nine sewed garments; one thousand two hundred and eighty-seven pairs of socks and fifty-five carpets and coverlets.

The most urgent need of the present moment which we have not as yet undertaken to meet is that of a hospital. Negotiations are already on foot, and we hope that in a few days we may see this need met in a simple way. There is greater danger of widespread epidemic breaking out as the result of so much exposure, insufficient food and unsanitary housing, and we are alive to the duty of using every means of preventing trouble.

We have acknowledged with gratitude the receipt in total of $12,136.61. Of this sum, $5,763.80 was received from England through the Woman's Armenian Relief Committee: $136.40 from the American School, Smyrna; $500 as the advance guard of the *Christian Herald* Fund; $2,815.16 from the sale of goods manufactured to the Sassoun Commission, and the remainder from various sources, public and private, in America. To *The Outlook* is due thanks for a considerable sum in this balance, but, owing to the censorship of the mails, I have not been apprised of the exact amount.

The expenditures reported to October 15 amounted to $3,066.98. From October 15 to January 1, $3,252.61 has been expended for raw material; $2,758.80 for wages; $3,064.07 for the bakeries and supplies of wheat; $104.72 free aid (fuel, etc.); $87.20 administration, rent, fuel, postage, and telegraphic expenses, etc.; $668.80 notes payable; leaving a debit of $866.57, January 1. As against this indebtedness we have the assurance of $10,000 from the *Christian Herald* Fund and other promises of help.

In closing I cannot sufficiently express my admiration and gratitude to the various agencies and individuals in England and America through whose untiring efforts all this relief work is being done. I should fail in my duty, as well as deprive myself of a pleasure, were I to omit to render heartiest thanks to the Woman's Armenian Relief Committee of England and to the New York *Christian Herald* of America for their distinguished services.

But generous as have been the sums received in the past, we must still beg for renewed efforts and larger gifts to avert famine and death through the remaining months of winter, and with the opening of spring to supply the villagers with the seed and implements necessary to enable them to take up their self-supporting life again.

Grace W. Kimball

Forum,[117] vol. 21 (June 1896): 449–59.

Armenia's Impending Doom: Our Duty

M. M. Mangasarian[118]

As an Armenian, I have no sympathy with the sweeping denunciation of the Turks, much less with the unqualified encomium of the Christians of the Orient. Nothing is gained by giving to the facts a partisan twist, by depicting the Mohammedan as an incorrigible devil and the Armenian as an incomparable angel. Though my own immediate relations have suffered unspeakable horrors during the recent outbreaks, still no one could be more reluctant than myself to credit the charges of astounding inhumanity, nay, of bestiality, brought against the Kurds, the Turks, and the Circassians. I have not only hailed with enthusiasm the reports of fraternal devotion and hospitality, of compassion and chivalry, shown by individual Turks to their Armenian neighbors, but I believe in them implicitly. In the cities of Trebizond, Caesarea, Gemereg, Egin, Sivas, and Aintab, not a few Moslems risked their own lives by offering an asylum to the Christians. The example of these noble Turks not only helps us to be moderate in our judgment of the Ottomans, but in a time of moral skepticism it also helps to confirm our wavering faith in human nature. Men everywhere are better than their creeds, and, in its essentials, human nature is something like the divine.

The Armenian is so well-armed in his cause that there is no reason why he should resort to a wholesale defamation of the Mohammedan in order to engage the sympathy of Christian nations. Moreover, these exaggerated attacks upon the Turk are bound to produce, sooner or later, a reaction in his favor. The truth about the Turks and the Armenians is so easily within the reach of every candid investigator that there is no excuse for confusing the issues. Both have their full share of the virtues and vices of Oriental races.

In forming an estimate of the Armenian character, we must not lose sight of the fact that the Turks are the masters and the Armenians the slaves. Notwithstanding this vital difference the Armenians are, to say the least, intellectually and morally the peers of the Turks, and if they cannot compare favorably with the free peoples of Europe end America, it is due to five centuries of uninterrupted oppression and persecution to which they have been subjected. Under these circumstances, it would be unreasonable to expect of the Armenians all the virtues of Englishmen and Americans. By that stupendous obstinacy with which the Armenians, in spite of unparalleled hardships and misery, have refused to forsake the country they call their fatherland,—a country which, from time out of mind, has been the tramping-ground and the battle-field of the devastating armies of Nebuchadnezzar and Alexander, of Genghis Khan and Timour, of Shah Abbas and the Arabs, of the Seljuks and the Ottomans, and by that equally marvelous tenacity with which, since the close of the third century of the Christian era, they have, as a nation, clung to the faith preached to them by Gregory, surnamed "The Illuminator,"—the faith in which their King Tiridates was baptized twenty-seven years before the Emperor Constantine had issued the famous Edict of Toleration and which they have so successfully defended against the fire-worshippers of Persia, the caliphs of Arabia, and the Tartar conquerors,—by all these things they have won for themselves a place in history which cannot be taken away from them. It is to be deplored that Europe and America know so little of what it has cost the Armenians to remain Armenians and Christians in a land where Islam is without a rival and where every inducement has been offered and every severity practised to make apostates of them. But I do not despair of the civilized nations of the world, for when they study the history of this martyr-nation,—to-day the only representative of civilization and Christianity in Turkey,—and of the Vartanians, Levonians, and their noble brethren who died to stem the torrent of Persian and Ottoman fanaticism; and when they realize the ineffable sacrifices which the Armenians to-day are making to protect their homes and honor, they will not hesitate to do a little for the people who have done so much for humanity.

On May 29, 1453, Mohammed "The Conqueror" ascended the wonderful throne of the Bosphorus. From that day to this the crescent has mocked sun and breeze from the minarets of St. Sophia. During the five centuries following the capture of Constantinople by the Turks, there has taken place a wonderful intellectual and spiritual awakening, as well as an unparalleled industrial progress in Europe and in America. The Renaissance in Italy, the Reformation in Germany, the Revolution in France, and the Emancipation Proclamation of Abraham Lincoln, bear dates subsequent to the fall of the Eastern Empire. But these centuries of activity and movement for the Occidental nations have been centuries of deterioration for the Mohammedan Orient. Once the empire of the Sultan had an extent of more than 100,000 square leagues in Asia, Africa, and Europe, a magnificent territory with the finest harbors, richest islands and mines, and with a soil the most fertile in all the world. But this vast area has been gradually reduced, until to-day Sultan Abdul-Hamid II has lost his hold on Europe and is proving himself unworthy of ruling his remaining possessions in Africa and Asia. That splendid empire which the Turks inherited five hundred years ago has been reduced to a state of intellectual and industrial pauperism. The traveler in Turkey is everywhere reminded, by innumerable ruins, of those nobler and sturdier races that once called the country their own, and made it the cradle of culture and religion. The Sultan and his sluggish Turks tread on a ground under which sleep the Greek and Roman sires of modern civilization. With the exception of a few mausoleums and mosques, the Ottoman Turks have not built a single town or city, or created a single industry or institution, or in any way improved the condition of the peoples they have conquered and converted. The Ottoman Government, since Solyman "The Magnificent," has been in a comatose state.

Nor is it because the Turks are Mohammedans that vandalism has been their profession, or that government "a la Turc" has been synonymous with organized brigandage: the Saracens were Mohammedans, too, but they produced scholars, and were for four hundred years the intellectual teachers of Europe; the Seljukian sultans have left monuments to their love of art and science; the Persians have given to the world Hafiz and Sadi; but the Ottoman Turks have not produced a writer or a statesman whose name will live. The saying that "wherever the Sultan's horse hoofs tread, there the grass never grows again," has been fully corroborated by the recent reports of pillage, rapine, and murder which have reached the ears of the whole world. When the Czar, Nicholas I, called the Turk "the sick man of Europe," he not only made a correct diagnosis, but be also led the civilized world to anticipate with pleasure the speedy demise of "the sick man." And though this event has been delayed, there is every indication that the time is ripe for a European coalition, a concert of civilized nations, to drive the Turks, bag and baggage, beyond the desert and steppes of that darkest Asia which was their original home.

To those who still hesitate to credit the accumulating charges against the Ottoman rule, I suggest the present deplorable condition of Armenia. Though one of the fairest lands under the sun, and inhabited by a hardy, industrious, faithful, and frugal people, Armenia is to-day what California was under Mexican rule—the home of banditti and cut-throats. From the southern shores of the Euxine to the ancient Ararat, and from the snow-capped mountains which feed the Euphrates and the Tigris and the Aras, to that undulating sweep toward Western Asia which the Armenian calls his native land, the besom of fanaticism has swept within the past few years more than 50,000 men, women, and children to the most agonizing death; crowded the mountain fastnesses and caves with fugitives, and left in the villages and cities only fragments of what was once a proud and independent nation. What the Turks are doing to-day to the Armenians, they did to the Greeks in 1821, when more than 40,000 were put to the sword in the island of Chios; to the Nestorians in 1843, when the rocks and plains were covered with "the scattered bones, bleached skulls, long locks of hair, plucked from the women's heads, and torn portions of the garments they had worn";* to the Syrians, when the streets of Deir-el-Kamar and Zableh "ran with human gore in which men waded ankle deep";* to the Bulgarians, when in 1876, according to the American consul-general, Eugene Schuyler, and the English Blue Book, more than 16,000 were butchered in the first two or three days under the very eyes of Europe. Happy Bulgaria! She did not shed her blood

---
*See Layard's "Nineveh."
*See Van Lennep's "Bible Lands: Their Modern Customs and Manners."

in vain. But what was Bulgaria's salvation proved to be Armenia's danger. The Mohammedans, driven from Sofia, Varna, and Rustchuk on the Danube, crossed the Bosphorus and settled in Armenia, their swords still reeking with blood. Nor were they slow in avenging their humiliation. Just a year after the Bulgarian atrocities came the report of the total extermination by the Mohammedans of the Armenians in Bayazid. The Moslem refugees from Europe, with the memory of their defeat burning in their veins, converted Armenia into an amphitheatre of plunder and murder. "These Armenians," said the government officials to the Mohammedans, "are trying to expel you from Asia, just as the Bulgarians expelled you from Europe." It is not at all strange that the fanaticism of the Turk and Kurd, once aroused by such a fear, has become uncontrollable.

If I were to enumerate the causes which are responsible for the anti-Christian feeling in Turkey, I would not hesitate to say that the religious animosities between Moslems and Christians are most to be blamed. The Oriental Christian, I am sorry to say, is as intolerant of Mohammedanism as the Moslem is of Christianity. But the Moslem is in power and can give expression to his hate, while the Christian is weak and cannot strike back. It is true, however, that Christianity as a religion is more susceptible to the "Zeit-Geist" than Mohammedanism, and this fact must influence, as it certainly has done, all the nations that have professed it. Mohammed gave to his followers a sword, Christ gave to his disciples a cross. Christianity, too, has been guilty of persecution in the past, but the progress of the ages has elevated, broadened, and sweetened it, while Mohammedanism continues in spirit and in doctrine just what it was almost fourteen hundred years ago. From the mosques in Cairo and Constantinople, the faithful pray to Allah to "destroy the infidels . . . make their children orphans . . . defile their abodes . . . and give them and their families and their households and their women . . . and their possessions . . . as booty to the Moslems." Several passages in the Koran directly instigate the Mohammedans to exterminate the unbelievers:

> Verily the worst cattle in the sight of Allah are those who are obstinate infidels.
> When ye encounter the unbelievers, strike off their heads until ye have made a great slaughter among them.

> Oh, prophet, wage war against the unbelievers and be severe unto them, for their dwelling shall be hell.
> Oh, true believers, wage war against such infidels as are near you; and let them find severity in you.

I gladly admit that there are passages of ravishing beauty in the Moslem scriptures, but those which I have quoted exert a greater hold upon the ignorant and fanatical rabble.

Some color is given to the statement that a "djihad" (a religious war) has been proclaimed against the Christians by the fact that during the progress of the recent wave of hate and lust which, starting in Constantinople, reached as far as Diarbekir on the Tigris, wherever an Armenian appeared at his windows with a green or white turban on his head and announced his conversion to Islam, his life, his wife, and his goods were not only spared by the mob, but protected by the troops. It is the same old cry that is raised in Armenia to-day, "the sword or the Koran." I am assured in private letters that a multitude of Christians have been converted to Islam under compulsion. Men young and old have been prostrated on the streets and subjected to the Moslem rite, and no mercy was shown to those who offered the faintest resistance. The Sultan may not have directly ordered the massacres, although Lord Salisbury in his last speech admitted that "among those who say it are men who have the opportunity of judging," but there is very little doubt that as the spiritual head of the Mohammedan world, he expressed the wish to see the unbelievers converted to the true faith. Such a wish would increase his popularity with the softas, who would not hesitate to resort to any measures to realize the pious hopes of their Caliph. Moreover, to the Sultan the Islamization of the Armenians is the only practical solution of the Armenian question. If the Armenians, by remaining obdurate, are killed, their women violated, and their homes and villages looted, it is their own fault, when by embracing Islam they can not only save themselves and their homes, but they can also command the full protection of the government. What more could a gracious sovereign do for his subjects? This is, without doubt, the reasoning which makes the Sultan proof against all the scruples of conscience. Thus the Armenians are killed, not because the Sultan wants them killed, but because they refuse to be converted. In a large sense, therefore, the bloodshed in the East is in the name of religion. The age of the crusaders is over, but the age of the "crescentaders" is here with all its ancient vigor and rigor.

Of course the attempt on the part of the Armenians to improve their political condition has intensified the religious hate of the Moslems. There has always been a religious element in the political, and a political element in the religious wars of the Moslems; and it is when these two blend in equal proportions, as in the present instance, that the fury and the thirst for blood develop to an appalling degree. It must be admitted that there is a revolutionary party among the Armenians, to which belong some of the young "hot heads" who have unquestionably resorted to desperate measures, verging upon those of rank nihilism, with the hope of forcing the Great Powers to come to their rescue. These Armenians find encouragement in the example of the Greeks and the Bulgarians who, assisted by Europe, succeeded in shaking off the Turkish yoke. Besides, the traditional interest of Russia in the welfare of the Christians in the Ottoman Empire,—as shown by the treaty of San Stefano, and the treaties of Paris and Berlin in which the six Powers of Europe united to extract from the Turk a promise to protect his Christian subjects against the predatory tribes,—led the Armenians to count upon the intervention of Europe in the case of an uprising. While I am not of the number of those who cherish the chimerical hope that Armenia—which is at present no more than a "geographical expression"—can speedily become an independent kingdom, I cannot find it in me to be severe upon those who, goaded to exasperation by the scorpion scourge of the tyrant whose lust the Armenian is compelled to satisfy by giving his goods and his daughters, have begun to imitate their oppressors in their act of plunder and murder. There is a limit, even to prudence, as well as to endurance. Revolution is the shadow that accompanies despotism. It is foolish to hold the shadow responsible or to attempt to strike at it. It is only when despotism is overthrown that its shadow will disappear. Without wishing to justify the questionable acts of a few of the revolutionists, I profoundly sympathize with the heroic struggle of the educated Armenians for the past thirty-five years to ameliorate the condition of their people. The liberty-loving nations of the world should be the last to blame the Armenians for their political aspirations. Those wretched and persecuted people in their distant mountain homes have caught a strain of freedom's paean, and are making a brave effort to snap their chains and to rise to the rank of the world's free nations.

Aside from the above causes, which are of a religious and political nature, there is still another. The Turks are jealous of the Christians because of the comparative prosperity of the latter in all the principal cities of the empire. In times of peace and security the Greeks and the Armenians, who are by race and religion more European than Asiatic, easily outrun the slow-going Turk and drive him out of the markets of commerce and finance. The superior and more advanced education which the Christians receive in their schools qualifies them for important diplomatic posts from which the Turks themselves, by reason of their unfitness, are excluded. For many centuries the Greeks and the Armenians have filled high political offices in Turkey, Persia, and Egypt. It is unreasonable to blame the Oriental Christians for their mental and moral superiority to the Turks. Merit will win, even in Turkey, and it is merit—not cunning and craft, as has been insinuated by some Turkophile newspaper correspondents—which has helped the Christians the world over to become the leaders and masters. Turkey lost Europe because it found itself unable to cope with the Christians, and for the same reason it has lost the commerce of Asia. The frequently repeated charge that the Christians of the Orient are usurers who have shorn the innocent Turk of all his possessions, is a pure invention. In the interior of Asia, the people who toil and think are the Christians; the people who walk the streets, their hands folded on their back, and who crowd the cafes to smoke their long pipes the livelong day, are the Turks. In spite of the unfavorable conditions, the Armenians and the Greeks are to-day the civilizers of the Orient—the manufacturers, the inventors, the builders, the doctors, the lawyers, and the teachers. They are the first to adopt European manners, to build their houses after Western models, to introduce English and French text-books into their schools, to translate the foreign authors, and to study the intellectual and industrial movements in Europe and in America. It is not derogatory to the Christians that the Turks cannot keep up with them.

This is but a cursory review of the principal causes which culminated a short time ago in the frightful massacres, the reports of which have startled the civilized world. The sudden outpouring of a volcano with its heated streams of lava could not have produced a greater destruction than this violent eruption of Turkish and Kurdish fanaticism and lust. Children and women, as well as men, have been disgraced and tortured to death. To this very day the officials lay the blame entirely upon the Christians. But, with the exception of a limited number, no one either in Europe or in America places any confidence in the official despatches of the government.

But why does Europe hesitate to stop the bloodshed, to terminate the blight of Turkish misrule in Asia? There is no doubt that the hereditary fear of Russian aggression is still the bugbear of Europe. It was the opinion of Napoleon that without the Turkish government in Constantinople, Russia would overrun Europe and Asia, and the Cossacks, by unseating the Saxons and the Celts in Europe, would become the masters of the world. The following conversation is reported to have taken place between Sultan Mahmoud, the grandfather of Abdul-Hamid, and a European ambassador:

"I am left alone to defend Europe against Russia, and Europe aids the Russians. But, after me, Europe will fall a victim to these Russians," said the Sultan.

"You are right," answered the European, "but do not despair of Europe. It will some day recognize the importance of Turkey as a bulwark against the Russians."

"God is good," replied Mahmoud, "let His will be done."

Turkey, therefore, has been regarded as the "advance guard" of the liberty and civilization of Europe, the only country that can hold Russia at bay. With the Czar at Constantinople, it is feared the Black Sea would be converted into a Russian dock whence his ironclads would proceed to possess the earth. But the world has been changed since the days of Napoleon, and it is impossible today for any one power to overrun the whole earth. No one was better fitted to become a modern Caesar than Napoleon, and no country was more popular than France at the beginning of this century. Notwithstanding, Napoleon was crushed at Waterloo, and France has become a republic.

I fear that the true secret of European sympathy for Turkey is a commercial one. England and Germany manufacture the articles which are sold in the bazaars of Constantinople. The army of the

Sultan is clothed, shod, and capped by Europe. Turkey manufactures nothing, builds nothing, digs nothing out of the soil; it must import everything. It is to the interest of commercial Germany and England that there should be a Turkey where they can sell their "shoddy." With the Greeks or the Armenians in power in Constantinople, there would immediately spring up native manufactories, the mines would be in operation, railroads would be built, and the people, able to supply their own needs, would stop importing to the same extent from Europe. Turkey, therefore, is a tolerated government owing its existence not only to the political jealousies of the Powers, but also to the commercialism of Europe.

But is the civilized world under no obligations to the Armenians? In my humble opinion, it is the duty of America and Europe to intervene for good. The doctrine of non-interference is dangerous and unworthy of our religion and civilization. The Turks do not hesitate to kill in order to propagate their faith and to maintain the rule of their prophet. It is the duty of Europe, by interfering, to check their power for further evil. But Europe hesitates; and, while it is trying to make up its mind, reports of fresh outbreaks come from every direction. In this policy of stolid indifference and hesitation, Russia appears to me to be the greatest sinner. It is impossible for the Russians to forget that England, during the war of the Crimea, entered into an alliance with two despots, Napoleon III and the King of Sardinia, to save a third despot, the Sultan of Turkey. And now Russia is showing the same consideration for the tyrant of the Bosphorus. Moreover, the interests of Russia require that there be no independent or autonomous Armenia, for that would disturb her own Armenian subjects, and further, it has been the unerring policy of Russia to obstruct all reform measures in Turkey, lest "the sick man of Europe" should recover his health and prolong his days.

Germany and France take their cue from Russia. We have not heard of a single protest from official Germany against the Turkish atrocities. From a moral point of view, the conduct of Germany in this respect has been a great disappointment. Germany, considering her power and intellectual greatness, has done less for the cause of the oppressed and the down-trodden than any other nation in the world. Few peoples are more devoid of chivalry than the modern Germans. When have they made the cause of the persecuted their own? When have they hastened to the rescue of the weak and the oppressed? When have they made a sacrifice worthy of their heart and brain in the interests of justice and humanity? And France! The home of the Revolution, the most chivalrous nation of Europe, the land of Rousseau and the Girondists—she is dumb with the fear of Russia. Russia has hypnotized France, and her ministers are to-day receiving decorations from the Sultan.

After all, England is par excellence the moral nation of the world. Behind her driving commercialism is the English conscience. Above and beyond diplomatic England are the English people, as above its fog and mist are the everlasting skies. The first appeal of the oppressed of the world has always been addressed to the conscience of the English-speaking world—a conscience the most sensitive and the most uncompromising. With all her faults, England is still the apostle of civilization. Her Government's double-dealing with the Christians of the Orient deserves all the upbraiding it has received from the pen of William Watson, who has won the poet laureateship of humanity:

> Never, o craven England, never more
> Prate thou of generous effort, righteous aim!
> Betrayer of a People, know thy shame!
> . . . What stays the thunder in your hand?
> A fear for England? Can her pillared fame
> Only on faith forsworn securely stand,
> On faith forsworn that murders babes and men?
> Are such the terms of glory's tenure? Then
> Fall her accursed greatness, in God's name!

These are scathing words, but in what other country has there been raised a voice so pure and sonorous, so mighty and moral? The Armenians are hopelessly doomed unless the English-speaking people hasten to their assistance.

A word to those Americans who are lending the influence of their voice and pen to the support of the Turkish Government. While I could myself repeat a thousand favorable things of the Turkish people, I find it impossible to say one good thing of the Turkish Government. Do the friends of the Turk know that Turkey to-day is one of the slave markets of the world? Do they know that in Turkey, where the scurvy, leprous dogs of the street are religiously cared for, women are debauched in the harems? Is it not in Turkey that Circassian, Georgian, and Armenian girls in their teens are sent as presents to the pashas and the Sultan? Has not the Turkish Government made puppets of women and tyrants of men? Do our prominent society women, bankers, and diplomats wish to be known as the friends of such an institution? Can they respect themselves when they try to discredit the accumulating charges against so villainous a government? To labor in America for the emancipation of woman, but to see no wrong in the systematic rapine of Christian women in Turkey; to defend the reform of abuses here, but to stay away from all meetings which demand justice to the sufferers in Turkey, are flagrant contradictions—something to be really afraid of. When I think how some of our best men and women maintain a studied silence and turn a deaf ear to the cry of agony from the cities and villages of Mt. Ararat, a terrible sadness comes over me. My hand shakes so that I cannot write; the tears fall hot upon the page before me; I feel a stifling sensation in my breast, something like a lump rises to my throat, I shudder and gasp for breath!

If we fail to save the starving Armenians, they will perish. But that is not such a dreadful thing after all. Something worse than that will happen to *us*; we will die a moral death. If Armenia's wrongs cannot provoke the righteous indignation of the civilized world, then nothing can. To turn our back upon this nation struggling for the simplest rights, namely, security to life, property, and honor, is to forfeit our claim to civilization. If we can wink at the Turkish atrocities, then alas for us! for no crack of the lash upon our moral epidermis will ever sting us into action; but withdrawing from the great arena where truth and falsehood, liberty and oppression, clash and clang with "blows of death," we shall live on like a herd of swine, bent upon growing fat, and deaf to the bugle-call of humanity.

Turkey in Extremis

E. L. Godkin

The Cretan trouble was growing in gravity so rapidly that it alone threatened the Turkish Empire when the recent riots occurred in Constantinople. The Cretans have been in insurrection for a year, owing to the total breakdown of the Cretan constitution accorded in 1867 by the Porte, which included a "General Assembly," composed of both Christians and Mussulmans, but which has never met, or not more than once or twice, owing to the fixed belief of all parties that its resolves would have no effect. In fact, the indefinite retention of Crete by the Porte has been impossible since the Treaty of Berlin. The success of the Servians, Bulgarians, and Rumelians in securing complete or partial independence, and of the Montenegrins and Greeks in getting an extension of their territory at that time, has rendered peace impossible in European Turkey, for it has produced among all classes of the Turkish population the conviction that the end is near.

The Cretans are being powerfully assisted by their brother Greeks of the mainland, with both arms and men, and the Turkish navy is quite unable to prevent these accessions of force. It has been so evident for some time that it would be impossible to suppress the insurrection as long as this went on, that some of the Powers which are engaged in holding Turkey, foremost among which is Germany, some weeks ago proposed to blockade the island; but Lord Salisbury, to his honor, refused to concur. It was bad enough not to interfere on behalf of the Cretans, but to interfere against them would have been worse. Accordingly, there is now no danger of it. Remonstrances addressed to the Greek Government have proved equally useless. It cannot, if it would, prevent the dispatch of aid to the Cretans. The population is thoroughly aroused, and the islands are so numerous and the coasts so extensive that effective surveillance is out of the question. Moreover, in these Turkish wars regulars are not necessary. Both sides fight through massacre and pillage and from behind walls and ditches, and the Greek volunteers, though nothing but armed peasants and fisherman, gave a good account of both the Mussulman inhabitants and soldiery. The longer the disturbances last, the more difficult their suppression becomes. The whole mainland is in a state of excitement, particularly Macedonia, and the Montenegrins are straining in the leash. They killed Turks manfully and successfully for three hundred years as a condition of their existence, but for the last twenty years their occupation has been gone. The young men find it hard to grow up under the new conditions, and long to seek out their ancient enemy.

The supporters of Turkey were, therefore, at their wits' ends about Crete alone when the troubles in Constantinople began. But they are inevitable. Contempt for the Sultan's authority has at last reached the centre, after having so long prevailed in the provinces. The Christians have been made furious by the Armenian massacres and by the hopes raised by the trouble in Crete and Macedonia, and the Mussulmans are enraged with the Sultan for not killing more Christians. This readiness of the Turkish Government to make massacre the penalty of all sorts of sedition is difficult to comprehend if one does not remember that, by the Mussulman law, Christians live by sufferance under all Mussulman rule. The Sacred Law gives them their lives and property solely on condition of their remaining quiet and not complaining. Death is to the Mussulman the natural and proper punishment for a Christian who makes a disturbance. Therefore, when there is a rising anywhere, it seems as natural to the Mussulman that all the Christian men, women, and children in the neighborhood of the trouble should be killed as it would seem to us that the ringleaders should be arrested. Never since the Turks took Constantinople has a Christian rising been suppressed except by massacre, and, as a rule, no massacre has stopped until Christian powers intervened. The Turks, therefore, look on the slaughter of Christian families in disturbed districts much as we looked on the arrest and trial of the Chicago rioters—that is, as an act of vigor on the part of the authorities.

The riots in Constantinople are at last likely to bring matters to a head. The powers cannot allow that city to be given over to anarchy, however unconcernedly they may look on Armenia or Crete. They must maintain order there, owing to the size and wealth of the European population and the importance of the city to the civilized world. But if they interfere to maintain order, they virtually dethrone the Sultan. The protection of a sovereign by foreign force in his own capital means that his rule is, to all intents and purposes, at an end. To this complexion it has come at last, and to this complexion it was certain to come within a year when the massacres were going in Armenia. They were largely intended to act *in terrorem*, nearer home. For these shocking scenes of pillage and bloodshed which have disgraced our civilization during the past year, the European Powers are as much responsible as the Porte. It committed them, but they could have stopped them. For this disgrace we are largely indebted to the good understanding between Germany and Russia, and above all to Germany. Lord Salisbury probably would have interfered if he could. He probably might have interfered had he been the strong man people supposed he was, but small obstacles cowed him and drove him into subterfuge.

Nothing in modern politics is stranger than the changed attitude of Christian Europe towards the Turks. When they were really a strong power and able to set Europe an example in both civil and military virtue and administration, it was considered a pious duty in Western Europe to fight them. Now that they have lagged behind the civilized world, and descended to the lowest depths of barbarism and incompetence, it has become the fashion among a certain class of politicians to preach the possibility of their regeneration and the danger to peace and good order of interfering with any brutalities that may seem good to them.

The Constantinople Massacres

D. Kalopothakes[119]

Athens, September 18, 1896

Twelve hundred Armenian refugees, nearly all of them men and boys, are now here and at the Piræus, a few in houses hired for the purpose by the Local Relief Committee, but the majority huddled together in army tents which the Greek Government has provided, and which have been set up in the open fields at New Phalerum. At Syra there are 300 more, at Patras some sixty or seventy. Only 250 of those here have found work; the rest are entirely dependent upon the local committee, which draws its funds from private philanthropy.

Each refugee's account of what he himself saw during the first three days of the massacres throws abundant light upon the complicity of the Turkish authorities in the atrocities committed. One, a coal heaver, relates how he escaped from the coal depots at Lower Pera, when all his fellow-Armenian coal heavers, some forty-four in number, were suddenly surrounded by a Mussulman mob, headed by some twenty-five policeman, and butchered to a man. The mob then rushed to their victims' lodgings, which they plundered and destroyed. Another was in a house opposite Fundukli's Khan, a large four story building, which was besieged by a crowd of over four hundred Softas, headed by soldiers. The iron gates were forced. Some fifteen Armenians, who were employed in the building as porters, sought safety on the roof, but were pursued even there, and each one, after receiving several stabs, was hurled down from the roof into the street, while the crowd below yelled, "Long live Sultan Hamid!" Two refugees depose that they saw two other

Armenians caught by a Turkish butcher and his assistants, and, after being suspended by the feet from the meat-hooks in front of the shop, literally hacked to pieces by the butchers with their meat knives. Another eye-witness relates that an Armenian priest, while walking in the street, was followed by a Turkish mob, and, on attempting to take refuge in the house of a Frenchman, was dragged out by his robes. When the inmates of the house expostulated in his behalf, a Turkish officer in the crowd replied that the Government had issued an order that all Giaours should be slaughtered. The priest was therefore dragged off towards Galata-Seraï, but, after only a few steps, his head was split open with an axe by some one in the crowd. A well-dressed Armenian was eating in an open restaurant when the night-patrol passed; the officer in command, knowing him to be an Armenian, ordered him to come to the police-station. He asked to be allowed to finish his food, but was dragged out promptly, and bayonetted to death on the sidewalk in front of the restaurant. At Bahdjè-Kapoù two Armenians were discovered hiding on a roof; the policeman rushed into the house and hurled them down into the street, crying, "Long live Sultan Hamid!" At Feri-Koï, a well-to-do Armenian on horseback was seized and knocked off his horse by the police, who then told the mob to cut his head off, which was promptly done.

In many cases Turks accepted money from the Armenians to hide them, took them to their own houses, and then hastened to inform the police, who never failed to come and drag them off to slaughter. Two of the refugees saw thirty of their fellow-countrymen slaughtered in quick succession, in the space of a few minutes. An Armenian was knocked down by a Bashi-Buzuk and left insensible, whereupon an officer approached, drew his sword, and stabbed the fallen man through and through the body, until he was sure that he was dead. In front of the Swiss Legation a young Armenian milkman was butchered. A passing corpse cart refused to take the body, on the ground that, according to orders, it must first be dragged by the feet to the nearest police-station, as an example to Giaours. The day before the outbreak an eye-witness relates that, in front of his shop, a water seller was asked by a policeman for a glass of water, which was given; but when the man asked for payment the policeman glared at him, and went away without paying. Next day the same policeman returned with several others, caught the water seller, and hacked him literally to pieces before the shop, crying, "Giaour! Yesterday you wanted money for a drink of water; now we will drink your blood!"

Testimony of a special importance was given by another refugee. He was sitting in a café with some Greek friends when a servant of the Grand Vizier came in and, being personally acquainted with one of the Greeks, sat down with them and related how his master's cook, an Armenian, had been summoned on the day when the troubles broke out, and paid, and told that he must leave. The poor man begged to be allowed to remain a few days longer, until quiet should be restored, but the Grand Vizier refused. The man then begged for at least a safe-conduct, upon which his master gave him in charge of a Turkish fellow-servant, who, acting upon orders, conducted him to the Galata-Seraï, where, at a sign from him, the policeman cut the Armenian down and rifled his body.

Another eye-witness, who was employed in the Feri-Koï beer-garden, on the road leading to the Armenian cemetery, testifies to having counted, from 10 P.M. on Wednesday until Thursday noon, 28 ox-carts and 136 ordinary carts full of dead bodies, passing up the road from Galata and Pera alone, while 71 cart-loads came from the Haskoi Road. Near the cemetery there were some ice-houses, with great trenches, where the ice is stored in winter, and now empty. Here the bodies were thrown in pell-mell, by a force of 58 Turks (according to witness) who were employed by the authorities, who forbade any Armenian or Christian to have any share in the work. Another witness testified that on Wednesday and Thursday nights, from dark until morning, a continuous file of carts full of dead bodies was moving up the road to the cemetery heights above Pera.

The refugees speak enthusiastically of the friendly attitude of the Persian Mohammedans of the Shiz sect, who protected and succored many an Armenian at peril of their own lives, against the infuriated Softas. The Jews, on the contrary, were zealously engaged in marking with a cross all doors where Armenians were to be found. It is note worthy, that, according to the unanimous testimony of all the refugees whom I interviewed, the Turkish mob, while engaged in slaughter, and even the Turkish officials at Galata-Seraï would cry out, at each act of butchery, "Long live England!

See what England does for you! Take that from your friends the English!"

But the crowning testimony is that of a young Armenian of barely twenty-one, whose splendid physical proportions and frank, ingenuous face attracted my notice. I found that I had, to use Cicero's words, "stepped into a history." This young fellow belonged to a body of twenty-five firemen and porters attached to the Galata-Seraï (the chief police station of Constantinople). Only four of their number were Kurds and Turks, and they disappeared just before the outbreak; the remaining twenty-one were all Armenians. When the massacres began, only eleven of them happened to be at the café, or public house, near the entrance to the Seraï, where they lodged. My informant was among the eleven. About 2 p.m. on Wednesday, when cartloads of dead bodies began to arrive at the Seraï, the Chief of Police sent for them, and set them to sorting the dead Turks from the Giaours, as the Moslems consider it unclean to handle a dead Giaour. In this first instalment of dead only five or six were Armenians, the remainder being Turks, probably soldiers, but all were naked. When this task was over, the porters were ordered back to the public house, and told not to stir out on pain of being shot. At the same time strict orders were given and guards posted about the public house to prevent these men from being molested.

From this tavern the porters could see all that passed in the Seraï, and counted over 300 Armenians brought in under arrest by the police and troops. Soon they were sent for again from the Seraï, and found a horrible piece of work awaiting them. The arrested Armenians were all crowded into a large hall; a door opened into a broad passage, terminating at a steep flight of stone steps leading down into a courtyard. Each of the arrested Armenians was called out by an officer into the passage, which he found lined with officers and soldiers, the latter carrying fixed bayonets on their muskets. He was ordered to walk forward, and as he reached the top of the steps he received a stunning blow on the head with a cudgel, and a bayonet thrust on either side, through the ribs. The body falling down the stairs was taken by the Armenian porters, who were waiting at the bottom, and dragged out into the courtyard and down into the cellars. Their butchery lasted for three hours and a half, an uninterrupted succession of blows and bayonet thrusts, the bodies falling down the steps almost without a groan. The porters were soon covered with blood as they had to pile up the bodies in the cellars; one of them, the captain of the fire brigade, fainted away at the fifth corpse that he lifted, and a Turkish officer standing by gave orders to have him removed and restoratives applied. When the sickening work was over, the porters were ordered to wash themselves, but they were so saturated with blood that the soldiers had to turn the fire-hose on them to wash them off. My informant showed me his broad linen girdle, which, though washed since them, bore distinct traces of blood. Then they were ordered to wash down the steps and the courtyard, after which they were ordered back to their tavern, and told to be on hand for night-work. After their return to the public house, they saw a large number of carts loaded with dead bodies brought to the Seraï.

In the evening they were again sent for, this time to drag out the corpses which they had piled up in the cellars that afternoon, and to load them upon carts. Nineteen cartloads of eighteen or twenty bodies each were thus sent off successively, each under charge of one porter and two soldiers, to the Armenian cemetery. My informant said: "While piling up the corpses we saw many an eye open and close, and heard an occasional groan or sigh, but it was night, and we were working with a band of sentinels and officers over us, and could do nothing for any unfortunate wretch who was not quite dead." At the cemetery each cartload was emptied into the trenches, and the cart drove back at once with the porters and guards, leaving the rest to the Turkish laborers stationed at the cemetery, no one else being allowed to approach. Everything was under strong military surveillance. The Seraï was crowded with troops under the command of higher officers in full uniform. After the carting was finished, the porters once more washed out the courtyard and were dismissed for the night. Next morning (Thursday) very early they heard the noise of fighting and killing in the neighboring streets renewed. They were soon called out under strong military escort to drag into the Seraï the corpses with which the Grand Rue de Pera and the adjoining streets were thickly strewn. My informant saw his sister's son, a youth of eighteen, set upon by the police and cut down, but not before the lad had drawn a revolver and shot two of his assailants dead. Our friend had been obliged to drag his nephew's body by the feet into the Seraï like all the rest. The bodies were again piled up in the cellars, awaiting transportation by night. This bloody work lasted from early morning until about half an hour before sunset; then the porters were once more dismissed and not called out again that night.

During the following twelve days they were employed in various less outrageous ways about the Seraï, but were never allowed to go one step beyond the outside sentinels, while within strict orders had been given that no one should lay hands upon them. Finally, my informant, who was trusted more than his fellows, was given a letter by the head commissioner to carry to one of the islands, and, after delivering it, he determined to escape. A police officer of the Seraï was at his heels who had a long-standing grudge against him, and it was evident that he was bent upon getting the porter into some corner and killing him. As the Armenian was passing the Greek embassy, he succeeded in darting through the open gate, in spite of the cries of the policeman. He was kindly received by the Greek Ambassador, who himself had him put into a carriage and sent, under the charge of a cavass, to the Greek steamer, which brought him and many others safely to Piræus. I may add that I have succeeded in obtaining a list of the Turkish military and police officers who assisted at this infamous butchery in the Galata Seraï, but must refrain from publishing it, out of regard for the safety of the other ten Armenian porters who are still imprisoned there and employed about the premises. Besides, it is only too evident that all these officials, high and low, were but executing the orders of the "the great assassin."

The Massacres at Van

Many who read Dr. Grace Kimball's account of the relief work at Van as published in our April number were doubtless the more keenly interested in the newspaper reports of the atrocities committed there by the Turks less than three months later. Miss Kimball's own story of these outrages has been graphically told in several recent publications. We quote below from her article in *Lend a Hand* for September.

> Van's turn came at last. The disturbances were brought about by the worst element from among the revolutionists—scamps from Russia and Bulgaria—men who had no local interests, no families, and no lands or property at stake, but who came as absolute dictators of the destiny of the entire community. The Armenians were too broken spirited and hopeless to oppose this energetic band of criminals under the guise of heroes and patriots, and it is hard to say of whom the people stood most in fear, the incensed Turk, on the one hand, or these men, on the other, who insisted, under threats of murder—which were several times carried out—on quartering themselves on the peaceful inhabitants and demanding money and other assistance from them. So great was the terror they inspired that even in the relief work the native helpers were afraid to advise as to who should not receive assistance, lest they incur the animosity of these men. For many months they used every means to force the young men to join, furnished them with arms from Russia and Persia, and dressed in a wild, striking sort of uniform, went back and forth by night, from one rendezvous to another, frequently meeting the Turkish patriot, and thus adding constantly to the smoldering fire of Turkish hatred and fanaticism. During the spring one of these bands met the patrol, was challenged, shots were exchanged, and Turkish soldier killed. The authorities with difficulty calmed the wrath of the soldiers. Since Bahri Pacha's dismissal the local government, under Nagin Pacha, has honestly and successfully labored to defend the

town against outbreaks, and the advent of this lawless band was, therefore, doubly unfortunate and fatal to the interests of the community at large.

When the snows disappeared the revolutionists began, in spite of the warning and advice from the Governor-General, the British Vice-Consul, and the American missionaries, to send armed bands against the Kurds, to avenge the wrong done the Armenians in the fall. So the government saw that no compromise was possible and that the city must be cleared of the revolutionists; their haunts were surrounded and searched by the police, but such is the configuration of the town that it was perfectly easy for the rebels to elude their pursuers. Finally the storm broke; at midnight on Sunday, June 14, an encounter took place at the edge of the town between the Turkish patrol and an armed band, the Armenians say, of Kurds smuggling salt; the Turks say of revolutionists. A soldier and the officer in charge were badly wounded. By noon the long expected outbreak was well under way. In all quarters of the town, where the population was mixed, Turkish and Armenian, and in quarters abutting on Turkish neighborhood, crowds of hundreds of low Turks, Kurds, gypsies, and irregular soldiers and gendarmes arrived with guns and swords and every kind of weapon, and broke loose on the utterly defenseless and unsuspecting people. They swept from house to house, from street to street, from quarter to quarter, killing all whom they could reach, pillaging the houses of everything, and, in the case of better houses, destroying them by fire. It was, I think, due to the fact of the excessive poverty of the Turks, and especially the soldiers, that the pillaging engaged their attention most largely, and for this reason the killing was not so great as might have been expected from the terrible animosity existing. The greater part of the Armenians were able to save their lives by flight. Probably about 500 were killed, while many were badly wounded. The riot continued for eight consecutive days. When the affray was well begun and the revolutionists took up fortified positions, and stood siege by the mob. Twelve of fifteen of these men, well armed, easily withstood all assaults, and inflicted severe loss on their opponents; probably 150 or 200 Moslems were thus killed, and for every Moslem killed the wave of fanatical frenzy rose higher. Soon after midnight of the fifth day, one or two mountain guns reduced these strongholds, and their doughty defenders sought refuge in the compact Armenian quarter, which had been protected by the British Vice-Consul. The government, acting in consultation with the British Consul, offered them the most easy and merciful terms of surrender, and these were urged as the only way to restore confidence and save their co-religionists from further violence and plunder, but the whilom leaders were too much impressed with the desirability of insuring their own lives to listen, and now that they had precipitated the avalanche of destruction, they, with the arms they had brought with them, left from the mountains and personal safety across the Persian frontier. Thanks to Major Williams' herculean efforts, the compact Armenian quarter—something like a mile square—was largely saved, and for days the American mission, protected by the Union Jack, gave refuge to something like 15,000 people.

At the time when Dr. Kimball wrote, shortly after the outbreak, her relief department was giving out daily rations of bread or soup to over 15,000 people, fully 10,000 of whom were homeless and destitute.

Dr. Kimball throws much blame on the revolutionary party of the Armenians. Notwithstanding the savage and brutal character of the Turks, Dr. Kimball says that the local government acted well, largely because of the influence of the British Vice-Consul, Major Williams, who was probably the means of preventing a general slaughter of Christians.

America's Duty to Americans in Turkey

In an open letter to Senator Sherman published in the *North American Review* the venerable Dr. Cyrus Hamlin, for many years a missionary in Turkey, replies with crushing force to the implication in one of the Senator's speeches that American missionaries in Turkey are beyond protection from their home government. He shows that existing treaty provisions are ample to secure all the rights accorded to "the most favored nation."

> Had our country defended the treaty rights of her citizens as all the nations of Europe have defended theirs, the massacres that blot with innocent blood the last pages of the century would never had been perpetrated, as I shall briefly show.
> The present Sultan, Hamid, came to the throne with an inveterate dislike to all Armenians who would not apostatize and thus follow his mother's example. He began his career by displacing them from office. Many hundreds of them were in various offices of government. He next began to oppress their schools with new and vexatious requirements and to spoil their school-books by an absurd censorship. Many schools were closed, many school-books destroyed

for containing forbidden words, such as "courage," "patience," "patriotism," "progress." In this work he encountered our schools, school-books, and teachers, and began cautiously his war upon them. He has destroyed our school-books printed and issued by the authority of his government and owned by Americans, an invasion of rights perpetrated upon Americans alone. Our government was often appealed to for redress, which was generally promised in the sweetest and most gracious words, of which our diplomats have been very proud. But no penalty was ever exacted, no promise was ever fulfilled, excepting the case of Mr. Bartlett's house, in which the moving force was the threat of an ironclad. Now every outrage thus treated during the last few years has been a distinct permission to go on to greater outrages upon property and personal rights. The Sultan has seen that it is a safe thing to perpetrate every indignity upon Americans and their property, until now the destruction of American property has amounted to nearly $200,000. Not a dollar would have been destroyed had our government from the beginning protected our rights as all the governments of Europe protect their citizens.

It must be remembered that the destruction and the looting of the buildings at Harpoot, Marash, and other places were done in the presence of government officials and troops, and the plea "done by a mob" cannot be accepted.

It must also be remembered that every building destroyed had been built in strict accordance with all the laws of building; their plans, measurements and proposed uses had all been laid before the proper authorities and received their sanctions. The government in destroying such buildings and looting them of all their contents of furniture, food, and clothing has gone back upon itself in its eagerness to show "its contempt of America and Americans." In all this the Sultan is backed up by Russia. No indemnity has been exacted or if any demand has been made it is understood that some high Russian diplomat whispers that now is not the proper time to enforce it, and it is dropped. Thus the "Great Republic" is justly the derision of other nations and cowers before a poor Sultan who cannot pay a piastre of his public debt, nor make the smallest loan in the money markets of Europe.

No Turk has yet been punished for robbery, pillage, murder, rape, rapine, torture unto death of women and children, and the horrid work still goes on. Why should it not? The nations, our own nation especially, have for two years been giving the Sultan *carte-blanche* to do as he please; and his pleasure is the extermination of all Armenians who will not Islamize, the expulsion of the American missionaries, the destruction of their property, and the showing of himself as superior to all treaties and to all the claims of truth, justice, and humanity toward all men of the Christian faith.

The Eastern Ogre; Or, St. George to the Rescue, 1878 and 1896

W. T. Stead[120]

The above heading was the title of the first pamphlet I ever published. It is twenty years since it made its appearance, followed by a prompt disappearance. I kept a copy or two as a kind of memorial tablet, such as we erect over the grave of the dead. Such in those old Bulgarian days were the high hopes which we of the Agitation dared to entertain. What a bitter commentary upon that parable of things to come were the things that did actually occur!

How St. George Went to the Rescue in 1878

For St. George, instead of rushing to the rescue, spent a whole twelve months threatening to attack the Russians, who were locked in a death grapple with the Ogre. Then at the last moment, when the Assassin, gasping for breath, was compelled to relax his hold upon the provinces he had devastated with the revelry of hell, St. George stepped in, restored the Ogre's sovereignty over Macedonia, destroyed the guarantee exacted by the Russians for the protection of the Armenians, and then, to make his infamy complete, picked the Ogre's pocket of his Cypriote handkerchief, and strutted round Europe as the champion of peace with honor.

Of Accursed Memory

All that and more was done by Lord Beaconsfield, of accursed memory. No greater shame ever covered the head of any nation than that which descended upon Britain when, alike in the festive halls of the city and in the legislative chambers at Westminster, Lord Beaconsfield, with Lord Salisbury concealed in his sinister shadow, proudly received the plaudits of his countrymen for the crime of Berlin and the three card trick of Cyprus. The indelible infamy of that performance clings to us like the shirt of Nessus. It paralyzes us to-day, and will paralyze us until we pluck up sufficient courage to undo his evil work and sacrifice the booty which is the symbol of our shame, and a standing reminder to all Europe of the trickiness and dishonesty of *"perfide Albion."*

England's Responsibility for the Assassin

During the last few weeks England and Scotland have at last made a somewhat tardy but unmistakable national expression of their indignation at the reign of massacre established *en permanence* on the Bosphorus. It is well that this should be so. A nation that did not feel moved to say "Damn" and say it out full-mouthed in the hearing of God and man, on seeing the slaughtering that has gone on, and is going on, in the dominions of the Grand Turk, would be a nation without even a semblance of a moral sense. But in the midst of our indignation there has been very inadequate recognition of the fact that the guilt really lies at our own door. If the Assassin reigns—

> ... reseated in his place of light,
> The mockery of his people and their bane,

it is England who placed him there. We sent our fleet through the Dardanelles to protect him against the Russians, who, after incredible hardships heroically surmounted, were in a position to have hurled him into the Bosphorus. We summoned the Berlin Congress in order to re-establish his authority and consolidate his empire. It was England and none other that canceled the clause in the Treaty of San Stefano giving Russia right to compel the Turks to guarantee the Armenians against outrages and massacres. And it was England, through her accredited representatives, who, while re-enslaving Macedonia and Armenia in the name of public law and the independence and consolidation of the Ottoman Empire, filched like a footpad the island of Cyprus under cover of a fraudulent convention which binds us to defend the Assassin against his executioner, but which is to this day unrecognized by the public law of Europe and repudiated by the moral sense of our own people. A pretty St. George, indeed! Even Dick Turpin would have recoiled from such a piece of petty larceny as that which made England appear as the piratical Pecksniff of Europe.

"The Insane Covenant"

From that day down to the present moment of writing England remains branded with the black and burning shame of that transaction. We may laugh in our sleeves at the simplicity of the Turk, who imagined that we meant to fulfill the obligation to which we solemnly affixed the signature of England. But the Anglo-Turkish Convention stands. It has no force in international law, but is a binding document between the Assassin and the Queen of England. There have been, of course, various threatening speeches. With many shakings of the head and solemn frowning, the Turk has been told by ministers and others that unless he mends his ways he can no longer expect any support against the Russians. But the convention has never been denounced, and Cyprus, which was the sign and seal of that covenant with Hell, remains in our occupation to this day. As long as the British flag is flying over that island without the sanction of the European concert, in flat violation of all the principles of international law, upon which our intervention in Turkey has been defended—I do not say justified—so long will it be impossible for us to appeal with any confidence to the other powers for joint action against the Eastern Ogre. Hence, it seems to me that the present agitation which has done honor to the heart of Britain is much less complimentary to her head. For what is the use of vociferation on a thousand platforms that St. George must go to the rescue, when the one thing which renders action impossible is the deep conviction that dominates the policy of all the powers, uttered or unexpressed, that St. George's one object in going to the rescue is to repeat on a larger scale the Cypriote larceny?

The Precedent of Bulgaria

It is no use for eloquent and impassioned orators, confident in the integrity of their own hearts and the sincerity of their own intentions, to fume and bluster against this plain and straightforward exposition of how the land lies. Those who are running the Armenian agitation, from Mr. Gladstone downward, are no doubt perfectly honest when they declare that they are animated by a disinterested desire to secure the protection of the Armenians from the hands of the Assassin. No one denies that they mean what they say; but the very same set of men said very much the same kind of thing as to the disinterested desire of England to help Bulgaria twenty years ago. Russia undertook at her own cost to liberate the Bulgarians. After she had spent £100,000,000 sterling, and sacrificed the lives of 100,000 of her noblest sons, England, acting through her ministers—whom our agitators were powerless to arrest—re-enslaved one-third of Bulgaria, delivered over Armenia to the uncovenanted mercies of the Sultan, and then ran off with Cyprus as their wages for a crime almost unparalleled in history for its combination of Pharisaism and theft. Therefore we have no reason whatever to marvel that every European, and especially every Russian, expects that we shall act in the same way again.

How the Russians Argue

But "Once bit," say the Russians,

> twice shy. It is all very well for English agitators to clamor for armed intervention on behalf of the people whom English ministers have handed back to the Turk. We all know what that comes to. In a year or two the agitation will die out, and when we have spent all our money, and sacrificed the flower of our army, then we shall have to face England as an enemy, and see her running off with the tit-bits of Turkey. Lord Beaconsfield took Cyprus in 1878; we should find Lord Salisbury or some one in his place attempting to seize Constantinople or Gallipoli in 1898. History repeats itself. National characteristics do not disappear in twenty years. As England tricked us then, so England will trick us again. You can never can trust the English excepting to look after the main chance for themselves, and to leave every one and everything else, including their principles, in the lurch when the time comes for laying their hands upon their neighbors' goods.

Is There No Place For Repentance?

This may be a brutal way of putting it, but if we look the facts fairly in the face, it is exactly what every Russian feels, and feels most keenly; nor are there many Frenchman, Austrians, or Germans who would dissent. But what then? "Are we to sit with hands folded and do nothing," I shall be asked,

> because Lord Beaconsfield committed a crime twenty years ago? Is England's voice to be silent forever in the councils of Europe because the nation unwillingly acquiesced in the antics of Lord Beaconsfield in 1878? Is it not our duty, the more we have sinned in 1878, to make what reparation is possible in the year of grace 1896? And if we enslaved the Armenians and Macedonians in the year of the Anglo-Turkish Convention, is it not all the more reason why we should send our ironclads through the Dardanelles, and let the Bosphorus resound with the roar of our great guns as our blue-jackets shell the Sultan out of his place at Yildiz?

Such are the questions which many impatient, unthinking, good men and true ask throughout the length and breadth of the land. But to all these questions there is one sufficient answer.

First-fruits Meet for Repentance

By all means let us make such reparation as is possible for the crime of 1878. We were then strenuous for the tyrant and the Assassin; let us now at least defend the cause of his oppressed and slaughtered subjects. But if so, before doing anything else, as the indispensable preliminary to any act of reparation or of penitence, we must denounce the Anglo-Turkish Convention and clear out of Cyprus. Nothing short of that can suffice to convince the powers—with whom we must act if intervention in Turkey is not to make things far worse than they are now—that we have repented of our evil deeds, that they have now to deal with a nation that has given a pledge of its disinterestedness, and that they may at least have a reasonable foundation for the belief that John Bull has amended his ways and means to act quite straight.

"Qui Bono?" the Answer

It is true that even if we clear out of Cyprus tomorrow, and send the Turkish ambassador packing from London with the shreds of the Anglo-Turkish Convention in his pocket, many Continental cynics would shrug their shoulders and talk about death-bed conversions. But we have no reason to complain of these gibes. We have merited them all too well. What we have to do now is to set about the discharge of a plain duty, which we owe to our own national self-respect, to the subjects of the Assassin, and even to the Assassin himself. If, when we have done all this, we should still find our steps dogged by inveterate distrust, it would be deplorable, but we should no longer feel that we had neglected the one indispensable step which lay well within our power to take, by which we could have given proof of the sincerity of our penitence.

Prince Lobanoff's[121] Last Words

A good deal of this, and more in the same strain, I wrote in the *Westminster Gazette* in view of the recent visit of the Czar to Balmoral. I did not then know what Madame Novikoff has since brought to the knowledge of Europe—namely, that Prince Lobanoff had explicitly declared in Moscow during the coronation festivities that the attitude of Russia in relation to Armenia was governed by the fact that England was committed by the Anglo-Turkish Convention to defend the Sultan against Russia should she take any action whatever to protect the Armenians against their oppressors. The very last recorded utterance of Prince Lobanoff on this subject is thus reported by Madame Novikoff:

> At one of the coronation balls at Moscow I chanced to meet Prince Lobanoff, who, in reply to some observation of mine as to the difficulties between England and Russia, replied very seriously:
>
> "You refer to the terrible Armenian question, I see. But how can we Russians ignore the meaning and importance of the Cyprus Convention, which compels England to oppose Russia whenever a serious danger threatens the integrity of Turkey?"
>
> I protested that the English had changed their minds about the sacredness of that treaty.
>
> "No doubt," he replied, "I am not so badly informed as you suppose. I know all about that healthy change for the better. But, nevertheless, that treaty still exists. Do you suppose for one moment that if England were to rescind her obligations under that treaty we should fail to immediately respond with proposals for a new departure?"

Prince Lobanoff is dead. But the ideas of Prince Lobanoff remain, nor can we wonder if his successor resolutely refuses to move a step in the direction of an armed intervention in Turkey until we have hauled down the British flag which was hoisted at Larnica as a menace that no Russian intervention would be permitted on the Asiatic frontier of Turkey.

England's Proper Attitude toward Russia

In the course of the agitation, I regret very much to have seen many expressions of irritation and of indignation at the conduct of Russia—Mr. Gladstone himself not being altogether guiltless in this respect. It is a case in which we should do well to take the beam out of our own eye before raving at the mote in the eye of the Russian. In view of the evidence now patent to all men as to the real essential nature of Turkish rule, England's attitude toward Russia ought certainly not to be that of resentment or of indignation. Granting that, for the moment, the policy of reserve and of inaction adopted by Russia is most deplorable in the interests of humanity, it is but a passing episode of a few months at the most. But England's attitude for fifty years has been just that which Russia has adopted within the last twelve months. Let us grant, if you please, the worst that can be said against Russian policy, the effect of which has been to secure the twelve months longer lease of immunity to the Assassin of Stamboul. What is that compared with the guilt which we have incurred by our persistent support of the Turkish misrule, a support persisted in for generation after generation, and that not merely by the adoption of a passive policy of non-intervention, but by an active armed intervention on behalf of the Assassin and his predecessors?

The Convert of the Eleventh Hour

England stands guilty before the world, and especially before Russia, for the continuous crime of her traditional policy in the Levant. No doubt, so far as the majority of our people were concerned, it was a sin of ignorance. But that was not true twenty years ago, when the policy was deliberately re-affirmed and enforced by Lord Beaconsfield in face of the angry and passionate protest of the national conscience, which, however, was powerless to prevent the execution of the mischief that he did at Berlin. Therefore, I hope we may hear no more execrations addressed to the Foreign Office at St. Petersburg. The worst that Prince Lobanoff did was to adopt passively, at a remote distance, the policy which the English nation pursued ruthlessly and actively for over fifty years. We have now repented, genuinely I have no doubt, but in the fervor of our conversion it would be more fitting if we were covered with shame and humiliation, and sat silent and abashed before Russia, rather than to venture on the strength of this conversion of the eleventh hour to behave ourselves unseemly and to hurl contumacious words against Russia, who has borne the burden and the heat of the day all these years. This, surely, is the dictate of decency. It is none the less prompted by every consideration of expediency and policy.

England, Austria and Constantinople

Those good souls who are shouting themselves hoarse in favor of an isolated intervention by England talk like children. Not less childish, although equally well meaning, is the inane persistence of some journals who seem to imagine that the one way of securing Russian co-operation is to bribe her with an offer of Constantinople. What Russia wants is not to plant herself upon Constantinople, but to be sure that England, or England's ally, Austria, will take advantage of any upset in the East to establish herself here. To convince Russia that such is not our little game, we must clear out of Cyprus. It is driveling folly to talk of offering Russia Constantinople as the price of her alliance. Constantinople is not ours to give, nor would Russia accept it as a gift if it were. There is reason also to believe that we are at this moment bound by a secret treaty to Austria and Italy, which would compel us to support these powers in making war against Russia if she tried to seize Constantinople. Such, at least, is the assertion stoutly made by those who were in the confidence of the Italian Minister by whom the arrangement was concluded—for it is a misnomer to speak of it as a formal treaty.

"Peace, Imperfect Peace"

Still, leaving that on one side, those who talk about giving Russia Constantinople forget that what Russia wants is not to bring about a general overturn, but to keep things going without a catastrophe.

"Anything for a quiet life" is the motto of Russia. "Peace, imperfect peace, rather than no peace at all" is the cry of the Czar and his ministers. Nicholas II is as desirous of earning the title of "The Prince of Peace" as was his father before him, and it is adding insult to injury to assume, as is constantly done in such well-meaning journals as the *Spectator*, for instance, that all that holds him back from active intervention on behalf of the Armenians is a doubt whether or not we would object to him appropriating Constantinople as his share of the swag. Single-handed intervention by England would, in the opinion of the European nations most concerned, mean that we saw a chance of seizing some coveted position in the East.

The Jingo Song of 1878

The echoes of the Jingo song with which England vibrated in 1878 have not yet died out of the Continent. The Russians, indeed, have good reason to remember the insolent swagger of the music hall braves when they boasted that they had the ships, the men and the money, and the Russians should never have Constantinople. That rough music hall ditty is believed to express the unchanged traditional policy of Great Britain. It was emphasized in 1878 when our ironclads forced the Dardanelles and anchored almost within gunshot of Constantinople. At that time it was an open secret that plans were prepared for holding Gallipoli, so that England, having command of the sea, might hold the Dardanelles in force. Now, it is just as well to recognize the fact that any move in that direction will be regarded by Russia as practically equivalent to a declaration of war. It might be deferred war, but any attempt on our part to seize the Dardanelles would be regarded in Russia and on the Continent generally, not as a means adopted solely in order to execute justice on the Assassin, but simply as the seizure of what we intended to keep. In order words, England would have begun the game of grab by seizing the first and most valuable booty for herself.

The Dardanelles Song of 1896

It is not very pleasant for our national self-complacency to recognize the fact that this would be the natural conclusion that would be drawn the moment the first British redcoat landed at Gallipoli, but the fact is so. Nor need we be very much surprised that such should be the conclusions of our neighbors, when we see the kind of thing that is held by some of the more vehement of our agitators.

There is, for instance, Mr. William Allan, M.P. for Gateshead, one of the best fellows in the world, enthusiastic, sincere, and full of generous sympathies for the oppressed subjects of the Sultan. But what, we wonder, does he think would be the conclusion which the "Frank and Muscovite" will draw from the warlike ballad which he contributed last month to the *Newcastle Daily Leader*:

SEIZE THE DARDANELLES

We fear not Frank nor Muscovite
When Liberty is calling,
With British pluck for those we'll fight,
'Neath Moslem vengeance falling:
Cease your preaching! Load your guns!
Their roar our mission tells,
The day is come for Britain's sons
To seize the Dardanelles.

We need no help from other powers,
When Duty's path pursuing,
To save the weak alone is ours,
And shall be Britain's doing:
So cease your spouting! Load your guns!
Their might no power excels,
It is the hour for Britain's sons
To seize the Dardanelles.

Have Britain's sons forgot their sires,
Who fought for freedom ever?
And faced a thousand battle-fires
All tyrant hordes to shiver:
Come cease your prattling! Load your guns!
Not words for them, but-shells,

> And ready now are Britain's sons
> To seize the Dardanelles.
>
> Why longer wait when Murder's hand
> May victims still be seeking?
> Its shadows hover o'er the land
> With blood of thousands reeking:
> Cease your babbling! Load your guns!
> Hope in their thunder dwells.
> The signal flies! Up, Britain's sons!
> "We'll seize the Dardanelles!"

Now, it is well for us to seriously face the facts and to recognize that all this kind of thing is the veriest nonsense. We are not going to seize the Dardanelles. And we are not going to take any isolated action of this kind. We are not going to do so, because it would make matters infinitely worse for every one concerned, including the Armenians. We cannot do so because we are universally distrusted, and rightly-so long as we hold Cyprus. The first thing, therefore, for us to do is to tear up the Anglo-Turkish Convention, and to intimate to all the powers our readiness to evacuate Cyprus the moment they can agree upon the future government of that island.

The Future of Cyprus

Of course, to surrender to the uncontrolled sovereignty of the Sultan any territory or island where the inhabitants have for twenty years enjoyed the benefits of a civilized administration is not to be thought of. The Sultan, besides, has forfeited, not to England, but to Europe, all right to any of his dominions in Europe or Asia, and it would therefore be quite justifiable for the European powers to mulct him in Cyprus as a fine for his contumacy, to hand it over to Greece, or to make any other disposition of it that may seem good in their own eyes. But there is no necessity for taking such drastic measures. There would be no difficulty in restoring the Ottoman sovereignty in Cyprus, subject to such provisions as existed in Eastern Roumelia before the sub-Balkan province was merged in Bulgaria. It would be a profitable experiment for the powers to have to dispose of this little fragment of Turkish territory, which might help them to deal with the rest of the Sultan's possessions, which will sooner or later be placed in liquidation.

What Ought to Be Our Eastern Policy

But, it will be objected, suppose we clear out of Cyprus, what then? Then we should have taken the first step toward re-establishing in the concert of Europe on a basis which would render it possible to arrange for joint action. But joint action for what? Surely it is necessary to envisage the Eastern Question as a whole, and if you are to make sacrifices in order to put in motion this international machinery, you ought to have some definite idea as to the use to which you are going to put it. To what end do you intend to work? What is your policy, in short? To all of which, first, I make a negative reply. My policy is not to propound any of those grandiose schemes of partition which find favor in the eyes of amateur diplomatists writing in the monthly magazines, who propose to precipitate that general division of the Sick Man's dominions which would be the letting loose of all the jealousies and all the animosities—in other words, of bringing about the general war which every statesman in Europe regards it as his first duty to postpone. What we have to do is much more simple.

Enforce the Treaty of Berlin!

We have simply to take our stand upon treaty obligations to which we ourselves are parties, and which, if thoroughly fulfilled, would avert the cataclysm. The treaty of Berlin governs the whole position. All our present trouble has arisen from the fact, as it was everybody's business, it was nobody's business to see that the Sultan carried out those reforms for which written security was taken in the Berlin treaty. It is now generally recognized, even by the most impulsive and headstrong of those who are clamoring for action, that the Russians were perfectly right in objecting to any scheme of reform limited to one corner of Asiatic Turkey, merely because that happened to be marked Armenia upon the map. The Armenians, as Madame Novikoff reminded us twelve months ago, are everywhere, and local reforms limited to three vilayets on the eastern frontier would leave more Armenians exposed to the Sultan's fury than it would shield from his vengeance.

For the Armenians

What then must be done? The answer is written at large in the clauses of the Berlin treaty. To begin with, we have the Armenian clause, which runs thus:

> The Sublime Porte undertakes to carry out without further delay (this was agreed to on the 9th of July, 1878) the ameliorations and reforms demanded by local requirements in the provinces inhabited by the Armenians, and to guarantee their security against the Kurds and Circassians, and will make known periodically the steps taken to this effect to the powers who will superintend their applications.

The first step should be for the European concert to appoint one thoroughly capable, energetic, upright man as superintendent of the Armenian reforms. The six powers cannot each undertake the superintendence of the reforms.

A European Superintendent of Reforms

Why then not appoint one high official, who would represent the whole of the six powers, and be armed with their authority, who would be presented to the Porte in the name of the six powers, deputed by them to undertake the task which was eighteen years ago imposed upon all the signatories of the Berlin treaty? Some may doubt the possibility of the six powers agreeing upon any official, but the answer to that is that it depends upon England. If England is honest, and desires to see the Armenians protected—those of them still left alive—she cannot desire a better opportunity of proving the sincerity and disinterestedness of her Armenian enthusiasm than by taking the initiative in the European Concert in proposing that the superintendent delegated by all the powers to superintend the execution of the necessary reforms in the provinces inhabited by the Armenians shall be a Russian. If England and Russia are agreed upon this point, France will certainly make no objection; and if England, Russia, and France are agreed, the other three powers of the Triple Alliance will be not less unanimous.

Who Must Be a Russian

Therefore, we take it that if we are but in earnest of our desire to work with Russia for the amelioration of the condition of the Christians in the East we have a very good opportunity here of proving it. Considering that it is openly asserted that our government would have no objection whatever to a Russian occupation of Armenia, it would be difficult to see what objection they could make to the much milder measure of appointing a Russian superintendent of reforms, acting in the name and with the authority of all Europe.

Eastern-Roumelianize All the Rest

But when that is agreed upon, it by no means disposes of the whole question. Fortunately, our part is still plainer in reference to the other provinces of the Empire. By Clause 23 it is expressly provided that local autonomy shall be given to those provinces. By this clause the Sublime Porte undertook to introduce reforms into the other provinces, which, in order to make them correspond to the wants of every province, should be deliberated upon by commissions, in which the respective local elements were to be prominently represented. But the final settlement of these reforms was to be left to a European commission.

Now the commission met years ago, and decided as to what ought to be done in Macedonia. The practical effect of this was *nil*, although, fortunately, a preliminary discussion proved that there was no difficulty on the part of the powers in arriving at a practical agreement as to the nature of the autonomy in question. But there the matter rested. Macedonia, for whose benefit this autonomy was specially devised, remains to this day as she was when the Russians evacuated the territory, and left the Turks to re-establish their authority over the province which Russia had freed but which England had re-enslaved.

How to Dry up the River Euphrates

What ought to be done, therefore, for all the provinces outside those inhabited by the Armenians, is simply to take this clause and insist upon Turkey giving effect to the provisions of the organic statute for Macedonia drawn up by the powers nearly twenty years ago. There would be no disruption of the fabric of the Ottoman Empire. We should simply, to use the phrase familiar to students of prophecy, provide for the quiet "drying up of the river Euphrates." In each province local autonomous governments would come into existence under governors practically appointed by the powers. Nor would there be any objection, although there is no specific treaty obligation to do so, to appoint a superintendent charged with the superintendence of the application of Clause 23 in the provinces other than those inhabited by Armenians.

For Constantinople the Status Quo

There remains the question of Constantinople. But this question is the very last that needs to be raised, for it is as yet utterly impossible to arrive at any agreement as to who shall be put in the place of the Sultan, and therefore the Sultan must remain there. Nor need we be in the least alarmed about this. If there is an efficient European superintendent seeing that reforms are carried out in every province where the Armenians live in Asia, and if the autonomous constitutions promised by the twenty-third clause of the treaty of Berlin are being established in all the other provinces of the Ottoman Empire under the superintendence and guarantee of Europe, the Sultan can be allowed to continue to reign over the shadowy outline of the empire which his predecessors conquered by the sword. His power for evil would be ended, but he would remain as useful a custodian of the Straits as any one else who could be named. In short, the true solution of the Eastern Question—at any rate, for the present—is to smash no diplomatic crockery whatever, but while preserving the semblance of a Turkish Empire, to draw the teeth of the Turk by enforcing the treaty which constitutes the charter of his existence.

How to Bell the Cat

There remains the question of securing the adoption of those reforms by the Sultan. If matters do get so far as we are supposing—*i.e.*, if the Anglo-Turkish Convention is torn up, Cyprus placed in the hands of the European powers, a Russian superintendent for Armenia ready to enter upon his duties, and similar arrangements provided for securing the application of Article 23 in the other provinces, then it is evident that the powers would no longer be laboring under their present fever-fit of mutual distrust, but would believe that, for the time being at all events, they all meant playing "on the square." If that were so, the Sultan would bow before their will with the fatalism of his race. If, however, by any possibility he refused, the ambassadors of Constantinople could easily secure his deposition and the installation of his successor without any more trouble than was necessary to depose Abdul Aziz. But admitting, for the sake of argument, that the Sultan would not submit, and that the usual resources to revolution had failed at the moment when it was to the interests of every one, including the Turks themselves, that they should succeed, there still remains the last argument of force.

How the Sultan Can Be Coerced

How that force should be applied is a matter for the decision of admirals and generals. But I cannot for a moment admit that the powers are shut up to the alternative of shelling the unarmed city or being defied by the crowned Assassin. The methods of coercion that are available under the circumstances are numerous. The simplest and most obvious would be the stoppage of supplies. Constantinople occupies a magnificent position which can be held against great odds, provided that its occupant has the control of the sea; otherwise, the ruler of Constantinople is like a rat in a trap. Constantinople is not a city that feeds its own population any more than London. It draws its supplies from Asia on the one side, and from Russia and the Balkan peninsula on the other. The Russian fleet in the Black Sea, with the international fleet which would force the Dardanelles, and cut off communication between Asia and Europe, would very soon suffice to starve the Sultan into submission. The only military operation that might be necessary would be the landing of a small force to occupy the railway and the high road by which supplies might be poured into the country from Andrianople. For the Sultan to talk of resisting the will of Europe while, without firing a shot, Europe could starve him into submission, is too absurd.

The Situation in Armenia

Grace N. Kimball, M.D.

The situation in Turkish Armenia is such as to make it the solemn duty of every one calling himself Christian to obtain definite information in regard to it in order to arrive at intelligent, well-founded convictions.

For not only does the solution of this question mean very much in the progress of European civilization and prosperity, but it is also to have a wide-reaching effect on Christianity itself either for better or worse.

One who has not been in Armenia (and by that I mean, not Constantinople, but in Armenia itself), however well read or interested he may be, can have very little idea of the actual situation at the present time.

The Government, from the Sultan down to the petty local official, is thoroughly imbued with the idea that the Armenians are rebels, are plotting and working toward a revolt, and are hoping to establish themselves in autonomy, and to drive out the Moslems, or in their turn to persecute and to massacre such as may remain in their borders.

So fiercely have the fires of the characteristic fanaticism of the Turks been fanned by official action that they simply refuse to accept the most convincing proof of the innocence of the mass of the Armenian people—wishing rather to believe, and to act ruthlessly on the belief, that the opinions and plans of the few are shared by the many.

The common people, Turks and Kurds—even more fanatical and ignorant than the official class—only too eagerly follow the initiative given, having the common motive with their rulers of reaping a rich but short-lived harvest of pillage and despoliation. Many of both the official and non-official class feel that the last days of Turkish domination have come, and that whatever of personal gain is to be snatched from the crumbling ruins must be snatched quickly.

On the Armenian side, out of the estimated 2,000,000 of that nationality in Turkey, not less than 100,000 or 1–20 of the whole population, have either been killed or forcibly converted to Islam. A few thousands have secretly or openly succeeded in leaving the country, and all who possibly can do so are following their example.

The death-rate from endemic and epidemic diseases, made a hundred-fold more virulent through the untold hardships and unnatural conditions imposed upon the people, is rapidly increasing. At the same time the marriage and birth rates are falling off still faster. All these factors aid very materially to bring about that consummation so devoutly desired by the Turk—Armenian extermination.

Of the uncomputed remnant of the Armenian people, it is perfectly within the truth to say that not one out of a hundred know or care anything about revolution, or the political situation in any of its phases. Their one and only desperate desire is peace and reasonable security at any price or from any quarter. They are perfectly willing to remain under Turkish rule, and only inarticulately beg for the permission to live and work. I am aware that this statement may be challenged by some, but I make it carefully, and as the result of close contact with practically the whole population of one of the largest and most typical of the provinces of Armenia. But very much in evidence to the Turkish Government, and increasingly so to the general public, is that small but active and often ill-advised body known as the Armenian revolutionary party. This, so far as Turkey is concerned, is an extraneous and invading body, with a by no means strong following in Turkey itself—a following composed almost entirely of men under thirty, a large percent under twenty years of age. Whatever hot-headed demonstration has characterized the revolutionary policy—to agitate with a view to attracting, or rather forcing, the attention of Europe and England—these demonstrations have met with quite as bitter condemnation from the great mass of localized Armenians as from the Turks themselves.

And herein lies the atrocious guilt of the Sultan and his Government, that thousands of innocent lives have been ruthlessly sacrificed, while only the clumsiest effort has been made to seek out the real offenders, and comparatively few have ever been brought to justice.

The political infidelity of the few has been made a pretext for carrying out a policy of absolute extermination of an innocent and most valuable people, in obedience to a mad and inexplicable prejudice against them in the mind of the supreme ruler.

So we have, at the present moment in Turkey, the Government and the Moslem population utterly alienated from and fanatically suspicious of the Armenian minority. They are ready at the slightest pretext in any part of the country, or in all the country, to go off into one of those oft-repeated debauches of butchery, restrained only partially by the undecided menaces of the European Powers, and by the ever-increasing precariousness of domestic politics and finances.

On the other hand we have the Armenian people, decimated, demoralized by fear, and impoverished to a degree that is inconceivable to the Western mind, every department of trade and labor closed, and with, at best, but momentary security to life and property.

This condition of things has existed for two years and three months—each month worse than the one before—witnessing more than the realization of the worst fears, and seeing hope of rescue or relief ever growing fainter.

Still the European deadlock holds. And still the Sultan, with a hopelessly bankrupt treasury, with an utterly rotten and demoralized bureaucracy, with his Moslem people excited to unquenchable fury against his Christian subjects, with thirty to forty thousand Hamidieh Kurdish cavalry, fully armed and equipped, ready at any moment to declare autonomy if they are punished for murdering and pillaging their Christian neighbors—still Abdul Hamid II *talks* of reform and *means* extermination.

Meanwhile 200,000 Armenian families, robbed of everything, and, by the conditions which obtain, cut off from the ordinary means of earning a living, and are looking to the Christian West for the meager necessities of life this winter. Probably 75,000 breadwinners have been lost to their families during the past two years, leaving approximately 300,000 helpless and destitute women and children. How can we Americans help in this situation, which, without doubts, appeals to everyone?

First, there is the power of the influence of our great Christian Government to be thought of as a factor in bringing about a radical and permanent solution of this question; for, after all, it is the solution that the world groans for, and not the cheap palliations that have been supplied at such enormous outlay of life and money.

England ought to feel—it is a disgrace to our Christianity that she has not already felt—that the United States Government is with her, heart and soul—and *fleet*, if need be—in the defense of humanity. And this does not mean the demolition of the Turkish Empire. It should mean the constituting a power strong enough to either reinforce or restrain the Turkish Government in such an effectual way as to make life once more possible for all right-minded and innocent people in Turkey, be they Christian or be they Mohammedan. For it is not generally appreciated, perhaps, that thousands of the Mohammedan population, as well as the Christian, are reduced to great want and suffering by the general social and economic demoralization. I am quite aware of the great delicacy of the international situation and of the futility of merely spasmodic outcries from press and platform. But it is a question for our National conscience how far we as a people are justified in pursuing a policy of selfish non-interference, when our National influence and prestige can unquestionably do so much toward a safe issue from this intolerably cruel situation.

Our representative at Constantinople should be a trained diplomat—the best we have. Our consular service should be so enlarged and strengthened as to become adequate to our Minister's needs for supplying information and for enforcing his demands for the protection of American interests. A Minister in Constantinople must have consuls in the interior, else it is virtually impossible for him to know the conditions under which his constituency is living, or to aid them when in danger or difficulty. Ever since British consulates were established in the interior of Turkey, American citizens in that country have been very largely pensioners on British consular service for protection, and for the transaction of all consular business. This great accommodation and benefit has been generously given by the British Government and by its consular representatives.

Is it not time, and is this not the time, that our own flag should mean power and protection in Turkey?

Again, as to our fleet. I have myself many times been an eye-witness to the wonderfully reassuring influences on all classes of a foreign gunboat. Russia has for months kept one or two naval ships in each of the Turkish Black Sea ports. And while we know this is not for humanitarian reasons, yet the panic the population experiences when the ships withdraw shows clearly what a great factor for protection and peace their presence is. Why can we not keep a strong squadron in the eastern Mediterranean, not as a menace to Turkey, perhaps not even to add to the Sultan's already sufficiently distracted condition by pushing indemnity, but to be there, adding strength to our diplomatic standing, giving the English Government the benefit of its co-operation, and acting, as it undoubtedly would, as a "steadier" to the general situation? No power on earth can for a moment can suspect us of ulterior motives.

Thus we see that to really help the Armenians we must contribute to the forces which shall bring about political relief. But we must at the same time alleviate their immediate moral distress.

It is quite safe to say that from Constantinople to Persia, from the Caucasus to Mesopotamia, nine-tenths of the Christian inhabitants of every city and village are reduced to dependence on outside aid for daily bread, clothing, and fuel. Orphans by tens of thousands are wandering homeless and helpless. Thousands of widows have no refuge or protection against the evil intentions of their Turkish neighbors.

These make crying demands on our human and Christian sympathies. Money may be sent safely and expeditiously to Constantinople, and thence to the various centers of relief work. At each of these centers there is a body of experienced men and women, missionaries and British consuls, who will distribute the relief in the wisest possible way. Two or three cents daily, will feed one person, while $1 will go a long way toward clothing an individual or furnishing the winter's fuel for a family. The condition of the widows and orphans, however, is one which appeals most strongly to our sympathies, as it offers a most a useful avenue of Christian benevolence, an opportunity of relieving desperate present need. Moreover, the establishment of orphanages under missionary supervision would utilize our large mission plant and put our work on a footing difficult of attack by either Turk or Russian. Twenty-five dollars will take one of these poor, hungry, shivering children out of the street or from some hovel where he finds precarious shelter, and put him into a comfortable Christian home. The same sum or less annually will enable a homeless widow to become self-supporting, and to care for her own or others' children in these orphanages.

It is to be earnestly hoped that all who have given in the past to the relief of the Armenians will continue their gifts through this winter, remembering that, much as their gifts were needed last year, they are more generally and even more desperately needed this year. It is to be hoped also that all societies, clubs, and collecting agencies heretofore working for this purpose may reorganize with redoubled zeal.

It is also worth remembering that all aid so given means not only material relief to these sorely tried people, but in a very real way it means a moral support without which they would well nigh lose faith in God and man.

Vassar College, Poughkeepsie, N.Y.

The Immediate Future of Armenia: A Suggestion

W. K. Stride

At a time when the antagonism between Christian and Mohammedan in the East has again reached the acute stage, circumstances happen to have directed the attention of the writer of this article to the subject of the Military Brotherhoods of the Middle Ages, and thence he has been insensibly but almost inevitably led to consider some of the resemblances and differences between the age of the First Crusade—in which the Military Brotherhoods had their rise—and the present time.

In several respects the two eras are alike. The eleventh century, like the nineteenth, opened with expectations of vast changes; and the anticipated advent of the Millennium, with its new heaven and its new earth, hardly excited more visionary and extravagant hopes than the reign of universal fraternity which the French Revolution appeared to be ushering in. Later in both epochs, when these bright hopes had paled and faded into the wan reality of evils uncured and the continued strife of nation against nation, there came for both centuries a time when the sun seemed struggling through the clouds; and the proclamation of the Truce of God as a remedy for the misery of the peasant is perhaps comparable—at any rate as a protest against oppression—to the philanthropic legislation in England which has lately produced the Truck and Factory Acts. About the same time too, in both centuries, a new power seemed to have arisen to effect the unity of that somewhat vague collection of peoples, which one age has called "Christendom," and the other, "the civilized world": Hildebrand's lever was to be the universal authority of the Church; while that of the doctrinaire economists of the middle Victorian era was to be universal Free Trade. Furthermore, toward the end of both centuries Mohammedan cruelty to Eastern Christians kindled in Western nations a fierce resentment, and the Bulgarian and Armenian atrocities of our own time were foreshadowed eight hundred years ago by the renewal of the massacres of the pilgrims at Jerusalem. And lastly, just as in the present century there has been a greater development of philanthropy in the establishment of humanitarian institutions than the world has ever before seen, so the eleventh, if it were remarkable for nothing else, would be gratefully remembered as the foster-mother of a particular class of such institutions; for it was about the year 1020 that some pious merchants of Amalfi founded that brotherhood for the relief of the sick and poor at Jerusalem which was afterward transformed into the illustrious Order of the Knights of St. John.

It is not necessary to detail at any great length all the differences between the two ages. A dozen will at once occur to the reader. The most noticeable points of contrast are, perhaps, the difference between the position and power of Mohammedanism then and now, and the change from the mediaeval to the modern conception of the necessary connection between design and execution. The Turk, who then was, and for centuries after was to be, the dread of Europe, is now its scorn, and his continued occupation of Constantinople is only possible for a single day because of the inability of the Great Powers to arrange to their general satisfaction the division of his Hellespontine territories. Yet enormous as this political change is, it is no greater than that intellectual change which has remodeled our ideas of the relation between the means and the end. Mr. Bryce observes in his "Holy Roman Empire" that, "In the Middle Ages men's impulses were more violent and their conduct more reckless than is often witnessed in modern society, while the absence of a criticising and a measuring spirit made them surrender their minds more unresistingly than they would now do to a complete and imposing theory."

In fact the child-nations of the earlier age have now become men and learned to look before they leap; and an enterprise far less difficult than that which the Crusading hosts undertook—as by one impulse, and almost, we are tempted to imagine, without one thought—has within the last twelvemonth been definitely abandoned even before the full cost had been reckoned. With us the question is not merely, Is the end attainable? but, Is it, even if attainable, worth the means to be employed? With them the question was simply, What is the end? Once clearly recognized, that end was attained or attempted in a Balaklava-like spirit which, if not war, was at least magnificent.

Seldom has the modern attitude been more explicitly stated than by the present British Under-Secretary for Foreign Affairs. Mr. Curzon observed, during the debate on Armenia in the House of Commons, that "Crusades to-day must bear not only a chivalrous but a practical aspect." The declaration marks the distance which separates Mr. Curzon or even Mr. Gladstone from Peter the Hermit or Walter the Penniless, for nothing is more striking than the fact that eight centuries ago the practical aspect was far more completely ignored by Christendom than even the chivalrous aspect is at present. Without military leaders, organization, transport, commissariat, or any clear idea whatever, except that of pressing onward to the rising sun, a vast crowd of 60,000 persons streamed on in motley disorder in the tracks of the goose and the goat which strayed onward before them. Thousands died by the way in Germany, Hungary, and the Eastern Empire, and the rest were cut to pieces almost as soon as they had landed on the shores of Asia. Even the more organized armies which followed that first mad rush had notions but little clearer of the means of attaining their object, and of the 700,000 men who mustered on the far side of the Bosphorus, not one in twenty reached Jerusalem. But though "the aggregate of human suffering and the waste of human power" thus displayed seem terrible to us who have just reluctantly come to the conclusion that the "Armenian atrocities" are not worth a great European war, we cannot, even at this distance of time help feeling a thrill of emotion at the heroism which could inspire and endure such sacrifices for the sake of an idea. Despite Burke's famous utterance, the age of chivalry is not passed, and the very fact that hostile operations against Turkey were, and to some extent still are, seriously contemplated shows that it is not. All we require now is that, before we give it free scope, our chivalry shall be practical,—that is, that it shall have at least a chance of achieving its object, and that the object shall be to the general benefit. For this kind of chivalry, it seems to the writer, there is still room in the world, and it is toward a definite object that he would like to see it directed.

Political prophecy is notoriously hazardous, and even an opinion which is held by a large majority of dispassionate observers is often ill-founded. But it does sometimes happen that the writing on the wall is distinct enough, not only to need no prophet to interpret it to the king, but to be intelligible to all who see it. When Lord Salisbury uttered his memorable warning, that persistent and constant misgovernment must lead the Power that followed it to its doom, it must have been plain to all Europe that Abdul-Hamid had been weighed in the balance and found wanting, and, though a little longer time in which to put his house in order might still remain to him, his kingdom seemed already to be divided among other nations. In other words, the inevitable has become the immanent, and there is undoubtedly an enormous preponderance of opinion to the effect that before the first quarter of the twentieth century has elapsed, the Empire of the Sultan as we know it to-day will have been broken up.

Such an anticipation will arouse feelings of regret or delight, of dismay or triumph, according to the political and religious prepossessions of different persons. But in one sentiment almost everyone will join—in grave apprehension for the safety of the Christian subjects of Sultan. In Turkey in Asia and Turkey in Europe together there are some 4,000,000 Christians under the direct government of the Porte, the Armenians alone numbering over 2,000,000; and one of the strongest arguments in favor of nonintervention in the internal affairs of Turkey has been that such interference, whether successful or unsuccessful, would immediately stir up against these the relentless revenge of the dominant race. The Moslem, fanatically cruel in the hour of victory, is doubly so in the hour of defeat, and if the Ottoman Empire goes down in that "tempest of blood and fire" which has been predicted for it, the consequences to its political and religious foes will be terrible. In European Turkey the Christians are accustomed to act together, and they have powerful nations within hail. The struggle there will be on somewhat equal terms. But in Asiatic Turkey, between Mohammedan Kurds and Mohammedan soldiers, the Armenians might be almost blotted out in a single week. Here then, if anywhere, is a field for the practical chivalry of this later age—the protection of Christians in the East.

"Chivalrous," it may be urged, "but hardly practical!" "Ships," as Lord Salisbury has said, "cannot operate in the mountains of Asia Minor, and before troops could arrive in the interior, the massacres of Sassun might have been repeated in twenty different places." There is considerable force in the objection. It has never been accounted useless, however, to lock the stable door *before* the steed is stolen, and the object of this paper is to suggest a means of averting the evil.

Few more striking instances of complete change of ideal could be given than that afforded by the history of the Military Brotherhoods of the Middle Ages. Remembering a few passages in "Ivanhoe" or "The Talisman," a few denunciations by Carlyle, or a few sarcasms of Voltaire, we are in the habit of regarding them as successively haughty, despotic, unprincipled, wealthy, luxurious, useless, and finally mischievous Orders, about whom when we have admitted that they were brave, we have said almost all the good we can. Yet, if they deserved such a description at all, it was only in their later stages and when they had lost sight of their original ideals. Indeed, they were at first for the most part purely charitable organizations, founded for the relief of poor pilgrims, and it was only when they extended their work of mercy from the hospital to the battle-field that they took up arms and became the terror of the infidel and the solace of the Christian. But even then their work was by no means exclusively military or therapeutic. Lands accrued to them in every country in Europe, and their priors and preceptors became stewards of great estates. In two instances too—and this more nearly concerns our present purpose—an Order took possession of a large tract of country for its own occupation. The Knights of St. John found the island of Rhodes a wilderness and left it a garden: the Teutonic Knights found East Prussia a swamp and left it a fruitful field. Yet all the time they kept the maintenance of their faith, whether against Moslem or pagan, steadily in view, and were always as ready to attack the infidel as to defend the Christian.

To-day the Turk needs no attacking: the "Sick Man" may be left to meet his approaching dissolution. But during those last hours the Christian may need protecting, and as it seems hopeless to expect any help from the Concert of Europe,—while the intervention of a single nation seems equally out of the question,—it is only from some voluntary organization that help can come. To be strong enough, such an organization must be military; to be imposing enough, it must be non-national, or rather open to, and supported by, the Great Powers; to be above suspicion, it must work without thought of gain, and whatever surplus there may be of income over expenditure must be devoted to the further development of agriculture and industry. An institution—call it a Brotherhood, a Society, a Company, or what you will—conducted on these lines would have at any rate the chance of great usefulness.

"This is all very well," it may be urged, "but how are you going to construct such a Society, and how in constructing it are you going to avoid arousing political jealousies which would shipwreck the whole scheme at the start?" The answer is that such a Society exists to our hand; for in England, Germany, Italy, and Spain there still survive fragments of the Order of St. John of Jerusalem; the French "langue" has only recently been suppressed; and in Russia, even in this century, not only has a new Priory been created, but the Czar has accepted the position of Protector of the Order.* If these fragments could be brought into touch with each other there would be at once, ready-made, the ancient framework on which a modern Brotherhood could be built up.

Metaphor at times deceives us, and we are often led to trace an analogy, which does not exist in fact, between the corporate life and nature of an institution and the corporeal life and instincts of a man. Yet if ever there were an excuse for such argument by analogy there would be an excuse in the case of the Order of St. John, which has at times seemed inspired with a conscious life of its own and whose history during seven centuries has been one continual and on the whole successful effort to adapt itself to altered circumstances. Before the First Crusade, as has been said above, it had its origin as a hospice for sick and poor pilgrims, whose nurses and monks were already engaged in their works of mercy when, just eight centuries ago, the trumpet tones of Peter the Hermit were summoning Europe to the defence of the holy shrines. With the first successes of the Christians in the East the Order was reorganized and became a military and a monastic as well as a charitable Order. Till the end of the thirteenth century its Knights, with those

---

*Porter: "Knights of Malta."

of the Temple, formed "the regular militia of the Holy Land," and when Palestine was finally lost to Christendom, it found—first in Cyprus and then successively in Rhodes and Malta—an opportunity of carrying on its self-imposed task. Its occupation of Rhodes undoubtedly saved Rome from the fate of Constantinople, and its possession of Malta proved a great check upon the pirates of the North African coast, for both islands were fortified with such skill that for ages all attacks on them failed; and thus possessing an impregnable citadel, the Order was able to extend its maritime supremacy over the whole of the Eastern Mediterranean. It was only when the hurricane of the French Revolution was uprooting the firmest institutions in Europe that the destruction of the Order was apparently accomplished; and yet since then it has again adapted itself to its environment and shown signs of life in various countries. In England it has thrown out one branch which has developed into "The National Society for the Aid of Sick and Wounded in War," and another which has become widely known as "The St. John Ambulance Association." In Germany the Bailiwick of Brandenburg, under its better known name of "the Johanniter," not only did notable service to the wounded on the field in the wars of 1866 and 1870, but took a prominent part in carrying out the Geneva Convention. In Jerusalem, however, is to be found at once the most ancient and the most modern development of all, viz., the Ophthalmic Dispensary, where a wholly non-sectarian work is being performed by the same society, on the same lines, and in the same place, as when it was begun 850 years ago.

The framework is already to our hand, then, and in being international and charitable it fulfils two of the three necessary requirements. The third or military side of its constitution it could reassume to-day even more easily than it assumed it in the eleventh century, for there is more enterprise and ardor seeking vent now than even at the time of the First Crusade.

Nor would such an enterprise be any real novelty. It is not necessary to lay much stress on the ancient connection between the military orders and the Christians of Asia Minor, though it had important consequences in the Middle Ages. Yet in the last twenty years history has been repeating itself, and the establishment of Military Consuls in Armenia and Anatolia may be regarded as a tentative stop in the direction of European guardianship against Mussulman injustice.

The establishment of Military Consuls, however, did not have a fair chance. They only began their labors in the summer of 1879, and in 1881 they were recalled. But in that short time they showed that great possibilities of usefulness lay before them. Mr. H. F. Tozer,—till lately a Fellow of Exeter College, Oxford, and a well-known authority on Eastern matters,—when traveling in Asia Minor seventeen years ago, formed great hopes of the success of the new system. They were not, he says, fixed like ordinary consuls in any one city, but held a roving commission within a certain area, and were to collect information, especially as to commercial matters, as well as to be a continual protest against wrong-doing. In Kaisariyeh he found the new consul "occupied all day and every day in investigating all kinds of grievances." An American missionary in Kharput in the course of a conversation with him "thought that they might in time assume the position of 'residents' or authoritative advisers, and thus gradually become possessed of a more definite control." Even the news of their coming excited great expectations of real reforms, some of which might by this time have been carried out if the consuls had been able to acquire any administrative control.*

Mr. Tozer's reflections on the subject of the industrial future of the country are worthy of careful consideration. After noticing the extraordinary fertility of the soil—a matter which Colonel Burnaby* had emphasized a year or two before—and pointing out that it affords "ample openings for colonization," he touched on the corruption of officials and the ignorance of the government—which disgusts even the Turks,—and proceeded to inquire for a remedy.

---

*"Turkish Armenia and Asia Minor," by the Rev. H. F. Tozer, pp. 3034.

*"We rode over rich soil which had been left fallow for miles around. 'There are not inhabitants enough to cultivate the land,' was the guide's answer to a question on the subject. He was doubtless right. Asia Minor needs a three-fold population to develop its natural wealth. . . . It could supply the whole of Great Britain with corn, and the mines of coal and of other minerals would prove a source of immense wealth to the inhabitants" ("On Horseback through Asia Minor," p. 172). "It surprises a traveller to find that the Turks make so little use of their mines. In the course of my ride I passed through a country apparently abounding in iron, and with many traces of coal. At Madeh there is copper and silver. With intelligent engineers to explore the mineral wealth, Turkey would be able not only to pay the interest of her debt, but to become one of the richest countries in the world" (*Ibid.*, p. 168).

THE IMMEDIATE FUTURE OF ARMENIA

The presence of a few consuls, however vigorous and able, was inadequate. A native government was impossible, because of the antagonism of creeds. Political jealousy must prevent any European state from undertaking the administration. A fourth suggestion—"the formation of an independent state by the combined action of the Great Powers"—seemed "outside the sphere of practical politics.* Later in the book, however, he suggested three remedies which would at all events ameliorate the condition of the people; namely, the appointment of a Christian governor, to secure the inhabitants against speculation and oppression; formation of a local militia, to protect them against the Kurds; and the expenditure of the revenue on local objects, to develop their resources.* Now it is important to note that these three would all be attained by, and indeed if summarized would almost imply, the establishment of some such institution as has been suggested above.

It would be foolish to ignore the difficulties in the way of putting such a scheme into practice. Leaving aside for the moment the arrangement of details, we have the political difficulty to face. Jealousy, as Mr. Tozer well says, must prevent any European nation from being allowed to undertake the enterprise single-handed, and his further criticism, that the formation of an independent state by the combined powers was outside the sphere of practical politics, seems justified by obvious reflection that Russia would not permit any military occupation of the country. Yet it may be doubted whether such a reflection, though obvious, is correct. Russia has already as large an extent of territory as she can comfortably control; her orthodox rulers know well enough that they would be likely to have as much trouble with the Monophysite Eutychians of Armenia as they had with the Catholics of Poland; and, most important of all, her real interests do not at all lie in Asia Minor or in Armenia. The possession of the Bosphorus, the Dardanelles, and a ten-mile strip round the Sea of Marmora are worth more to her than the whole of the ancient kingdom of Rûm, with Armenia and Kurdistan thrown in. The reason is evident. Between the Black Sea and the Mediterranean runs a great mountain-barrier, through

---

*Ibid., pp. 185–94.
*Ibid., pp. 418–19.

which no stream passes, and from which no river of any importance, save the Hermus and the Meander, flows southward or westward into the open sea. At the general overturn Russia, as some say, will, or, as others say, will not, get Constantinople. If she does, she will not want the added responsibility of Turkey in Asia; if she does not, its possession will be of no solace and of no use to her, for the mountains will still lie between her and her next natural objective—Mesopotamia and the road to the Persian Gulf,—as they lie now between Transcaucasia and the Mediterranean.

Yet even if the great Slavonic nation had the universal greed which English Russophobes attribute to her, she need see nothing alarming in the prospect of such an occupation. It is not suggested that it should be more than a temporary expedient with which to bridge over in safety a time of transition. No other European nation has any interest at all in Armenia except the interest of humanity, and Russia is near enough to anticipate any movements which may seem to threaten any interests which she has in that part of the world. Moreover, it would be a distinct gain for Russia—even assuming that she is to be the heir of the Asiatic possessions of the Porte west of the forty-second and north of the thirty-sixth parallel—that she should enter into the enjoyment of the vineyards and olive-trees which she planted not, rather than into the costly and laborious task of developing the resources of a country which for centuries has suffered from neglect, ignorance, and oppression.

It remains to put into shape the proposal to which all these considerations tend.

Ever since the Treaty of Vienna the Great Powers have claimed a gradually increasing right to regulate the affairs of the Porte—as Professor Holland* puts it, "to supervise the solution of the Eastern question, or, in other words, to regulate the disintegration of Turkey." "The Turkish Empire," he declares, "is placed as it were under the tutelage of Europe, while the claim of any single Power to settle the destinies of that Empire without the concurrence of the rest has been repeatedly negatived." In Greece, Egypt, Syria, the Balkans, and the Islands, as well as in Asia Minor, this

---

*Introduction to "The Eastern Question," by T. E. Holland, D.C.L., Chichele Professor of International Law at Oxford University.

right has been freely exercised, and it is now a truism of morals that the Great Powers have the responsibility of, as it has long been a truism of politics that they have the requisite authority for, the enforcement of good government. Yet good government has proved impossible of attainment, and there was never less promise of it than at this moment. In Article 61 of the Berlin Treaty the Sublime Porte undertook "to carry out without delay the improvements and reforms demanded by local requirements in the provinces inhabited by the Armenians, and to guarantee their security against the Circassians and Kurds,"—a promise which had previously been made to England separately, in return, not for the cession of Cyprus, as is so often alleged, but for the undertaking to protect Asiatic Turkey against further Russian aggression. The occurrences of the last two years show that no attempt has been made to fulfil these engagements, and the recent confession of the mingled impotence and disinclination of the Great Powers to enforce them makes one despair of their being any more conscientiously observed in the future than in the past. There is thus on the one hand no question of the right of Europe to insist that Turkey shall take whatever steps the Powers may agree in considering necessary for that purpose, and on the other very little of its inability, perhaps even of its disinclination, to ensure that those steps shall be taken.

Yet if the nations, as political units, are shy of meddling in the matter, there are in almost in every nation many individuals who would gladly see it dealt with, and to whom the news of the state of things prevailing in Armenia came with a shock of horror and humiliation. They are of all ages and all classes; some of them young and some old, some of them rich and some poor, some of them hotly adventurous and some more coolly philanthropic; but they represent—in England at least, and probably in more than one other country—a large proportion of the nation. In politics—more especially in foreign politics—they are not apt to interfere, but their dissatisfaction is none the less strong for being suppressed. To such a class of observers, and I believe it to be a very large class, this paper is addressed. International action may be impracticable from the impossibility of securing a cordial international agreement. National action may be impossible just because it is national. But action of some kind must be undertaken unless the Armenian massacres are to be repeated at the first unlucky opportunity. National and international action having failed, there remains voluntary action, and for voluntary action to be effectual, it is not in this case necessary that it should be initiated by national or international intervention. That weapon would be in the background, and could be employed with far more force on the occasion of the very first dispute.

It may seem that the mission of this "Brotherhood of St. John"—if I may so style this suggested society—would be in the nature of a forlorn hope, and that the society would be offering itself as a *corpus vile* for a risky though perhaps interesting experiment. If this were so, I do not think it would tell very strongly against the proposal: there are always volunteers in plenty for the forlornest and most dangerous of enterprises. But in truth it would not be so. It is not to be supposed that a few enthusiasts would recklessly scatter themselves over the provinces of Asiatic Turkey, and proceed to defend the oppressed and defy the oppressor on every possible occasion. The course of action would probably be of a very different kind. Starting with two or three seaport towns as their base, where they could purchase or construct buildings in strong positions, and where they could act in conjunction with, and as supplementary to, the European consulates, they might gradually extend their influence into the interior as their resources of men and money permitted, till a line of posts was established from sea to sea, with branches diverging laterally into the remote valleys of the interior. Each station would possess its own force of militia or police, and some sort of fortress capable of affording at any rate a temporary protection to fugitives as well as to the members of the Brotherhood; and at longer intervals there might be depots of more considerable size capable of holding out almost indefinitely against the attacks of any save regular troops. There would thus be existing, in the very heart of the now disturbed districts, cities of refuge, so to speak, which would not only be effectual sanctuaries in case of sudden local outbreaks but would be capable of arresting in some degree the torrent of anarchy which will be let loose in Asia Minor when that country falls or is forced from the grasp of the Turk. These stations would also become in the interval centres of trade and industry, and by being the pioneers of commercial and agricultural development would be the first to profit by every fresh extension of their sphere of influence; while, as they would not be working for their own enrichment,—and the appropriation to local improvements of all profits above a low fixed rate of interest must be one of the first of their rules,—they would be free from the temptations to which the promoters of less disinterested enterprisers are prone. Chartered companies are in bad odor just now, but even Mr. Labouchere would hardly condemn a chartered company whose object was genuinely philanthropic rather than financial.

For such a task the descendants of one of the proudest Orders of chivalry may seem but little fitted; but, in truth, the undertaking would hardly differ more from the ordinary conception of their work and constitution than their own ideal differed from itself at various periods of their history. Who, for instance, could have supposed that the nurses and almoners of the eleventh century would have developed into the valiant knights of the thirteenth, and that they in turn would have suffered such "a sea change" as to become the bold sailors of Rhodes or Malta? Yet the same sentiment underlies all these various manifestations—the eager desire to uphold their own religion and to protect its helpless disciples against "the infidel." It was only when they lost sight of that ideal, and became, as the Templars and the Teutonic Knights had successively become several centuries earlier, merely self-indulgent members of an anachronous caste, that the career of the Knights of St. John, like that of the Templars and the Teutonic Knights, seemed to have closed. At the very time of their apparent dissolution, however, they passed into yet another incarnation, and are probably at this moment in at least as flourishing a condition as they were eight centuries ago. The world may not be about to see another Crusade—though that is by no means certain—but the Brotherhood of St. John has reverted to its original character. If any human institution is capable of dealing with the perplexing and threatening condition of affairs in the East, it is probably an Order which has behind it so noble a history, and has so often proved at once its pliancy and its toughness.

Since the above was written affairs in Turkey have been going from bad to worse. The massacres in Sassun have been followed by the more dreadful, because more organized, massacres in Constantinople itself; and at the moment of writing comes the news of another outbreak of fanaticism at Kharput, in which 4,000 Armenians are said to have perished. It is evident that what is to be done must be done quickly. Fortunately, too, it is evident that a widespread and at the same time deep and fiery indignation has at last begun to stir the nations. In Italy, Germany, and France there are symptoms of a feeling which, despite the political exigencies of the moment, may force the hands of the mere *politiques*. England is humming like a hive of angry bees; a dozen meetings are being held nightly in the small as well as the large towns; and Mr. Gladstone, the great Achilles of the host, has been persuaded to come forth from his tent. Indeed, one English paper (the "St. James's Gazette") has gone so far as to suggest a new Triple Alliance between England, Italy, and the United States, for the purpose of dealing with the matter, in default of—or even in defiance of—the Concert of Europe. Now, therefore, if ever, is the time for action. If the storm breaks before some kind of shelter has been provided, the Christian inhabitants of the Ottoman Empire will be exposed to its full fury. It may be that the storm will be upon them—that the Ottoman Empire will be breaking up—before anything effectual can be done. On the other hand it may be that that empire will last some years yet. If so, we may be sure that the same raids, the same rapes, the same tortures, the same massacres will be repeated, till either the Armenians are virtually exterminated or some Great Power is shamed into forcible interference. The plan sketched out in this paper would then prevent some misery, be some check on the fury of the oppressor, and offer to at least a few indignant or charitable hearts the chance of defending the defenceless and of relieving the destitute.

The Armenian Question

Lyman Abbott[122]

> And the men of Ephraim said unto him, Why hast thou served me thus, that thou calledst us not, when thou wentest to fight with the Midianites? And they did chide with him sharply.
>
> —Judges viii*

The Children of Israel were not at this time a nation. They were twelve separate peoples, each with it separate territory. The Midianites, neighboring pagans, had oppressed some of these tribes. Gideon had gathered the tribes together and gone to war against Midian. Three hundred men had put the great Midianite army to flight. Ephraim had not been called on to share, and Ephraim complained. Why have you treated us thus?, said this stalwart, brave little tribe. We wanted a share in this honorable warfare. You have dealt with us unfairly.

Men tell us that this book of the Judges describes a barbarous time—and so it does; and that its notions are barbarous notions—so some of them are; but I think to-day, as one looks on the map of Europe and at the attitude of the so-called Christian Powers of Europe, he may well question whether Christendom in the nineteenth century might not learn something from Judaism in the days of Judges. He who is practically, though not nominally, the pagan of the East is persecuting Christians in Turkey with a rancor, a

---

*Sermon preached at Plymouth Church, Brooklyn, N.Y., Sunday, November 15, 1896. Reported stenographically by Henry Winans, and revised by the author.

bitterness, a devotion of hate absolutely never equaled before in the history of the world, and the Christian Powers are not taking counsel with one another how they may put a stop to it, but each Power is interfering with every other Power's interference; each Power, in its jealousy of other Powers, forbids war against the pagan for the protection of the Christian.

I have not spoken to you before on the Armenian problem because I have not wished to stir your emotions, or my own, fruitlessly, and speak to-day only because I think I have a little light in answer to the question; What can we do? and wish to point out to you, not what is the duty of England or Russia or Germany, but the duty of America and Americans.

In the first place, we ought to know the facts. The fact is that the persecution of Christians in Armenia is the worst, the most cruel, the most barbarous religious persecution the world has ever seen. It is estimated that two thousand Christians were slain in the persecutions of Diocletian; that between five and six thousand Protestants were put to death under the persecutions of Torquemada in Spain; that thirty thousand were slain in massacre of St. Bartholomew; that a hundred thousand Protestants were put to death in the wars of the Duke of Alva against the house of Orange—but that includes those who were slain in open battle. Those who have perished in Turkish Armenia in the last four years nearly, if not quite, equal the sum total of all those slain in previous executions. Eight thousand seven hundred and fifty is the number officially reported as massacred in three or four days in Constantinople itself, while some estimates put the total number of massacred men, women, and children at the present time since 1894 at one hundred thousand. And this is probably an underestimate.

I would not, if I could, recite the horrors of these persecutions; I would not repeat the tale of blood; I would not recount the monstrosities, the cruelties, which have accompanied them. I am not here to stir your blood to feverish heat. I try to keep my own moderately and reasonably cool while I speak to you on this crime of the centuries. I desire to give light, not heat.

In the second place, we ought to know that this persecution is not the result of sporadic acts of mob violence. We ought to know that it is a definite, pronounced, established policy, patiently, persistently, remorselessly pursued. We ought to know that the causes of it are partly race hatred, partly trade jealousy, partly religious animosity. We ought to know that the Turk in Turkey is not synonymous with the Mohammedan, any more than American is synonymous with Christian. The word Turk is significant of a race; the word Mohammedan is significant of a religion. Most Americans are Christians—that is, they are not pagans; and most Turks are Mohammedans—that is, they are not Christians; but the Turk may or may not be a Mohammedan, as the American may or may not be a Christian.

In his birthplace and cradle the Turk is Asiatic. He came to Europe centuries ago with his drawn scimitar. He came murdering and to murder, plundering and to plunder. He came a barbarian, a robber, a brigand, and he has stayed in Europe ever since, a robber, a murderer, and a brigand. He is as barbaric to-day in the heart of him as he was in the centuries gone by. Whatever evolution has done for other races, it has not done anything for him. He is a Turk still. The Turkish Empire is composed of heterogeneous populations under the subjection of the scimitar of the Turk. He has never made any attempt whatever to affiliate these populations, to bring them into fellowship with himself, or to do them equal justice: he has simply held them by the throat with one hand, while he has rifled their pockets with the other. The Turkish Empire has used its power simply in taxing them; and it has taxed them, not that it might give them a good government, but that it might rob them for its own purposes. It is true that the Turkish order is a government, and it is true that the American order is a government, but it is a misnomer to use the same word for both. The object of the American government is to protect the life and liberty of all its citizens. That is not the intent of the Turk. The idea of the Turk is the idea of the old Roman imperialism—subjugate the province, that you may take as much out of it as possible.

Now, this Turk has seen in successive years these subject populations improving in spite of them. They have grown wiser, more intelligent, more virtuous, more prosperous. He has seen the Greek and the Nestorian and the Syrian and the Bulgarian, and now the Armenian, enter into places of profit, of industry, of advantage, and his race hatred has been intensified by his trade jealousy. This massacre of the Armenians is not a new thing in Turkish history. "In 1822 not less than 50,000 Greeks were massacred in the Islands of the Ægean Sea; in 1850, 10,000 Nestorians were butchered around the head-waters of the Tigris; in 1860, 11,000 Maronites and Syrians perished in Mount Lebanon and Damascus; in 1876 upwards of 15,000 were slaughtered in Bulgaria." That is the Turk. That is what he has been doing all the time.

And this race prejudice, this trade jealousy, have been intensified and embittered by what we are pleased to call his religion. What is religion? If it is consecration, devotion, enthusiasm, regardless of the One to whom the consecration is made, regardless of the object of devotion, regardless of that which excites the enthusiasm, then the Turk is religious. Then the Phœnicians, who inspired themselves to lust by their religious rites and caused their own children to be sacrificed to their cruel gods, were as religious as the Israelites. Then Torquemada, in lighting the torch and presiding over the tortures of the Inquisition, was as religious as the men who burned beneath the flames or were tortured on the rack. Then the Duke of Alva, with his unsheathed sword putting thousands and tens of thousands to death on the plains of Holland, was as religious as William of Orange fighting for patriotism and his native land. Then Catherine de Medici summoning to *Te Deums* over the slain was as religious as the massacred martyrs whose bodies filled the streets of the European metropolis.

Religion is of two kinds—the aggressive and the non-aggressive. And of the aggressive religions there are two—the Mohammedan and the Christian. The Jewish religion did not seek to make converts; it simply built a wall around itself and protected itself from other religions. The Brahmanical religion does not seek to make converts; all the Brahmans desire is to be left alone. But the Christian and the Mohammedan religions do seek to make converts. The one does it by the cross, the other by the sword; the one by love, the other by hate; the one by assimilation, the other by subjugation; the one does it for the purposes of service, the other does it for purposes of selfishness. Now, you may call them both religion if you like, but they are as far apart as heaven is from hell.

Says James Freeman Clarke in his account of Mohammedanism: "When God—so runs the tradition—I had better said the blasphemy—resolved to created the human race, he took into his hands a mass of earth, the same whence all mankind were to be formed, and in which they after a manner pre-existed; and, having then divided the clod into two equal portions, he threw the one half into hell saying, 'These to eternal fire, and I care not,' and projected the other half into heaven, adding, 'And these to paradise, and I care not.'" That is the theology of the Mohammedan. That is the God who is the center of their religion. Calvinism was serene and lovely and flowering spring as compared with the theology of Mohammedanism, which is based upon a faith in a remorseless God who cares not whether this half of the human race lives in eternal torment and this half in everlasting paradise. The Mohammedan religion knows nothing of the fatherhood of God, and it knows as little of the other fundamental truths of Christianity. "Stress is laid on prayer, ablution, fasting, almsgiving, and the pilgrimage to Mecca. Wine and gaming are forbidden. There is no recognition, in the Koran, of human brotherhood. It is a prime duty to hate infidels and make war on them. Mohammed made it a duty for Moslems to betray and kill their own brothers when they were infidels; and he was obeyed in more cases than one."

Thus we have these three elements together in the Turkish heart: first, race prejudice; second, trade jealousy; and, third, religious rancor and hate. The Mohammedan knows only one way by which to extend his religion—this: kill the men, kill the women, kill the older children, and educate the babes into Mohammedans. Mohammedanism has never varied from its first starting-point in Asia. It has always run this one consistent course: a persecuting power because it is an aggressive power, believing in a God of indifference, making a worship of lust and cruelty.

Now, we ought to know these facts. We have no right to shut our eyes to them. We have no right to be ignorant of them. And, knowing them, we ought to be intolerant of all apologies, excuses, distinctions, or eulogies. I mean exactly what I say—*intolerant*. I hate the intolerant that is indifferent respecting moral character and moral distinctions. I hate the tolerance that knows no difference between virtue and vice, cruelty and humanity, honor and dishonor, courage and cowardice. Purity ought to be intolerant of impurity. Honesty ought to be intolerant of dishonesty. Heroism ought to be intolerant of cowardice. Love ought to be intolerant of hate. Consider for a moment the defenses offered for the murdering, massacring Turk. The Armenian has provoked it all: it is all his fault. Oh Æsop, come to life again, and tell us the story of the Lamb and the Wolf! I have heard this charge: negroes provoking the massacres of the Ku Klux Klan in the South, and always the negroes the victims, and always the white men safe. How many Turks have been killed by Armenians? Whose sword is red with blood? The lamb has devoured the wolf. The lamb has muddied the water the wolf was drinking. The Turk is a gentleman! Ah, this Turk is a gentleman! I have met that, too, before. This corrupt politician, it is true, bribes congresses, buys votes, manipulates primaries, miscounts votes—he does all that; but then he is a good husband, he does not beat his wife, and he does not maltreat his children! This Turk has killed Christians—unoffending Christians—by the thousands and tens of thousands, but he is a gentleman. Yes, so Mephistopheles is a gentleman. So the Duke of Queensberry was a gentleman; in his veins putridity instead of pure blood, but he was one of the finest gentlemen of England. Probably the Duke of Alva was a gentleman. Doubtless Torquemada was a gentleman. O Rachel, Rachel, mourning for thy children and will not be comforted, for they are not, weep not. Herod is a gentleman! O Armenian exile, with thy cottage in ashes, and thy wife violated before thine eyes, be not wrathful: if he that did it was not a gentleman, he that set him on was one! O childless widow, who cannot close thine eyes in sleep without seeing thine husband brained before thine eyes and his blood spattered on thy robes, weep not; he that did it was a gentleman! And we hear these things and our blood does not boil!

But the persecutor is religious. And he has as much enthusiasm for his religion as the Christian has for his religion. The Christian missionary believes in his religion of the Cross, and this Turk believes in his religion of the Crescent. Why sit in judgment between them? Fanaticism harnesses its two steeds of lust and cruelty, flings the reins of self-restraint upon their backs, lashes them with the devil's own conscience, and as the wheels go over the crunching bodies of its victims, tolerance stands by the side of the course, takes off its hat, and honors—religion! We ought to know the facts, and in the knowledge of those facts we ought to be intolerant of every excuse and apology that is made for them.

We, as an American nation, can do something more than know the facts, and something more than feel rightly about them. We either ought with the whole power of our Government to protect American citizens on Turkish soil, or we ought frankly, publicly, openly, to declare that we have not the strength to do it, and call our Ambassador home.

Nations, like individuals, are sometimes too weak to do what they ought to do if they were strong enough. Poland could not resist Russia. But we ought to look the question fairly in the face. We have in Turkey over two hundred Americans, engaged in what is ordinarily regarded as lawful business. I know they are missionaries; I know they are teachers; I know they have not gone there to make money. They are not consecrated to the work of getting on in the world. That much may be said against them. But still Americans generally will recognize the fact that a man who has gone to another country, inspired by a desire to aid the men, women, and children there, is entitled to as much protection as the children there, is entitled to as much protection as the man who goes there to sell them scimitars or rum. I am not going to enter into the question to-day whether the missionary service is right and wise, or wrong and unwise. It is an honest and honorable vocation, and Americans have gone into it. We have 621 schools, including five colleges. We have 27,400 pupils in those schools. We are spending half a million dollars a year in the work of civilization. Those are American interests. I will not say Christian interests; I will not say missionary interests. They are American interests. And the men engaged in this work are entitled to have this country say one of two things—either, We cannot protect you, you are at your own risk, or else, God helping us, we will spend our last dollar and our last man, but we will protect you. And that is what I would like to have the United States say. We are strong enough to think of putting back on her throne in Hawaii a recreant Queen who had undertaken to tear in tatters the constitution. We are strong enough to say to Great Britain, The interests of Venezuela are our own; you must not encroach on them. We are strong enough to threaten war when there is a possible danger to a few American interests in a South American Republic. But we let our property be burned, our schools and colleges be closed, our men and women live in terror of their lives, and have as yet done nothing more than present a gentle protest.

In 1815 the Algerian pirates had for twenty years been preying on the commerce of Christendom in the Mediterranean Sea, and the Christian Powers did not dare to do anything to prevent them, because England had made a treaty by which practically she pledged herself not to interfere, that France might be injured. Each government was afraid to interfere with the *status quo*, and the commercial interests were helpless. In 1815 this then little United States said, We will stand this no longer. We had stood it; we had paid thousands of dollars in ransoms for the American. We had submitted because we could not help ourselves. But when the war of 1812 closed, we sent out one of our Commodores; we engaged the fleet of Algiers, we defeated it; we took the chief robber, the Sultan of Algiers; we made him there give his submission; we made him there pay back damages; and the robbers were swept from the Mediterranean Sea. O for an American like the America of 1815! I believe myself that if this American Government were to say to Turkey, You shall not threaten the peace, the prosperity, the lives, the well-being of American citizens on your soil—you shall not—I believe if America were to say that to the murdering, massacring Turk, America could do to-day what America did in the same section of the globe in 1815. And if a gun was fired at our flag, or a drop of American blood was shed, that gun would unite all America, as the guns on Sumter united the North, and that blood would cement in one great National party all Americans, as the blood that reddened the streets of Baltimore united all the North, and this Nation would move to the consummation of its purpose, unbroken, a united people; and the conscience of Europe would respond. It is not true that Germany or France or England or Austria would set itself up in armed defense of murder, when the United States Government, having no territory to acquire, no prestige to win, no advantage to gain, no balance of power in Europe to break, had interposed and said, "This crime shall go on no more."

There is another thing we can do. We can follow the precedent of 1824. In 1822 the Turks were massacring the Greeks. The Greeks were not like lambs led to the slaughter. They unsheathed their swords and rose in rebellion. There was a revolution against Turkish authority in Greece; and then, as now, all the Christian Powers kept off. Every Power was jealous of every other Power. Christian Powers, we call them! What is a Christian Power? You remember in "Faust" how men with raised swords in the form of a cross advance upon Mephistopheles, and before the raised cross he retreats and falls upon the ground, apparently vanquished by the mere symbol. Ah! it is a pretty picture, but it is not a true one. The devil does not retreat before the mere raised cross. A Power is not made a Christian Power because it has cathedrals with crosses on them, or crosses on the priests' robes, or crosses on the breasts of the women, or crosses on the covers of prayer-books. The cross in the heart and in the life makes a man a Christian; the cross in the heart makes a nation Christian. Only those Powers are Christian that dare risk something, that dare endure something, for Christ's sake and for humanity's sake. These Christian Powers did not dare in 1824; they do not dare now. Then it was that one of America's greatest statesmen pronounced one of his most statesmanlike utterances. He called on America to issue its protest against the wickedness that was oppressing Greece. I read from Daniel Webster:

> The time has been, indeed, when fleets and armies and subsidies were the principal reliances even in the best cause. But, happily for mankind, a great change has taken place in this respect. Moral causes come into consideration in proportion as the progress of knowledge is advanced; and the public opinion of the civilized world is rapidly gaining an ascendancy over mere brutal force. It is already able to oppose the most formidable obstruction to the progress of injustice and oppression; and as it grows more intelligent and more intense, it will be more and more formidable. It may be silenced by military power, but it cannot be conquered. It is elastic, irrepressible, and invulnerable to the weapons of ordinary warfare. It is that impassable, inextinguishable enemy of mere violence and arbitrary rule, which, like Milton's angels,
>
>> Vital in every part,
>> Cannot, but by annihilating, die.

Last spring our Congress passed resolutions of protest against the Turkish atrocities in Armenia. They were sent to the President of the United States. He was to communicate them to the Powers—the Christian Powers—of Europe. Is there any man in this audience who knows whether he has done it or not? If he has, he has not let his right hand know what his left hand has done. Those resolutions should have been so uttered to the Christian Powers of Europe that the sound of our voice would have gone round the world. We ought not to have spoken our condemnation of wholesale massacre in a whisper—we should have spoken it with thunder tones. At least we may speak to the consciences of mankind. It is time we did.

Finally, we can afford relief and succor to those who have suffered from this wholesale persecution. We can open our gates to all fugitive Armenians. I do not find fault with our Administration that it closed them the other day and left the fugitives waiting on Ellis Island until bonds should be given. It is not the business of the Administration to make laws or set them aside. But we should so alter our immigration laws as to provide clearly, definitely, and so positively that this land is the harbor for the politically oppressed of all countries, however empty their purses, and we ought to reach out a helping hand to the widows and the orphans on Turkish soil.

The American Board has indicated the presence of a statesman as its practical administrative head in its ready adaptation of its methods to the changed conditions. I received last week a letter from its Foreign Secretary, Dr. James L. Barton, saying that it is proposed to take the dismantled and unoccupied houses of the Armenians and gather in them, so far as it can be done, the orphans whom the Turkish scimitar has spared, under the care of Armenian widows, and thus save the girls from the harem and the boys from beggary, and both, by Christian education, to the faith of their fathers.

I am proud of the Christian ministry. I thank God to-day that in all this time of terrible torture and horrible experience not one single man or woman in the missionary service in Turkey has fled. Our own American Minister there has advised them to leave their posts; such counsels have gone to them from America; but one and all they have said, We will stay with those who are themselves martyrs for our faith; we will live with them; if need be, we will die with them. The Christian Church can at least do this: It can say to every brave Christian minister and every brave Christian woman in Turkey, You are right; stay where you are; our prayers shall go with you; our contributions shall go with you; our help to the enlargement of your work shall go with you. If I were both Government and Church, I would buy every house in Armenian Turkey that could be bought; I would wrap the American flag around it, or hoist the American flag above it; I would gather as many orphan children and as many widows into those homes as I could; and I would say to the massacring Turk, You lay your finger on one of them at your peril.

What will Plymouth Church do? How many such homes will it take? For how many orphans will it provide? What word of greeting will it send across the sea to its martyred kinsmen in Christ?

The Arena,[123] vol. 17 (March 1897): 652–62.

The Armenian Refugees

M. H. Gulesian[124]

"Might I choose from the world where my dwelling should be,
I would say, still thy ruins are Eden to me,
My beloved Armenia."

The Constantinople massacre brought the horrors perpetrated by the Turks upon their defenceless victims nearer home to Europeans and Americans than the number of nearly one hundred thousand innocent people in the interior of Turkey had ever done; for, during this massacre, thousands were able to escape by means of the foreign legations and by the foreign steamers anchored in the harbor. And the sight of these fleeing men, women, and children, at the very point of the Turkish bayonet, has brought a realizing sense of the condition of affairs existing in Turkey, even to the most sceptical. It is estimated that, of those who escaped during this massacre, twelve thousand went to Bulgaria, about one thousand to Alexandria, Egypt, about eight hundred to Greece, a few hundred to Marseilles, France, and various numbers to other countries. The graphic accounts given in the papers of the destitute condition of the poor exiles at Marseilles so stirred the kind hearts of Miss Frances E. Willard and Lady Henry Somerset, those noble women who are always ready to extend a helping hand, that they resolved to go at once to Marseilles to see what personal aid they could render. Miss Willard speaks of the scene which met their eyes as one of unspeakable pathos. She describes the men from all ranks and conditions as being huddled together on bare benches, utterly destitute and forlorn, with bread and water only for food, and a board to sleep on, in the dead and poisonous air of the great barn-like place in which they had found shelter. It will readily be seen that there was plenty of work for these noble women to do, and they performed it almost miraculously. In a short time they had so transformed the place as to make it fairly comfortable, and they then turned their attention to the task of making arrangements by which many of the refugees could be sent to the United States. After some difficulties, arrangements were made, and soon about four hundred were put on board steamers bound for the United States, with happy hearts that they would now, so soon, reach the long-desired land of freedom. But alas! the bitter disappointment that awaited them here. On arriving at Ellis Island they were detained two weeks, and told that they were to be returned to Turkey. After waiting anxiously for more than two weeks, every day expecting their release, I went to New York to interview the emigration commissioner. I had with me letters guaranteeing positions for about fifty, and these I presented to Dr. Senner, hoping he would be able to release that number at any rate; and although he pointed out most courteously that he could not grant my request, he yet gave me the satisfaction of saying that they should not be returned to Turkey.

After finishing my interview with Dr. Senner, in which I told him that it would be more humane to drown them in New York harbor than to return them to Turkey, I went to the pier where they were detained, and found a most forlorn and abject-looking set, believing that they were to be sent back to Turkey, or finally disposed of in the harbor. After making it known to them that I was one of their countrymen, and had come from Boston to look after them, they crowded up to the iron fence and begged me to do all I could to get them out of that place. They said they had heard talk of sending them back to Turkey, and did not feel sure but that the Turks were compelling the United States to send them back, the thought of which was terrorizing. They spoke in such a discouraged way of the uncertainty of their fate, when they thought they had finally entered a free country, that it could not but touch me to the heart. I talked with them for half an hour, assuring them that they would not be returned to Turkey under any circumstances. One thing that made my blood boil more than anything else during this detention of the refugees was the tyranny exercised by the petty officials, and the abusive language used both to the refugees and to me, in regard to landing the refugees, when it required my strictest attention to understand their broken language, and I could not help wondering how long it was since they themselves had crossed the ocean. In thinking over the whole transaction, I came to the conclusion that the intention of the immigration bureau was to make it as costly as possible, especially to the steamship companies, so as not to make it profitable for them to bring any more refugees over. They did not realize that these men were not paupers, or immigrants in the usual meaning that word suggests, but that they were refugees, who had fled here because their lives were in jeopardy in their own country. The bond of $500 each, required by law, was finally reduced to $100, and by that time a gentleman of New York gave bonds for $25,000, which procured the release of all. While these men were being thus detained, thousands of the refuse of Europe landed without any trouble.

After their release, the different organizations and individuals that had agreed to be responsible for a certain number took them to the different places prepared for them. This distribution was effected by the Salvation Army, the Armenian Relief Association, and Dr. Ayvazian of New York. Of those sent to Boston, forty-seven were sent to the Woman's Christian Temperance Union, and forty-two to Miss Blackwell, each of whom had agreed to be responsible for a certain number, though not for so large a number as were sent. Others came in small detachments at various times. A temporary shelter was offered in Revere by a gentleman, for the Woman's Christian Temperance Union to use for the accommodation of those in their charge, and I offered to Miss Blackwell the use of one of the floors in my factory. I then made it my chief work to make these poor people as comfortable as I could, and to make the place as homelike as possible during their short stay, while awaiting situations. I divided the room by a large curtain into two divisions, using one part for the sleeping-room, and the other for a living room. By a free use of flags and bunting in the American and Armenian colors, we made the room quite attractive.

Beds and bedding were freely contributed by many kind friends. Then I began my first experience in housekeeping, which I found quite exciting. Finding three rooms near the factory, suitable for kitchen, dining-room, and storeroom, I hired them. I then bought a stove, all necessary kitchen utensils, tables, tableware, chairs, etc. I also succeeded in procuring an Armenian cook, who made good Armenian bread and other native dishes.

On the arrival of each detachment they were met by Mrs. Samuel J. Barrows,[125] Miss Blackwell,[126] and myself. They were then conducted to 16 Waltham Street, where a warm breakfast was served them. We owe a great deal to the above-mentioned ladies, as well as to Mrs. Fessenden and Mrs. Baker of the Woman's Christian Temperance Union. Soon we had an organized systematic way of conducting the place. After a few days' trial, it was found necessary to transfer the men at Revere to Waltham Street, although they still continued under the charge of the Woman's Christian Temperance Union, Revere being found too distant, and too much time being taken in going back and forth to look after them.

When this transfer was made, the Woman's Christian Temperance Union paid twenty-five cents a day per head for their food. The refugees were mostly men, though some women and children were among them, and they told me that during the two months' journey, they had not had a change of clothing, or any food they could relish.

When their board and lodging had been arranged for, I felt it most important that they should learn as much English as possible while with me, and begin to learn American manners and customs. Several ladies kindly volunteered to come and teach, and four or five classes were taught every morning from 9 to 11.30.

In the evening they attended the evening school near by, and once, sometimes twice, a day, I talked to them on American customs and manners. Within a few weeks they had made great progress. They were all most eager to find some work by which they could support themselves. It has been observed by every visitor to the home that these men were bright, intelligent-looking, and in some instances highly educated, speaking three to six languages. Though these men were born in Asia and brought up under a less than half-civilized government, yet their intelligence and moral character surpasses the average foreigner from Europe who comes to this country. Nothing would have brought them here but to escape the massacre. Many of them had a profitable business and a happy home; and when they tell of these ruined homes, and of the killing and torture of their relatives and friends, it is too pitiable to listen to.

Soon after their arrival I was distributing some of the clothing which had been sent in, and I noticed a number of them with tears rolling down their cheeks. I stopped and inquired what the trouble was, and they told me of the destruction of their property and all their life's earnings, and said that three months ago they had a prosperous business, bright firesides, and happy homes, and now they were accepting clothing given in charity. The sad faces and tears of these strong men moved my already long pent-up feelings, so that I was unable to go on with the work of distribution.

The stories of nearly all were such as to make one weep as they would speak so sorrowfully and affectionately of a father or mother, wife or children. They did not know where these were, whether among the living or dead, whether captives in Turkish harems or sick and penniless and left to starve. Every day one or another would come to me, begging to know if there was not some way in which they could find out about their dear ones. One of the saddest sights I ever witnessed was that of one of the refugees, a promising young man of eighteen, for whom work had been obtained in Brighton, but who after two weeks was taken seriously ill, and had to be taken to the City Hospital. When on his deathbed, he expressed a desire to see me, and I immediately went to see what I could do for him. During our conversation I asked him if he could give me any clew to his parents, that I might send them word, and he began to sob, and said: "I cannot tell; they ran one way and I another. I do not know whether they are alive or dead." He had since heard that they were believed to be in Alexandria, Egypt, but the uncertainty of their fate and condition was terrible. He said he could die easier if he were only sure that his mother was safe and unharmed. As I thought this case over, and reflected that this was only one of thousands, the discouraging thought came to me, "Can God be living?"

Another picture that oft rises before me in this dreadful drama that is being enacted is that of the old men, a large number of whom have been exiled—men who had held high and influential positions among their people, who were looked up to with admiration and almost with reverence for their many acts of kindness, charity, and devotion to their people. Nearly all of this class who have not been

THE ARMENIAN REFUGEES

killed are now exiles, and I have met many of them in this country, friendless, homeless, and penniless. They have already once nobly performed life's mission, and now they are suddenly bereft of everything, with youth, strength, and ambition gone. The picture is too sad to dwell upon.

> Alas, ye poor Armenians!
>   In undeserved distress
> Ye wander forth to slavery,
>   In want and wretchedness.
>
> A myriad woes ye suffered,
>   Nor left your own dear home;
> But now ye leave your fathers' graves
>   In distant lands to roam.
>
> These waters sweet, these smiling fields,
>   Where cities fair are set,
> To strangers ye abandon them,
>   But how can ye forget?
>
> Nay, while you live, remember;
>   Be to your country true;
> Your children and descendants,
>   Bid them remember too.
>
> The holy name of Ararat
>   And many a sacred fane,
> Till the last judgment wakes the world
>   Shall in their hearts remain.
>
> Alas for thee, my country!
>   Alas for thee, for us!
> I would that death had sealed mine eyes
>   Ere I beheld thee thus!*

---

*Translation of an Armenian poem.

Then I think how all these sad scenes, and all the butchery, starvation, and martyrdom of the last three years, all the suffering,—suffering so terrible that even that of the Apostles cannot be compared to it, or even the physical suffering of Christ,—all might have been averted if they would have surrendered their faith. Yet all was endured for the sake of The Christ.

During the stay of the refugees at the temporary home, services were held every Sunday, much to the pleasure of the refugees, who greatly enjoyed them. They were also participated in by many American friends and Armenian residents of Boston. Different ministers were invited to speak to them every Sunday. At the third service, the minister came without his Bible. When he asked me for one, I said I had not provided any, as each minister had brought his own with him. As he seemed at a loss to proceed without one, the thought came to me that there might be one among the boys. So I stepped behind the curtain, where some twenty were assembled, ready for the opening of the service, and asked if any of them had a Bible. Whereupon eighteen out of the twenty replied that they had, and started for their scanty little bundles. They had hardly been able to take anything with them, and yet they had not forgotten to take their Bibles. The Rev. Edward Bliss, in his recent book on "Turkey and the Armenian Atrocities," says, in speaking of the Armenians: "They cherish the Bible as the most precious of their possessions, and guard it all the more sacredly when to do so involves the hazard of their lives."

In considering the average refugee, the young and middle-aged, it is wonderful to see how bravely they bear their heavy burdens, and how courageous they are in regard to the future. The following case is an instance: One of the young men whose picture I have in a refugee group, had a fine dry-goods store, and was doing a most prosperous business. When the massacre began, he hurriedly gathered up what cash he could, closed the store, and ran for his life. He intended running to one of the legations, but the Turks were gaining on him so rapidly that he ran into the house of a Greek near by, and was hidden. After hiding for forty-eight hours, and when the massacre had ceased, he went out, disguising himself all he could, to see what had happened to his store. He found the store broken into, and not a thing left. Even the old broom he had used to sweep the floor was gone. He calls himself fortunate, however, as he recalls the terrible fate that befell many of his friends and neighbors, who lost their lives or suffered bodily injury, as well as losing all the property they had. Now, when I go up to the room given up to them, with a letter in my hand, or some one with me, they know that there is a chance for one of them, and they all come to the front eager to go. We have succeeded in getting places for all of them,—123 *in toto*. Wherever they have had a trade we have endeavored to place them in the same, and have in all cases tried to adapt the men to the work offered, as far as possible. We have sent men as civil engineers, carpenters, masons, cobblers, barbers, blacksmiths, to shoe factories, to cordage factories, to farms, for housework, and other occupations. Two have been placed in schools. We have had many gratifying letters from the people where we have placed them.

The happiest feature of their stay while at Waltham Street was that of the Thanksgiving dinner, when all Armenians were invited to the feast, and 225 availed themselves of the invitation. Many Armenian ladies were among them.

What impressed me strongly, as well as others, was the character and behavior of these 123 men while they were with me. Realizing the restraint under which they had been kept all their lives, especially since the massacre, I made up my mind to give them as much liberty as possible, so that they might know what freedom was like. So I opened wide the door, regardless of religious creeds, and it was left wide open during all their stay for them to go out and in as they pleased. Not once was this kindness taken advantage of, and from the beginning to the end of the sixty-two days, during which they were with me, none of them indulged themselves in intoxicating drinks or in any other improper way, although they had to pass two bar-rooms every time they went out. Many of them even gave up smoking when I told them the disadvantage they would labor under in working for Americans.

In their home life, the Armenians are a most affectionate, home-loving people. Their family relations are held most sacred. When the sons marry, they bring their wives back to the old homestead. Thus, sometimes there are three or four families residing under one roof, yet there is seldom any quarrelling or jealousy. They are naturally a moral people, and divorce is a thing almost unknown. As old as our history is, dating back to Haig the great-great-grandson of Noah, polygamy and slavery are also unknown.

Two questions are continually being asked me: "How do any of the Armenians get out of Turkey?" and "Why don't they all come out?" It must be remembered that most of those who do succeed in getting here are from cities on or near the sea-coast. To get out of the interior is a much more difficult matter.

I will relate one instance which concerns myself personally, and will serve to show why more Armenians do not leave Turkey. The instance is that of my youngest brother, who, by a fortunate circumstance, saved not only his own life, but that of his parents also, in that third and most terrible massacre, which overran Marash. While sitting on the wall enclosing the house, talking with a Turkish boy of his own age, he saw a large band of Turks and soldiers bent on plunder, pillage, and murder, approaching the house. This Turkish boy, out of the friendship he had for my brother, and at his entreaties, jumped up and ran to them, begging them to go away, and assuring them that a previous party had been there and stripped the house of everything. Although this was not true, it served the desired purpose, and as he was the son of a well-known and influential Turk, they probably believed him, or else did not care to waste time in finding out, as there were plenty of other houses which they could as well plunder, and to which they immediately turned their attention. After this massacre was over, I sent a hundred dollars for this brother to come over here with. Of course, the first thing to do was to get a passport from the Turkish Government, which is a very difficult thing to do, and is only done by bribing the Turkish officials. Thirty dollars of this money had to go to secure his passport. He started on a pack-horse, with a caravan, each man carrying his own food and bedding, as there are no hotels or inns in the interior. He passed safely through the small villages, but when he came to the city of Adana he was arrested at once and put in prison. But by bribing some of the minor officials, and through the influence of some friends he had in the city, he was released, and he took the train from Adana to Mersin, at which place he was to take the steamer. As soon as he got out of the train, however, he was at once recaptured, and after a day's imprisonment at Mersin, he was sent to Tarsus for examination, and from there taken back to Adana, which is the capital of the vilayet. There he was put in prison again, without any trial, in a place not fit for the worst criminals. At the expiration of three weeks, influence of friends and more bribing got him out again, and this time, avoiding the train, he succeeded in getting to Mersin. Here he bought his ticket for Marseilles, and had just money enough left to bribe one more man to row him in his own boat out to the steamer. So he, too, like most of the other refugees, landed at Marseilles penniless and friendless. This is not an extreme case, but represents fairly the difficulties encountered by the average comer.

Some travellers and writers, here and in England, have misrepresented Armenians, not taking into consideration the woful circumstances by which they are surrounded. Some have called them sharpers, others cheats and liars, which I claim is a misrepresentation of the true inner character of the Armenian. I can see how these characteristics have impressed themselves upon travelers, who only see Armenians amid the Eastern customs. For instance, if a storekeeper in the East does not ask for an article three times as much as it is worth, he might just as well give up business, as the buyer never expects to pay more than a third of the price asked. I would like to emphasize particularly that there is no chance while living in Turkey to learn anything different. Having for many centuries been at the mercy of the rapacious Turkish officials, who have had a perfect right to extort all they could from the Armenians, no matter how unjustly, they have had to learn in self-defence to evade and deceive, or they could not have retained for themselves enough to live upon. Nearly every example that is set them by the Turkish officials is one of dishonesty and corruption, so the Armenians have had to meet Turkish rapacity with Armenian cunning. But if these traits have been observed in some cases, I claim that they are not in our blood, but in our bringing up. They have been cultivated for self-protection. Men who write thus blindly forget that there is nothing in Turkey to develop honesty or trust in one another. On the other hand, there is every reason why we should become corrupt and demoralized. From time immemorial it has been the aim of the Turkish Government to set the Christian races one against the other, to break up all union, fellowship, and patriotism; and to that end it has used all its skill. The Turkish Government is so full of bribery and corruption that the whole population has become infected. I venture to say that to-day, if you were to take the children of the wisest and best families of America and England, and put them in the places of the Armenians of Turkey, they will grow up the same. In Armenia the degree of education is most limited; there are no books or magazines, lectures or newspapers. These things which are for the development of mankind are forbidden. Some people have said that Armenians could never learn to govern themselves, as they would not agree, and could not bear to have one superior to the rest. I am now more than ever convinced that that is a false assertion, and one that can be positively denied. I have pushed certain points to the extreme to test this, by appointing one over the others in various ways, and am absolutely convinced that Armenians can work together as well as any nationality on earth. All they need is to be sure that there is no selfish interest in those leading them. Naturally, of course, they expect that there is some underlying selfish motive in every measure proposed, as that has been their experience in nine cases out of ten under Turkish rule.

If the chance were given and the yoke of the Turk removed, these writers would find that they were as mistaken as those were who, before the massacre, said that the Armenian Church and religion were more a religion of form and ceremony than anything else, and lacked the essential elements of Christianity. When the test came, they found out that the devotion of Armenians to the Christian religion was unequalled by the people of the Western world at any age. So, with our national affairs, if the chance were offered I am sure there are hundreds if not thousands of Armenians who would be found ready to sacrifice not only self-interest, but even life itself, in order to secure the unity of our people. Where Armenians have been given the chance to learn better things, how quickly they have raised themselves to the standard set them by civilization!

It may be interesting to the public to know what kind of citizens Armenians make in this country. They have proved to be sober, industrious, zealous in helping one another, and faithful. As mechanics they rank as high as those of any nationality; they have good business ability. Two years ago, when I made inquiries, I found there were none confined in the different penal and charitable institutions of this State. Now there are about four thousand Armenians in this State, and according to personal letters which I received this last week from the various wardens and superintendents of these institutions, there were only two confined in them all. At Long Island, where that immense institution is full of paupers, Dr. Cogswell says in his letter that he has never known of any Armenians being under his charge. When it is taken into consideration that these four thousand men in the State of Massachusetts are for the most part here without their wives or any family ties, and that the young men are destitute of any sort of family connections, it will be seen that they are laboring under tremendous disadvantages and hardships which no other nationality has to struggle under. It may be well in closing to refer once more to the Rev. Mr. Bliss, who says, "Those who know the race most widely and most intimately, esteem it the most highly."

Armenia's Desolation and Woe*

In many respects the most illuminating account of the state of affairs in Armenia that has been given to the public since the fearful massacres of the past two years, comes from the pens of Professor and Mrs. J. Rendel Harris.[127] These devoted and delightful English people are well-known in the United States, because for some years they lived in Baltimore, where Professor held a chair in the John Hopkins University. They have made an arduous journey through the afflicted parts of Armenia as the almoners of the relief fund raised by the English Society of Friends. From stage to stage in their progress through Armenia they wrote letters back to the English people who had sent them forth; and these letters, simple and unpretentious in form, but most valuable in substance, are now gathered into a volume. The immense value of the work of American missionaries and educators in Asia Minor is constantly noted by Professor and Mrs. Harris, and the splendid heroism of our American countrymen and women through the recent adversities of Armenia is glowingly set forth.

In this book we have the sign of the Turk writ large. There is no mistaking the handwriting, for it spells murder, desolation, and deceit. Professor Harris does not overload his letters with details of the massacres. He and his wife were in Armenia to distribute relief and they describe what they saw and what they heard on the spot.

"Our Sufferings Have No Respite, No End"

The late Patriarch M. Izmirlian, Professor Harris says, was brokenhearted over the sufferings of his people. He said: "There is no

---

*Letters from Armenia. By Dr. J. Rendel Harris and Helen B. Harris, 12mo, pp. 266. New York: Fleming M. Revell Co. $1.25.

parallel in history for such systematic and continuous persecution—by robbery, torture, imprisonment, exile and murder-of men, women and children going on for years. There have been Neros who appeared and flooded the world with blood like big waves, and then disappeared; but our suffering has no respite, no end." It is these sufferings which Professor Harris describes. Of this continual oppression he gives many instances. Take for example the following description of the country to the north and east of Mardin:

> It is a good country for studying the decline of the Turkish government, for the people are almost bled to death by their unjust rulers, and I found village after village either wholly deserted or reduced to a fraction of its original population, while the hillsides were full of the traces of ancient vineyards, and fruit trees were growing wild that must at one time have been carefully cultivated. There has been no systematic massacre over this region, only habitual oppression and local outbreaks and disorder. We passed through one village which had been raided a few hours before by the Moslems, who had carried off three hundred sheep; but these robberies ought hardly to be classed with what has been going on in other places, for they are probably as natural to the life of the people as the ancient Border Raids between England and Scotland.

A Blow at the Head

The whole land is covered with ruins, and the lament of the orphaned and bereaved fills the air. The material damage is immense, but what may be called the moral damage is incalculable. The recent attack on the Armenians, Professor Harris points out, was a blow at the head. Most of the leading men were killed, and many of the teachers. The Armenian is better educated than the rest of the community, and has made himself a power in the East owing to his superior intelligence. This advance of the Armenian is only of recent date, and is chiefly owing to the American missions. The question, therefore, of re-establishing the schools is of utmost importance unless the people are to relapse into the old barbarism of fifty years ago. Professor Harris, wherever he went, did all he could to put the schools on a firm foundation again, thereby insuring a future to the oppressed people.

He points out, truly enough, that the Armenian question is an American question more than anything else. He says:

The civilization of Asia Minor is American; it is recovered by a network of American agencies; there are good colleges and schools, medical colleges, and schools for training teachers. The same thing is going on as in Bulgaria; the Americans are training the future rulers of the country.

The result were that the Americans were getting wealthy, enterprising, full of skill and commercial activity, and thus provoked hostility of the Turk and furnished a seed-bed for persecution.

Hope for the Turks and the Kurd

The miserable story of Turkish atrocity is relieved here and there by the heroism of the missionaries and some conspicuous deeds of nobleness by individual Turks. Professor Harris does not think the Turk is bad at heart, and even has some hopes for the Kurds if well governed. He says:

> I believe with all my heart that there is good stuff hidden away in the ordinary Turk, behind a mass of evil. For he is a slave to those in authority, and to the cruel part of his creed, and these two forces hold him in bondage to that which is bad; under better auspices I believe *much good* would appear, and the same remark replies to the Kurds, only that they are more savage still.

The Result of Persecution

Persecution as usual has not accomplished its object, but has done more than anything else to bring the persecuted into common accord. The first result of these horrible massacres has been to draw together the various bodies of Christians, and to accomplish a religious unity such as no councils could ever have found a basis for. Professor Harris says:

> The way it has come about is like this: it is the result of three operating factors. First, the solidifying influence of an awful persecution. The Christians have been wonderfully drawn together by the trials through which they have had to pass. As one of the pastors said to me, 'We were like pieces of cold iron, but this persecution has welded us together.' The second cause which has been at work is the sympathy of the Western Protestant Nonconformity. The Armenians know very well how much sympathy has come to them from

the Old English and American Evangelicals, and they have drawn their own conclusions. They say, 'We understand the Protestants now, and know they are not heretics.' And, thirdly, since the alleviation of the sufferings of the people has largely flowed through the hands of native Armenian pastors, working with the Old Gregorian Armenians, the two poles of religious thought and life have been brought into such contiguity that sparks of love have been passing all the time.

A Commonwealth in Ruins

But these brighter touches only serve to make the gloom of the picture more oppressive and more unbearable. Two more extracts must suffice. Describing the condition of things at Harpoot, Mrs. Harris says:

> The mass of the humanity is so great, *some must be lifted off the rest*, or very few will be able to do what they else could to recuperate. They will crush one another. What makes Ourfa so much better able to make a fresh start than other places is no doubt that so many were killed outright, and those who are left have a chance to do something.

Professor Harris thus describes the state of the country after the Turk and the Kurd have worked their will:

> It is like putting together a clock that has been smashed: it is a piece of broken society, and you have to study the conditions of life, beginning at the bottom—food, clothing, shelter—working up. Suppose in one of our towns one-half the shops were looted, one-fifth of the population dead or wounded, one-fifth of the women widows, it would be very difficult to put it all together again. Whole trades have disappeared; you want to shoe a horse, all the smiths are dead; tools are stolen, and the workmen have nothing and cannot get them back. The social problem is therefore very difficult, requiring much adaptation and skill. What can we do? Put together those who belonged together—try to construct a commonwealth out of ruins!

An Interview with Sultan Abdul Hamid

The Honorable A. W. Terrell,
Lately United States Minister at Constantinople

On the nineteenth day of March last, while attending the ceremony of the Selemlik in Constantinople, near the Yildiz Palace, I was informed by a master of ceremonies that I would be received in audience by the Sultan of Turkey after he had finished his devotions in the mosque.

On entering the palace at the appointed time, attended by Munier Pasha, the introducer of foreign diplomats, and by Mr. Gargiulo, my official interpreter, my reception was cordial; and during a conversation which lasted more than two hours many things were said by the Sultan regarding the treatment of the Armenian race by the Turkish government which he desired should be made known to the people of the United States. An expression of that desire was renewed by him on the fifteenth day of June last, on the eve of my departure for home. He was assured that his wish would be observed in such manner and at such time as would be proper after my official relations with his government had ceased.

In now complying with that promise, it is deemed proper first to introduce to the reader Sultan Abdul Hamid, by quoting from an article in the January, 1895 number of the "Contemporary Review." That article was written by one who is recognized by missionaries, as the ablest and most scholarly American divine and educator in Turkey, and who has resided in Constantinople more than twenty years. The extracts are as follows:

He [the Sultan] has never failed to win the heart of any European who has been admitted to any degree of intimacy with him. All find in him the noble and attractive qualities, which they cannot help but admire. . . . Except in religion, he is more of a European than an Asiatic. . . . He is no more of an Oriental despot than the late Czar; and many of the fine qualities discovered in the Czar after his death are equally characteristic of the Sultan. In personal ability, I should say he was the Czar's superior. . . . It is true of the Sultan, as it was of the Czar, that his policy was not adopted through personal ambition or the love of power, but from a sense of duty to religion and country. . . . In Asia Minor the Sultan has had some excuse for the persecution of Armenians in the establishment of their revolutionary committees. . . . He deserves the highest praise. . . . It is a new thing in the world to see a Turkish sultan attempting to cleanse his empire from filth and disease, and rivaling the most advanced countries in the world in his efforts to care for the health of his people. . . . He has done more for the education of his people than all the sultans who have gone before him.

The tourist who visits Turkey finds in Constantinople a resident colony of fifty-two native Americans, all of whom are missionary educators, or Bible-hours people, except two, one of whom is a dentist and the other a saloon-keeper. None of these has ever been presented to the Sultan, or admitted to the Yildiz Palace, which few except diplomats ever enter, and which is, perhaps, more exclusive than any palace in Europe. Over thirteen centuries of fierce attrition between the crescent and the cross have not tended to develop among rival religionists a spirit of mutual love; but, on the contrary, have even made it difficult for them to speak charitably of each other. Whatever may be the cause, certain it is that published descriptions of the Sultan, and of his habits, which have appeared in the American press, usually contain as many errors as sentences.

The Sultan is over fifty years old, of medium height, with clear olive complexion, dark hair, high forehead, and large dark-brown eyes. The habitual expression of his face is one of extreme sadness. Though the pashas who attended his palace when ministers or ambassadors are entertained and decorated with regal splendor, he always appears in plain garb, wearing a red fez, a frock-coat and trousers of dark-blue stuff, and patent-leather shoes. A broad service-sword with steel scabbard, which he holds sheathed in his hand, completes the costume. Sometimes a single decoration is worn on the breast. When he is seen thus plainly attired in the throne-room of his palace, on the first day of the feast of Bairam, seated on an ottoman covered with cloth of gold, to receive the congratulations of his civil and military chiefs, who are all radiant in uniforms and decorations, the contrast is very striking. No Christians but those of the diplomatic corps ever witness this impressive ceremony, which is conducted with the order that distinguishes a military review, but with an Oriental servility that an American finds it difficult to understand. On such occasions Osman Pasha stands at the Sultan's left, holding a cloth-of-gold scarf, which all reverently kiss after saluting their ruler.

No sovereign in Europe is more courtly or refined in entertaining his guests, and few can be more agreeable in conversation. In his personal intercourse with foreign representatives he is alike free from that stilted dignity which repels confidence, and from that absence of real dignity, which invites familiarity.

When I first dined at the palace, the Sultan sat at the head of the table, with Mrs. Terrell at his right and myself at his left. Osman Pasha, Ismael Pasha, the former Khedive of Egypt, the Grand Vizier, and other ministers of state were the other guests.

Nothing could excel the excellence of the cuisine of which he partook with his guests, the table-service and decorations, the magnificence of the dining room, or the excellence of his wines, which always remain untasted except by Christian guests. Each pasha wore the insignia of his rank, blazing with stars and decorations, while the plain costume of the Sultan was alone in harmony with my own. No armed men stood guard at the palace doors, and except a detail from the Imperial Guard, who always salute a foreign representative on his arrival, no soldiers have ever been seen by me within the palace walls on any of the occasions when I have dined there.

I do not hesitate to confirm the opinions of General Lew Wallace and my other predecessors, that the Sultan of Turkey is a ruler of great intellectual ability. I regard him as the ablest sovereign in Europe. My opinion as to whether, and in what degree, he is responsible for the massacres that have desolated his kingdom, was given to Secretary of State Olney. It remains unpublished, and will not be repeated here.

Much of the conversations referred to at the beginning of this article related to the matters of a diplomatic nature, which for manifest reasons it would be improper to repeat. The Sultan remarked that he had been much gratified by hearing from Sir Ashmead Bartlett, a member of the British Parliament, that I had spoken in just terms touching his Majesty's action in what he termed the Armenian "disturbances"; and that he naturally expected this on account of the personal friendship between us, which enabled me to know that he did not have it in his nature to be willfully cruel.*

He said that the facts about recent disturbances in Turkey had never been faithfully reported by the press of the United States, and that he hoped that I would make known to the American people what he was then about to say. Continuing, he said:

> Early during the Ottoman conquests in Asia Minor, the Armenians, who were being crushed by repeated invasions of the Tartars and the Persians, emigrated in large numbers, and obtained protection from the Ottoman rulers. They were kindly received, hospitably treated,

---

*The conversation with Ashmead Bartlett to which the Sultan referred related chiefly to my letter of December 29, 1895, to a leading missionary in Turkey, while the massacres were progressing. The letter will be found in Part II of the Foreign Relations for the United States for 1895. The following is an extract:

> To you sir, to the consul-general, to the secretary of legation, and, I believe, to President Washburn, I expressed four months ago that my conviction that the so-called reforms would, when announced, be followed by a massacre of Armenians and a period of great danger to our missionaries. This view was not entertained by those above referred to, nor by my colleagues; but, acting on my own conviction, instant measures were taken for the security of our countrymen. A residence in the southern portion of the United States at the close of our late Civil War had prepared me to anticipate the fearful era through which we are passing here. I had seen the resentful violence of a proud, dominant race, caused by enforced reforms for a subject race, which was increased by the arrogance of the enfranchised negroes, and which resulted in Ku-Klux outrages.
>
> It was known here that at least one of the great powers would not consent to the use of force to make the reforms proposed for the benefit of the Armenian race effective. And so, on the 21st of October, when very many persons were rejoicing over the irade then issued, which proposed to arm and make officers of a race that had for centuries been subjugated and denied privileges, I demanded and obtained on that day telegraphic orders to every civil and military chief in the Ottoman Empire to protect American missionaries. Once before, in anticipation of the reforms, and four times since, like orders were obtained at the Porte by myself, such frequent repetition being deemed necessary to impress officials in the interior. . . . I know that the Department of State feels the utmost solicitude for the protection of all American interests. It had sustained me in every responsibility assumed which had that protection for its object; and I cannot, even by implication, concede that it has neglected the interests of your associates and yourself. It surveys the whole vast field of our nation's complicated embarrassments and duties. Our vision is circumscribed by our isolation. . . . I expressed to Sir Ashmead Bartlett the opinion that no Christian sovereign in Europe could have acted more promptly than did the Sultan in the protection of the lives of all American citizens in the Ottoman Empire.

and received benefits in the protection of their lives and property. No nation continually engaged in war can excel in industrial and commercial pursuits. Thus it occurred that while the early sultans were busy with conquests, all manufacturing and commercial interests were monopolized by Christian races, and chiefly by the Armenians. Their religion was also tolerated, for Mussulmans tolerate the religion of all men who worship God. Thus the Armenians prospered, and remained contented under Mussulman rule for over four hundred years. They became the manufacturers, contractors, and bankers of the Ottoman empire. They enjoyed their religion, openly worshiped for centuries in their ancient churches and monasteries, and built new ones when needed. Their patriarch could always present their complaints at the Sublime Porte, and they were always protected in the enjoyment of their own methods of worshiping God.

Four books are regarded as sacred by all Mussulmans, namely, the Koran, the book of Confucius, the Talmud of the Jews, and the Bible of the Christians. How could a Mussulman murder Armenians merely on account of their religion, when the Koran prohibits cruelty, and requires that all men who believe in God shall be protected, except during war?

One of my ancestors—Selim I, the grandson of the conqueror of Constantinople—once thought that his empire would be stronger if all of his subjects professed the same religion. Some disturbances raised by Christian races caused him to ask the Sheik-ul-Islam if it would be lawful for him to kill all Christians who refused to be converted to Islam. The Sheik issued a *fetva*, in which he answered that it would not be lawful, and that Christians who were peaceful must be protected.* So Selim respected the fetva. Fire-worshipers and idolaters alone have no right to protection, and Mussulmans are prohibited from eating meat cooked by such people.

The Sultan then cited many evidences of the favor and partiality extended to, and of the confidence reposed in, the Armenians by himself and by former sultans, to show that their religion was not the cause of their recent misfortunes. He said:

One Dadian, an Armenian, was given entire control of the imperial powder factory by my father, Sultan Abdul Medjid. He grew rich. He could make powder that would not throw a ball across the room. Thus he had the army at his mercy. Dadian lived at a village on the

---

*History confirms the statement.

coast near this city. I remember that my father took me and my brother, when we were mere boys, to Dadian's house, and we slept there two nights.

Kuetzgrolian, an Armenian, was employed to procure every article of furniture, jewelry, and clothing for the palace. He became a great favorite. He had a residence on the Bosporus at Tchenguelkein, on the Asiatic shore, and became very wealthy. To his house my father would go frequently when he wished to rest.

The entire charge of the imperial mint was in the hands of an Armenian named Agop Effendi. His opportunities for obtaining wealth were of course great, and he also became very rich.

Another Armenian, Gumushgerdan, was the designer and maker of female attire for the imperial palace. He still lives there, and is immensely rich.

The Balians, who are Armenians, have been in succession from father to son the architects of palaces and buildings for the Ottoman sultans for generations. They built the palaces of Dolma Bagtche, Tcheragan, Beyler Bey, Yildiz, Flamour, the Sweet Waters of Asia, etc., and one is now my imperial architect.

My father gave to Dadian a large house at Beshicktesh (a quarter of the city), in which Artin Pasha, my present under-secretary for foreign affairs, who is also an Armenian, now lives. My father, in order to please Dadian, gave him a block of land adjoining his residence, upon which Sultan Medjid built from his private means an Armenian church, so that Dadian in bad weather could go there and worship God without going out of doors. At that time the disposition of the administration was far from sanctioning such partiality, but the confidence reposed in Dadian by Sultan Medjid caused him to bestow that favor.

My present minister of state in charge of the civil list, Michael Protocol Effendi, is an Armenian. He has exclusive control of all public lands, and of all real estate belonging to me. Many Armenians are retained in office by him, with my approval. I will cause their names and salaries to be furnished you.

After all the favors bestowed on the Armenian race by my house, which enriched them, their ingratitude was shown by plotting and organizing to destroy the Ottoman Empire. The revolutionary movement has been sustained by wealthy Armenians.

You should remember an Armenian bookbinder who bound for you two beautiful albums. After the disturbances of August last in the city, that man became frightened, and fled to America. "He wrote back, saying that, being unable to speak the English language, he could find no work, and wished to return. I directed that he should be permitted to return in safety. He then wrote saying that he had no money. Now, Christian people will scarcely believe it when I say that, being convinced that he was a good man, I directed that one thousand francs be sent to enable him to return home.

The Sultan more than once repeated his declaration that no Christians had ever been persecuted by his government or people for their religious faith, and that their churches and monasteries, which have stood from the early stages of Christianity, had been respected, preserved, and worshiped in; that they had always selected their own patriarchs and bishops, and were always protected in the full enjoyment of their religious freedom.

Referring to the massacres, he said: "The truth, unfortunately, is never published in Christian newspapers about conflicts between my Moslem and Christian subjects. Though no true Mussulman will ever punish any man on account of his religion, if he worships God, yet when people bind themselves together by their religion, and then use it to destroy the Ottoman empire, a different question is presented. While Christian Europe was excited against the Ottoman empire about excesses committed by its soldiers during the Greek revolution of 1827, it had no sympathy to bestow upon the butchery of twenty-seven thousand defenseless Turkish men, women, and children, who where massacred in one city after its surrender."

I here informed the Sultan that my government had published[*] the revelation made by the aged missionary, Rev. Cyrus Hamlin, which first appeared in the "Independent" in December, 1893, to the effect that the Armenian revolutionists intended to commit atrocities on the Turks and fire their homes in order to provoke against their own people atrocious retaliation, and thus enlist the sympathy of the Christian world. I added:

> Though my government is quite satisfied that atrocities have been committed alike by Mussulmans and Armenians in Asia Minor, it has never been disposed to meddle with this Eastern Question in any of its phases. I have never expressed the opinion that your Majesty instigated or ordered the massacre of Armenians, but I feel sure that their repetition would prove most unfortunate for the Ottoman empire. Both English and Armenian historians have done ample justice

---

[*]Foreign Relations of the United States, Part II, 1895.

to Moslem magnanimity. They have all contrasted the terrible butchery of seventy-five thousand Moslem men, women, and children in Jerusalem, by Duke Godfrey, after their surrender, with the knightly humanity of Saladin when he recaptured the city, and gave even the soldiers the privilege of being ransomed.

When at Damascus, and looking at the splendid sarcophagus of Saladin, to which I had been admitted by an imperial irade, I remembered his bearing after victory, and when contrasting his humanity with that of Christian crusaders, felt like standing uncovered before his tomb.

The farce then being enacted in Crete, where Greeks fighting for better government had been fired on from the ships of Christian powers a few days before, being referred to, I remarked: "I really think your imperial majesty has much cause for self-gratulation; for you are the only sovereign the integrity of whose empire is guaranteed by the great powers. No power guarantees the integrity of the domains of France, England, Germany, Russia, Austria, or Italy; but all these not only guarantee the integrity of your empire, but have actually been killing Christian Greeks in Crete to prove that they are in earnest."

He calmly answered: "The desire to guard against a conflict among themselves is natural."

The Sultan referred with manifest pleasure to the success which had attended the culture of the Southern potato yam in the provinces of Smyrna and Mesopotamia, and which had been introduced by me into the empire. I answered that next to having been instrumental in preventing strained relations between our respective governments, I felt most satisfaction in having been the means of introducing a new food crop for the poor, which would make famine impossible where it flourished well. The sad face assumed a look of much benignity as he made the following answer: "To be good to one's fellow-man is the best religion. The Prophet once said that if a man is so mean to himself that he gets drunk and like a hog sleeps by his liquor and cannot get away, it shall be forgiven if he repents; but he who willfully breaks the heart of a fellow-man may never be forgiven."

Thus does the isolated ruler, who is regarded by very many persons as a throned assassin, give utterance to the noblest sentiments, in a voice low and musical, while the kindly and sympathetic expression of his face is a constant puzzle to those admitted to his presence, and who may regard him as cruel.

I am quite aware that much of the foregoing seems unimportant; it is given chiefly because the terrible events that during the last two years have disturbed the Ottoman empire have naturally caused much interest in whatever relates to the appearance or the utterances of the Sultan. During the audience he sat on a sofa richly upholstered with satin brocade. The same material covered the walls. A small table, inlaid in mosaic, on which were cigarettes, which he frequently smoked, was place between us; and during the audience tea was served in jeweled cups of gold. Munier Pasha, a refined gentleman, was present during the audience. The room occupied was richly furnished in the style of Louis XVI. Paintings, some of which were of great excellence, decorated the walls, and silk rugs and a Turkish carpet of unique design covered the floor.

When it is remembered that in addition to being the Sultan of Turkey, Abdul Hamid is the calif or spiritual head of the Mohammedan world, with its one hundred and sixty millions of people, one feels less surprise at the servile adoration with which his subjects approach him. No matter how often during a conversation with a Christian diplomat he may speak to the most exalted of his subjects who may be present, the hand of the person addressed salutes him by quickly and gracefully touching the left breast, lips, and forehead.

The Sultan always converses in the Turkish language, though while yet a prince he studied French; and an incident occurred one night at the Yildiz Palace, when a comedy was rendered in Italian by an Italian troupe, which indicated his knowledge of that language. Among the audience were the Sultan; Osman Pasha, the hero of Plevna; Munier Pasha; the young princes of the palace; and I. During a prison scene the Sultan abruptly ceased conversing and became an intent listener; then, turning to me, he remarked, "That always touches my heart."

His efforts to encourage manufacturing industries have been marked. Works for the manufactures of fine porcelain-ware, in which he takes much interest, have been erected within the palace grounds, under the supervision of Selim Effendi, a Syrian Christian of much intelligence, who is one of the imperial ministers. An imperial library has also been established at Yildiz, the shelves of which are loaded with the works of standard authors of the United States and the chief nations of Europe. Here are found Arabic manuscripts, written when Arabia was the seat of literature, of art, of science, and of poetry, and at a time when European nations were in dense ignorance.

No lovelier view can be seen in any land than that which one beholds from the palace heights. To the south, across the mouth of the Golden Horn, is seen the church of St. Sophia, built by Justinian, and still fragrant with the memories of the early councils of the Christian church which were held in its south gallery. Within its walls more than seventy emperors have been crowned. In full view to the southeast across the Bosporus, on the Asiatic shore, is the spot where the bishops who once ministered to our barbaric ancestors, and others from Asia and Africa, met at the Council of Chalcedon, in 451, to condemn the heresy of Eutyches. A few leagues beyond the lofty snow-crest of the Bithynian Olympus, which is seen on the other side of the Sea of Marmora, are the ruins of Nicæa, where that other Christian council met in the fourth century to condemn the heresy of Arius. To the south, through a dreamy haze like that in the Gulf of Naples, is seen Seraglio Point, so famed in history, in romance, and in song; while to east, on the Asiatic shore, is the ancient Chrysopolis, now called Scutari, to which Xenophon led his ten thousand Greeks after his expedition with Cyrus. To the north and east flows with rapid current the dark blue water of the Bosphorus, two miles wide and three hundred feet deep, which, rushing from the Black Sea, which is almost in view, has just laved the cyanean rocks, or Symmplegades, between which Jason steered in the quest of the Golden Fleece. Below, to the east and extending down to the shore, the eye rests on a forest in which is a pleasure-kiosk of great beauty, and near it are a cataract and a lake. Birds of varied plumage, and the roebuck and the soft-eyed gazelle, roam there at will. There the oleander and the magnolia waved their blossoms of crimson and white to remind me of home. There art everywhere so assisted nature in its arrangement of trees and flowers as to create a restful retreat of surpassing loveliness.

When it is remembered that the Sultan rules over a domain which is inhabited by nearly twenty different races of people, each of whom belongs to a different religious sect, and most of whom speak a language peculiar to themselves; that all except the Turks, having been long subjugated, are therefore restless; and that their discontent has been encouraged by European interference, one must cease to wonder at the race conflicts that have clouded the reign of the present Sultan.

Nowhere in Europe can be found a finer-looking class of men than are the Turkish subjects of the Sultan, or more refined and courteous gentlemen than one sees among their educated classes. Long subjugation must naturally tend to develop degrading vices in any race; therefore it is not strange that all Europeans who have resided long in Turkey bear witness to the fact that the Turks far excel all their subject races in truth, hospitality, fair-dealing, and courage. It is a race full of contradictions, for it is the most gentle and the most cruel; the most hospitable and the most exclusive; the most tolerant and yet the most fanatical that can be found in any land.

The ruler of this strange race has been called the "Sick Man." He has one million of improved magazine-rifles, has purchased one million more, and has trained to use them soldiers who are fatalists, and who see heaven through the smoke of battle. If he should ever be forced, in desperate extremity, to visit Seraglio Point, and give to the breeze the mantle of the Prophet which is there guarded, summoning to its defense all the one hundred and sixty millions of faithful, he would soon be regarded as the most vigorous invalid of modern times.

A Mother of Martyrs

Chalmers Roberts[130]

You would see only a small knot of people, say twenty; perhaps a flourish of wooden clubs in the air. Then the mob would move on, leaving the body of a dead Armenian behind. This was massacre. Not a sound signified the horrible business afoot. The shops were closed as if for a holiday; people, men and women, evidently all Turks, were quietly moving about the streets. The stillness of it seemed to me the most appalling part. One soon grew hardened to the sight of dead men. One came to expect that venerable Ulemas and ascetic young Softas, on their way from mosque to mosque, would kick the mangled bodies which blocked their paths, and curse them for dogs of Armenian traitors. The pools of blood in the streets, in some places actually dripping and trickling downhill, came in time, after you had stepped over and around a hundred of them, to remind you of some early visit to a slaughter house. Animal blood all seems the same: it was hard to realize that this had run in human veins.

Looking back upon those three terrible days in Constantinople, in August, 1896, when from seven to ten thousand Armenians were killed, it is difficult to believe that such things actually occurred. The first news of the outbreak came most unexpectedly. It found the diplomatic colony in the enjoyment of one of their delightful summers at Therapia. Both threats and entreaties had been received at the embassies from the Armenian revolutionary societies; but these had come to be so usual that they were not noticed,—so many threats had remained unfulfilled. Perhaps the culminating event of that season at this Oriental Newport was the very pretty *bal poudre* that was given at the British Embassy by the chargé d'affaires and his attractive American wife on the evening of August 25th. As our party separated in the early morning of the 26th, not one of us dreamed of what the day would bring. The passing of ten hours found some members of the party prisoners in the Imperial Ottoman Bank, at the mercy of a band of determined Armenian revolutionists, who threatened to blow up themselves and their prisoners with hundreds of pounds of dynamite. It found the rest of us hurrying, frightened, up and down the city, doing whatever we could to save them. It found the women weeping and terror-stricken, huddled together in small groups for comfort and consolation.

I did not go down to the city that morning. In the summer season, the presence of one of the members of the force in the American Legation each day was all that was necessary. As it happened to be the turn of Riddle, my colleague, the minister and I remained at Therapia, busily engaged with Washington correspondence. We had no news from town until about four o'clock in the afternoon; then one by one horrified messengers began to arrive. The first only knew that a general massacre was on; that the streets were filled with dead Armenians, and that bombs were being exploded all over town, especially wherever a squad of Turkish soldiery attempted to pass. Later came news of the taking of the great bank. Of course we had no details until days afterwards; at first we heard only that the bank was held by a band of twenty-five revolutionists, who threatened to blow it up with all of the two hundred employees inside, unless the Sultan promised immediate compliance with their demands. These called for the improvement of the political status of his Armenian subjects. Afterward we heard how two strange Armenians had come to the receiving teller of the bank that morning and announced that, as agents of a silver mine in the interior, they wished to deposit a lot of silver bullion. This was a common occurrence, and they were told to bring in the bricks. What seemed to be the ordinary hamáls (porters) of the streets were given free admittance with the bags of supposed bullion on their backs. Then came the sudden killing of two great Croatian porters, who stood in red and gold liveries at the door, and huge iron doors were swiftly closed and barred. In full possession of the bank, the alleged miners announced their terms to the frightened directors present, and sent out one of them as a messenger to the palace, bearing their demand and the fierce threat accompanying it. This was Wednesday afternoon. That night no one slept. Diplomatic launches were going up and down the Bosphorus all night. The ambassadors were sending their dragomans first to the bank, to parley with the revolutionists, and then to the palace, to insist there that immediate steps be taken for the release of the unfortunate men in the bank, and that a stop be put to the prevalent wholesale murder. Naturally, the women relatives of the directors and clerks in the bank were nearly distracted with fear. We caught ourselves listening for the sound of a great explosion. It was nearly day when Maximoff, the famous first dragoman of the Russian Embassy, brought the Sultan's promise of immunity to the revolutionists, as well as the immediate proclamation of the political reforms, if they would give up the bank. Surrendering, as they said, not to save their wretched lives, but to secure the desired irade (proclamation), they were taken, carefully guarded, to the French launch in the Golden Horn, and carried out to the private yacht of Sir Edgar Vincent, governor-general of the bank, anchored in the Sea of Marmora, to await there the coming of an outbound passenger boat which would take them to Marseilles. In this way the ambassadors secured their first point. The bank employees, save the poor doorkeepers who had been killed at first, came out uninjured, and told us wonderful tales of their fifteen hours' imprisonment. During that time a continual fusillade went on between the soldiers surrounding the bank without and the Armenians within. One of the band accidentally dropped a piece of dynamite, and was torn to pieces in the explosion which followed. He died after hours of stoic suffering, refusing all aid offered him by the clerks: he was glad, he said, to die for his country.

Next day we were early in town. In the clear August sunlight the outlook was ghastly. We stopped by the bullet-battered bank, on our way to Legation. We saw pools of blood dotting the cobble pavement, and lines of soldiers standing silently about. We were just concluding that the massacre had stopped when a rattle of shots attracted our attention to a side street, where a crowd of rough-looking Turks were gathered before a barred and barricaded house. We passed several similar scenes, all of them in front of Armenian houses. The shots came from the owners, who were vainly trying to defend themselves against the rapacious mob. The stolid Turkish soldiers, standing about meanwhile, acted as if they were wholly unconscious of what was going on. The only moving vehicles in the empty streets were carts and carriages loaded down with dead men,—the bodies piled in any fashion, arms and legs hanging out,—on their way to the cemeteries. There was prompt system evident in every direction. The dead were being taken out of sight almost before they grew cold; the battered Armenian shops were being closed up with rough boards; lines of patrol were established in all of the principal streets.

Everything was done save the one thing essential; no one raised his hand to save an Armenian life. Wherever two Turks, or even one, met a luckless Armenian or ferreted out of his hiding-place, they beat him over the head with the wooden clubs which all the Turks carried, and an Armenian never attempted to resist. With a submission that was wonderful, he bowed his head to the blows. Only when he was in his home, barricaded, and felt that he could kill several Turkish soldiers, did he ever make any show of resistance.

When we reached the Legation, we heard unnumbered stories of the day and night before. Many people, among them rich Armenian bankers and merchants, were gathered there for protection, and each had some terrible personal experiences to relate. Most of them had lost relatives, and all had lost friends. Lemme, our second dragoman, who lived over in Psamatia, the Armenian quarter of Stamboul, told of the awful butchery going on there, because the place was known as a hotbed of revolution. Many of the revolutionists were armed with dynamite, and were throwing bombs wherever Turkish soldiers tried to arrest them. He told how one band barricaded itself in a church, and kept off the soldiers for hours. Finally, by promising to surrender, they tempted the soldiers in, until the church was filled; then, exploding a great amount of powder and dynamite, they killed themselves and their enemies. Of course many of the stories were exaggerated. One, subsequently verified, was of ten Turks who, armed with wooden clubs, entered the general railway station in Stamboul and killed thirteen Armenians, who were working with iron crowbars upon the track. It was in a discussion that arose over this incident that I heard one of the most prominent of the Armenian bankers of the city say to the minister, who could not understand the sheeplike submission of a whole race to death, that every Armenian was ready to die, if assured that his death would arouse Europe to the extermination of the Turk. We had often heard this threat of national suicide, but could never before believe it. A letter from the venerable missionary, Dr. Cyrus Hamlin, published in our Red Book for 1895, quoted as coming from a leader of the revolution. Only after this experience was its appalling truth forced upon us.

As it was well established that the murderers were seeking none but Armenians, and were offering not the slightest injury to other Christians, we were also convinced of what it has been so hard for the Western world to understand. This is that these massacres were in no sense religious, but were wholly political. They had no connection with the Moslem church, except in so far as all political movements have their centre in the priesthood. Armenians were killed because the Turks were convinced that they were conspiring against the holy government; and they were permitted to be killed because that same holy government did not dare to add to its well-established unpopularity by interfering with its infuriated subjects. Undoubtedly the priesthood had much to do with inciting the murderers.

Thursday afternoon, convinced of the safety of all other Christians, Riddle and I, accompanied by Cabell, a young Virginian, a chance tourist in Constantinople, took a long walk, wholly undefended and unarmed, over in Stamboul, where we knew the massacre was still unrestrained. Here again we saw the silent groups and the dead bodies they left behind when they moved on. We also saw, to be perfectly just, bands of cavalry in the open places, dispersing the mobs with riding-whips. But never a Turkish soldier dared to fire on a ruffian. And the soldiers seemed totally blind to many murders that went on in the smaller side streets.

Thursday night the killing continued; so, also, all night long, the rattle of the death carts through the streets carrying the dead to the burying trenches. Not until Friday night did the continual pressure of the ambassadors force the government to issue orders to the soldiers to fire on all the mobs. Then the massacres came promptly to an end. A visit made on Saturday morning to the Armenian cemetery at Chichli gave the best idea of the awful extent of the deadly work. Here the American and the Belgian ministers estimated that they saw from fifteen hundred to two thousand bodies, laid out in long lines, awaiting the completion of the trenches. Many of them had been lying in the hot sun since Wednesday, and were so swollen that their arms and legs were thrust up stark and stiff into the air.

Is it to be wondered at that, after this experience, ordinary stories of death and suffering seemed trivial, and only the extraordinary moved us to attention? For weeks there was a constant stream of petitioners to the American Legation asking for protection and aid to leave the country. Since we had been directed by the government to give aid to all who could prove their American citizenship (many Armenians have secured naturalization from us, only to return home to live), as well as to the women relatives of Armenian citizens in America, the idea got abroad that we were befriending the whole race. Therefore hundreds who could establish no claim upon us were turned away, weeping and bitter. Every morning there were sure to be groups of them sitting about the hall of the Legation, awaiting the arrival of the minister. They all came to be of the same type, and to attract little of our attention.

One afternoon, on coming in from luncheon, I saw sitting just outside the minister's room, where so often I had seen the black-draped figures, widowed or childless, a large woman with a markedly strong face. She was not bowed down in grief, as many of them had been, but sat straight up, looking ahead as if she saw nothing of the passing visitors. If there was some ideal of incarnate motherhood about her, there was also a firm expression of self-reliance. Her story, I felt, would not be of the usual tearful type. Her clear eyes were of a sort that yields few tears. As she waited for an audience I watched her, convinced that hers would be no ordinary story.

I spoke to Lemme about her. Lemme knew all the prominent Armenians in town. "Oh yes," he said, "that is old Madame Manelian. I would have sworn that she was mixed up in the troubles in some way. She is a very famous character in Psamatia, and I heard the other day that all three of her sons were killed in massacres. Her father was Agop Agopian, one of the best known Armenians in this country under the reign of Abdul Medjid. He was one of the Sultan's secretaries, and for a long time one of those favorites such as we still have, and who, as you know, are often the real power. He once saved the Sultan's life, when a young officer, for some grievance, attacked his Majesty. Agopian snatched a gun and killed the youngster. He grew old and rich and, it was said, very corrupt in the service. His daughter, the lady there in the hall, married Manelian, a professor in the military school near St. Sofia. At the time of the deposition of Murad in '76 Manelian was charged with fomenting a conspiracy among the students, and was sent to die at work on the fortification somewhere on the frontier. Ever since then Madame Manelian has been very bitter, and does not hesitate to call down curses on the head of the present Sultan openly and everywhere. I wonder the authorities have not laid hands on her before this."

This determined me to hear her story, and when I spoke to her she replied, as do most Armenians, in bad Levantine French. Fortunately, a prominent Armenian came in for a visit to the minister just at this time, and she was enabled to tell her story fluently in her own language, which he interpreted, as she went slowly along, in perfect English. It was written down that night into a long memorandum, and I am therefore able to give it here almost in her own language:—

> I come to ask your Excellency to be so graciously kind as to assist me, as you have assisted so many of my poor people, to leave this burial ground of our race. If I were a man I would stay here and fight for my rights. But I am only a poor woman, sixty years old. I have given my husband and my sons to the cause, and what more can a woman give? The police know me and watch me, but they do not dare to hurt me. The bloody monster of Yildiz, base as he is, will not allow them to touch me. He remembers what his father, Abdul Medjid, owed to my father Agopian. He would have arrested me, but he is superstitious and therefore frightened. My father saved his father's life; he fears that he would lose his own if I were harmed. I am safe. But my strength is almost gone; I have no further sons to urge against him; my days are almost run, and I would die in peace. My only remaining child, a daughter, is married and living in Bucharest; I come, therefore, to your Excellency, to ask your protection in leaving, and a small assistance which will enable me to reach Roumania.

Questioned as to what claim she had upon the United States, she knew of none. She understood that we were giving assistance to all Armenians who wished to leave. Assured that this was a mistake, she seemed very much disappointed, though she gave no sign of the tearful pleading usual at this point. But in his kindness the minister promised to use his good offices for her, and to do what he could, unofficially, to assist her departure. Then, because he was anxious to gather all the information possible concerning the massacres, he asked her of her experience. Very slowly and calmly, with but slight punctuation of sighs, she told this remarkable story:—

I had no cause to raise my sons to love the Sultan. Their poor father was sent to cruel imprisonment and a slow death, only because he was a friend of the brave, good Murad, whose place this usurper now holds. They knew his history. But to save them I sent them away as soon as they had been properly educated. Serkis, the elder, went to Athens, where he followed his father's profession and taught. Hagop went first to Marseilles, then to Paris, and finally to Berne, where he was actively engaged in furthering the work of the revolutionary committee. But this, I assure your Excellency, was against my advice. Only Mardiros, their milk brother, the child of my sister, who died in giving him birth, remained with me. My daughter Anna was married two years ago. Almost before I knew it my boys became very much involved and very enthusiastic in the Huntchagist cause. The government knew it. The police came to see me and questioned me about them. They followed Mardiros, but he, poor boy, knew nothing of the cause until my sons returned.

I was ignorant of their plans until one night in July they knocked at my door. I should never have known them, they were so grown and changed. Both had heavy beards, and their oldest friends passed them in the street unnoticed. We sat that whole night through talking of their plans. They had returned for a grand demonstration in favor of the reforms. Mardiros was soon their enthusiastic companion. He helped to conceal their presence; and he gave it out among the neighbors that I had taken in two of his companions of the Regie [tobacco monopoly] to board. We thought we had completely deceived the police. Serkis and Hagop came and went undisturbed for a month. They were so brave and so unselfish. My pride in them was very great. I knew the whole plan. I had helped with my own hands to store the explosives in the cellar of my own house. They went out each night to the meetings of the revolutionists, and spent the day in the manufacture of bombs, which Hagop had learned in Switzerland, and which he soon taught to Serkis and Mardiros. They planned that one band, as had come to pass, should seize the bank in Galata. Another, on the same day, was to occupy the great building of the administration of the Ottoman debt in Stamboul. In this last party were my boys. I saw them go forth on the morning of the day, and kissed them good-by as proudly as if they went to battle. I had well nursed my hatred through the long years; I almost wished, old woman that I am, to go with them. Then I waited.

Now that I see more clearly than I did through the youthful enthusiasm of my boys' eyes, I believe that we are not a fit people for self-government. Long submission has propagated in us all the meaner vices, and the virtues have had little nourishment. I have long known we are a race despised by the world. My boys knew it also. They told me how the people in other countries judge Armenians; but they were filled with enthusiasm to prove their bravery and their honor, and I shared in their ardor. Now I have greater faith in the judgment of the world. In spite of the long cruelty of the Turks to my people as a race, in spite of what we have all suffered as individuals under the present reign, there were actually Armenians so base that for a little of the Sultan's gold they betrayed their brothers. Some there were who, attending all of the meetings, promptly made plain to the authorities all that passed. The government knew of the whole plan days before it came to be carried out. They could have prevented the whole demonstration. But it pleased them to permit the attack on the bank to be made, in order to justify in the eyes of the world a wholesale massacre. And they have well succeeded.

It happened that one of the chief traitors was to lead the attack on the debt building. He failed to appear at the proper time, and sent messengers postponing the attack and deceiving my boys, who were there ready. Then came the news, like lightning, of the taking of the bank. My boys hurried home and thought themselves still safe. They little knew, as I know now, that the police, thanks to their traitorous colleagues, had been watching them for days. On the evening of Wednesday one of the chief police of Psamatia, at the head of a squad of soldiers, came to my house and demanded my sons. By this time the killing was well on in the streets, and all of our houses were closed. I opened a window in the upper story and denied that my sons were in the country. He replied that I was lying, and then began to tell me how long they had been there, what they had been doing, and even where they had been in the morning. The boys, who were listening behind me, knew then that some one had proven traitor. I still denied their presence. Then the officer ordered the men to batter in the door. They struck it not more than once, when Serkis seized some bombs which were under the divan and began to let them fall among the soldiers. Two, I think, were killed. But as they began to shoot I could no longer watch them. I ran to aid Mardiros in bringing the bombs from the cellar into the second story. Before we had carried them all upstairs the soldiers came back reinforced and the battle began. One of their bullets made a fine hole for me to look through. How I rejoiced to see the bragging police officer, who was directing the attack, die! Three times during the night they returned, and each time went back carrying their dead with them. None of us spoke a word. We all remained at our posts without food and without drink. We saw them kill the neighbors. They even set fire to the near-by houses in the hope of reaching ours. But, for a time at least, God was with us and the houses would not burn. Though none of us said a word of it during all that night and the next morning, we all seemed to know what was to be done. I have often wondered how the same idea came into the minds of all three of my boys, though there had been no plans for this circumstance beforehand. Meanwhile we all worked with a will, repulsing each attack as it was made, and killing I should say at least ten soldiers and wounding as many more. Turks are brave. They never fear death. When I was not watching I was distributing the ammunition in three little piles behind each of my boys. I also watched for an attack on the back door. It never came. We had but to open the wooden shutter for a moment whenever the soldiers tried to enter the door and let the bombs fall. The noise was so great as completely to deafen me. I remember why the last made so little noise. There was a deep pit dug in front of the house where the bombs had fallen.

It was just at sunset on Thursday when the last attack was made. I had not thought of the time when our ammunition would give out, but the boys had. They did not tell me, perhaps thinking that I would oppose them. I was trying to count the dead from the last bomb when I heard a different and a nearer report in the room. My first-born, Serkis, had shot himself in the temple. Then I saw to my horror that all of the ammunition was gone. I heard the blows of the soldiers raining upon the door, as I ran to pick up my dying son. I had not noticed that Hagop had taken the pistol from his hand until another shot in the room took my eyes from Serkis. Hagop lay at my feet. He died immediately. None of us said a word. The blows came thicker and thicker upon the door below, but it was strong. I saw little Mardiros take the pistol out of Hagop's hand, and I did not try to stop him. He looked straight at me and smiled as he pressed the barrel against his temple. I did not seem to hear the sound of the shot that killed him, for there was a great crashing noise made by the falling in of the door. I heard them entering below with loud hurrahs and curses. Serkis' head was in my lap. As I heard them searching downstairs, I put out all my strength and drew my other dead babies to me, and, leaning my back against the wall, pillowed their heads in my lap. I was smoothing their hair with my fingers when the soldiers entered the room. It was nearly dark, and one held a lighted torch. Five or six of them came, but somehow they all stopped as soon as they saw us. They stood there for some time looking at me, saying nothing, and I spoke not to them but I smoothed the hair of my boys. Then one said, 'Leave the old she-dog alone with her dead puppies.' And they went away.

We all sat for some minutes in silence after the story was told. The desolate mother had the same clear look in her eyes, wherein was never a tear. She scarcely breathed a sigh, but the interpreter was weeping softly,—weeping, I suppose, over this fine remaining monument of his degenerate race. And surely such a one should leaven a multitude despised!

Germany and the Armenians

W. J. Stillman

West Bournemouth, England, April 16, 1899

The last item in "The Week" of the *Nation* April 6, on the German Emperor and his influence on Turkish affairs, leads me (as I happen to have been in a position to know the true inwardness of the Armenian question, as well as the present condition of things in the Balkans, which is the subject of comment in that article) to think that a plain statement of the facts may not be unworthy putting on record in your pages.

When Lord Salisbury determined, in accordance with the public opinion of England, to put an end to the malfeasance of the Sultan, he called on Austria-Hungary and Italy, under the terms of a convention established in 1887, shortly after Crispi became Prime Minister of Italy, to join England in a demonstration before Constantinople, with the alternative of deposing the Sultan or compelling effectual and immediate reform in the government of the Asiatic provinces. Crispi inquired at Berlin, the Emperor being at the head of the Triple Alliance, if Italy should take up the rôle to which she was called, and the reply of the Emperor was, "Yes, and on my imperial word of honor, I will support you to the last man." Crispi replied with alacrity by sending the fleet to Smyrna, and mobilizing a corps d'armée for operations in Asia Minor. Austria-Hungary, reluctant but compelled, made her preparations to support England and Italy, unwilling to run the risk of war for the sake of the Armenians, and a little irritated that Salisbury should have taken the initiative in a matter which concerned Austria-Hungary much more closely than England. Nevertheless, the accord was made, and if action had been taken instantly, there would have been no difficulty or danger of war, for the Dardanelles were not in a condition to resist the immediate entry of the fleets, not a gun being in position to fire. At this moment the United States Government brought forward the Venezuela question, and the Jingoes in the States put on their light gloves for a fight.

The position of Lord Salisbury was one of the greatest difficulty. To suppose that the English Government feared a war with the United States from purely military reasons is not to know the country and its resources, or our own as the Spanish-American war developed them; but a war between England and America could be carried on only by devastating our coasts, destroying our commerce, and preventing our farmers from exporting their grain, at the same time strengthening the defences of Canada. The bombardment and destruction of our coast cities and suppression of our trade were, in fact, the only measures which the military position permitted, and they would have been, therefore, imperative. But there is a large and influential element of the English people resolutely opposed to the aggravation of difficulties between their country and ours; not from fear of the results, but because they consider the establishment of permanently amicable relations between the two countries necessary to the advance of civilization, and a war between them comparable to murder in the family. Lord Salisbury had these (who form an important part of his support) to consider; and though the Jingo element in England would probably have met the defiance in the manner the whole nation would meet a similar attitude on the part of any European Power, the horror of an internecine war and the revivification of the antipathies of the generations gone by was heavier than the indignation at the childish and inconsistent provocations of the United States. The possibility, therefore, of a war with us, made probable by the fact that England might be in a moment engaged with one or more of the European Powers, compelled Lord Salisbury to settle our question before entering into any other. It was not the "business and heathenism" of the Emperor of Germany, but those of the President of the United States, which "dried up the fountain of European pity for the Armenians," and compelled England to desist from one of the most humanitarian efforts her foreign policy has ever proposed. I cannot, without a protest, permit this attempt to deprive our Jingoes of their greatest laurel to pass unnoticed.

Before Lord Salisbury had got the Venezuela difficulty arranged, the Dardanelles were in a state to offer effective resistance to the united fleets and make probable a loss in men and ships which would have been worse than the sufferings of the Armenians; and it must be remembered that the movement for the relief of Armenia was purely humanitarian, and would have given England no exclusive advantage or any profit to justify any loss of life or property. It was a project which did the highest honor to the hearts of Lord Salisbury and the English people, and the grief in England at its abortion was great.

But the position in which this failure placed the German Emperor was very difficult. His guarantee of immunity to the new Triple Alliance in their action at Constantinople put him practically in an attitude of hostility to Russia, which Power has the highest interest in neutralizing British influence at Constantinople. It was, in fact, forbidding Russia to support the Sultan by war, and paralyzed the Franco-Russian alliance for near Eastern matters, while allowing England to employ the entire military force of the Triple Alliance to carry out her plan. To re-establish himself in the confidence of the Czar was no easy matter for the Kaiser, and it was necessary to remain practically neutral in the questions arising in the Balkan provinces and in Greece, and allow Russia to arrange them to her satisfaction as long as the vital interests of Austria-Hungary in Turkey were not assailed, these being guaranteed by the terms of the Triple Alliance. The result was that a convention was made between Russia and Austria-Hungary, binding both Powers to abstain from assisting either of the provinces or countries in the Balkans, including Greece, in case they attempted to provoke a war of emancipation with Turkey, and to maintain, while the convention is in force, the present status. The policy of Austria-Hungary is to prevent the breaking out of any war between Turkey and the Balkan States, but to encourage their development by degrees to effective political independence, not only of Russia, but of Austria, forming in this way a buffer chain of little states between the two great empires, and preventing for the future the acquisition by either of them of any more territory in the Balkans, including Constantinople. The Bulgarians are now assured, as the Greeks were when their agitation began, that they will not be supported in any aggression or assisted in any war for which they make themselves responsible, and no doubt Russia will adhere to this convention till she is ready to move on Constantinople, the hope of Austria-Hungary being that, before that moment arrives, the states which are now forming will understand their true policy, and be ready to defend the interests they have in common with the dual Empire against any aggression.

The defection of England from the understanding with Italy and Austria, supported as it was by Germany-*i.e.*, from the Triple Alliance-naturally provoked great irritation in the mind of the Emperor, who, one will readily conceive, held her to account for the scarcely veiled defeat which Germany suffered, and for the more positive failure to establish a concert of action between England and the Triple Alliance which would have paralyzed the Dual Alliance and made a war in Europe impossible. England would have been the President of the Quadruple Alliance, and, Germany commanding the position by land and England by sea, there would have been no resisting this pacific combination. When Greece broke out in 1897, she had been fully and officially informed that she could count on no European Power for any intervention in any case, but that she must take the consequences of her initiative; but the fatuity of Delyannis and the King in refusing to believe the assurances of diplomacy that they would be left to themselves to fight it out, and that the spread of the conflagration they counted on would be forcible prevented, if necessary, forced the position and led to the disasters of the war. Germany was neither in the mood nor the situation to support the action or influence of England in the Greek question, owing to the retreat of Lord Salisbury, for which we must accept the responsibility, and not the "base and heathen" German Emperor. Our foolish stone on the English track has had the effect of throwing the entire European train off the line, with immeasurable loss to humanity.

The same conditions obtain for the Balkan principalities that held for Greece. It is impossible to permit a war to break out which will endanger the peace of Europe, for the parties are now so nearly equally divided that interference becomes most probable if fighting begins. It was possible to abstain in Greece, which is after a manner separated from other states, but in Bulgaria it may be impossible, and a war could not be assured to benefit humanity unless England and Germany, *i.e.*, the Triple Alliance, co-operated, as they would have done but for us in the Armenian question.

Contribution to the Armenian Question

Carl Albert Paul Rohrbach[131]

To compute the number of Armenians at present existing is one of the most difficult problems conceivable. The number in Russia has been established with tolerable accuracy, and that dispersed throughout Austro-Hungary, Egypt, India, and other distant lands, is also approximately known; but in regard to Turkey, where most of the Armenian people still reside, our information is practically *nil*.

To-day Russia contains about 1,000,000 Armenians, and Persia some 50,000. The Turkish Government, interested in reducing the figure to a minimum, states the number of Armenians living under the scepter of the Sultan at 1,000,000. The indications are, however, that 1,500,000 is a far safer estimate.

The boundaries of the territory designated as Armenia are difficult to define. In a general way, however, it may be asserted that the area comprehends the two sources of the Euphrates, the Sea of Wan, Mount Ararat, and in great part the course of the river Araxes—without, however, bordering at any point upon the Black Sea or upon the Mediterranean. Within these limits we have a total area about the size of South Germany or of the State of Pennsylvania. The country is bounded on the south by Kurdistan, on the west by Asia Minor, on the north by the Russian Caucasus, Georgia, and on the east by the Persian province of Aderbaijan.

It would be erroneous to assume that a line completely surrounding the above-mentioned region would also embrace the entire Armenian community, or that the Armenians dwelling there outnumber all other resident nationalities. Armenians have long migrated in all directions far beyond the boundaries of their native land; while Mohammedan intruders—principally Kurds, but also Turks in considerable numbers—have established settlements in the province. Indeed, there are few districts of any considerable extent where the Armenian element may be found compactly massed. A continuous emigration of centuries has gradually spread the Armenian element over a territory fully four times as large as the original province; and within the wider area the Armenians form a fluctuating minority of but 5 to 10 per cent of the entire population; the greatest density probably existing in Eastern Cilicia and in the adjacent southern spurs of the Taurus, around Adana, Aintab, and Urfa. Armenians are also well represented in the great seaports and commercial centres of Caucasia and the Levant—in Tiflis, Baku, Batum, Constantinople, Smyrna, and Odessa. Scattered colonies, ranging from two or three hundred to several thousand souls, may be found in the interior of Russia, as well as in Austro-Hungary, Poland, Bulgaria, Egypt, Palestine, and East India; while, during the last few decades, a great many have also emigrated to America.

To form a clear conception of the so-called "Armenian Question," a knowledge of the general features of Armenian history is necessary. The first reference to Armenians is found in the inscriptions of the Persian kings of the Achemenidian dynasty, and here they are already designated by their present title "Arminu." This title, however, is not employed by the natives, who from time immemorial have styled themselves "Haik" (plural of Haj), and their country, Hajastan. They trace their establishment to the earliest ages, and claim direct descent from Noah. This theory, however, is now no longer tenable; for modern scientific research has successfully demonstrated that the Armenians did not occupy their present domain until the sixth century B.C. Further, it has been shown that they came as conquerors from unknown parts (possibly from Northern Syria and Eastern Cilicia) and settled near the Wan Sea, where they subjugated a people calling itself "Chalder," presumably "Chaldeans" or "Chaldees," but designated by the Assyrians "Urartu"; and it is to this land of the Urartu that the Bible refers when it says the ark of Noah rested upon the mountains of Ararat. Not until the Christian era did the idea arise that this mount was synonymous with Massis, the highest peak of hither Asia, situated in the district of "Ayrarat" about midway in the course of the Araxes. It is significant that even at the present day, and within the country itself, this Mount Massis is known as Ararat only to scholars.

In all probability the Armenians long constituted a warrior caste among the subjugated Urartu, until, in the course of centuries, victor and vanquished finally became amalgamated. The former belonged to the Aryan or Indo-European stock, while the latter were probably identified with that earlier race, which, although it is the ancestral stock of several Caucasian peoples, is still enveloped in mystery. At all events, the language of the conqueror, which is related to the ancient Persian, became the dominant one, and has so remained to the present day.

Soon after this amalgamation of races was effected, Armenia became a province of the Persian Empire under Cyrus and his successors, and it was during this period, when the country was governed by a royal satrap, that Xerxes and his 10,000 made their famous march through it from Babylon to the Black Sea, after the battle of Cunaxa (winter of 401–400 B.C.). After the death of Alexander the Great, Armenia was incorporated into the empire of the Seleucide; and after the defeat of King Antiochus III by the Romans (190 B.C.), it revolted against the Roman authority and set up the first native king of Armenia to whom history bears witness—Artaxias. It was for this monarch that Hannibal, flying from the Romans and seeking shelter at the courts of Asia Minor, built the capital Artaxata—situated on the Araxes, in the plain of Erivan—the ruins of which are still known by the name of Ardashir.

During the civil wars of Rome, and until the advent of Pompeius, Armenia was one of the great powers of the world. Upon the revival of Roman prestige, however, it again sank to its former modest status, though it survived as a kingdom until the fourth century A.D. It was the first political community to introduce Christianity as the religion of the state, an event which occurred during the reign of Tiridates (A.D. 300).

In A.D. 387 Armenia was conquered, the Romans taking the western, and the Sassanid kings of Persia the somewhat greater eastern, portion of the kingdom. The province was held by the Sassanids until their downfall in the seventh century, when, together with all the other Persian provinces, it fell into the hands of the Arabian Caliphs, from whom it was again wrested by the celebrated

Armenian dynasty of the Bagratide, who emancipated their country from the Arabian yoke and reestablished the kingdom. It was at this time that an Armenian, Leo III, ascended the imperial throne at Constantinople—indeed, the tenth and eleventh centuries may be said to constitute the heroic age of Armenian history.

But the unity of the kingdom was destroyed at last incessant conflicts between the nobility; and thus, upon the invasion of the Turks and Mongols, all resistance was rendered nugatory; Cilicia alone maintaining a petty Christo-Armenian kingdom until the close of the fourteenth century. At the time of the Reformation, Armenia was divided between the Turkish and the Persian empires but in 1829 Russia seized almost the entire Persian province, including the monastery of Echmiadzin, at the foot of Mount Ararat, the seat of the Chief Patriarch of the Armenian Church.

As we survey the history of the Armenian people, we are impressed by their extraordinary national and religious power of resistance. Although completely surrounded by the tumultuous waves of Mohammedanism, Armenia has nevertheless succeeded, throughout 1,500 years, in preserving its national and religious integrity. Founded at the time of the first great Ecumenical Conference at Nicaea (A.D. 325), the Armenian National Church, now counting several million followers, has remained intact. In order to do full justice to the nation, therefore, we must contrast this fact with the fate of the other Christian communities in the Orient since the rise of Islam. What has become of the Syrians, of the Egyptians, and of the Christian sects of Asia Minor? In Syria and Egypt, countries that once possessed a far more extensive ecclesiastical establishment than Armenia, the Christian Church and the ancient national tongue have become completely obliterated by Mohammedanism and the Arabian language; while in Asia Minor not a vestige remains to remind one that at the time of the Crusades the region was still the abode of Christian communities.

The intellectual life of Armenia survived until the fourteenth century. Then, under the pressure of Mohammedan rule, it began to stagnate. A condition of intellectual torpor ensued; and Armenia and the Armenians completely disappeared from the horizon of Western Christendom. The old historians and theologians, who, by their splendid works, had created the classical Armenian tongue, were faithfully transcribed in the monasteries, while their ritualistic formulas, and lectures from the Scriptures, were read in that language; but gradually the people ceased to understand them. Turkish and Persian idioms encroached more and more upon the language; until, finally, the contrast between the corrupt popular dialect and the language of the Church and of literature became as pronounced as that existing between the English of to-day and the Anglo-Saxon speech of the time of Alfred the Great. In consequence of this deterioration, the language of the Bible gradually became incomprehensible to the layman. Indeed, even among the priesthood, many were actually unable to understand what they read from the pulpit on Sundays; and this condition, with a scarcely noticeable improvement, has practically remained unchanged to the present day.

Until a few decades ago, the condition of education in Armenia, religious and secular, was not distinguishable from the prevailing in other Oriental countries; and there were few who could boast of an acquaintance with the splendid historic and literary traditions of their people. But three distinct agencies have lately cooperated in effecting an improvement. As early as the beginning of the eighteenth century Petrus Mechitar (i.e., the Comforter) founded the theological congregation known by the name of Mechitarians—a union of Armenian monks aiming at the scientific resuscitation of the National Church. As the work undertaken, however, was entirely without precedent in Armenia, and as the lack of experience was painfully felt (the Greek Church being no better off in this regard than the Armenian), a close union with the Church of Rome was rendered imperative—more particularly as the congregation, expelled from Turkish soil, was compelled to remove its headquarters to foreign territory. Since 1717, the Mechitarians, united with the Church of Rome, have been domiciled in a monastery upon the Isle of San Lazzaro near Venice; and, since 1810, a branch has also been established at Vienna.

The labors of these men in behalf of the Armenian nation have been very considerable, and, notably within our own century, very successful. In 1734, they published for the first time a printed edition of the Armenian Bible; and this was followed by a great mass of works, comprising editions of old Armenian writers as well as original contributions to the history, language, literature, and religion of the country. In course of time, however, the Mechitarians have gradually become estranged from their national church; and to-day, notwithstanding the continuance of scientific and literary activity, the separation between this priesthood, now thoroughly Roman Catholic, and the Gregorian Church is practically complete.* Nevertheless, the labors of the Mechitarians still operate as a potent factor in the intellectual life of the whole Armenian people, and constitute an invaluable guide to the study of Armenian antiquity.

The second factor in this intellectual progress was the Russian acquisition of Persian Armenia in 1829, which brought to the new Christian subjects of the Czar such culture as Russia could supply. The Russo-German University of Dorpat, in Livonia, was especially popular with Armenian students, while the splendid Lazarew Institute for Oriental Languages at Moscow (endowed by Armenians for the purpose) furnished excellent opportunities for the study of the Armenian language. It now became fashionable for wealthy Armenians to provide scholarships for talented youths of their own nationality, that these might be enabled to extend their intellectual horizon; and it became common for these students to aspire beyond the confines of Russian colleges to the more fruitful sources of scientific inquiry in the Occident. As a result of their efforts, the last generation records, upon the one hand, an extensive system of journalism and a new and prolific secular Armenian literature, and, upon the other, the establishment of a great number of public schools, which, like an intricate and ever denser network, are gradually overspreading the entire Russian province.

When we consider the conditions prevailing until the middle of the present century we must confess that these schools have accomplished wonders. In 1850, reading and writing were still rare accomplishments among Armenians; whereas, among the younger generation in Russia to-day, mastery of the mother-tongue in word and print is the rule. Unfortunately, the Russian Government, several years ago, found it necessary to close all Armenian schools in order to destroy the intellectual independence of the Armenian element, and to promote that process of Russification which has recently been extended also to Finland.

---

*The "Gregorian Church," so called after Gregory the Enlightener [Illuminator—editor's note], the apostle of Armenia about A.D. 300.

The third factor in the intellectual revolution of Armenia is the influence exercised since 1831 by the American missions in Turkey, the activity of which has ever been fundamental in character. At first the Americans attempted to prosecute the religious propaganda in union with the Armenian Church. Within a few years after the establishment of the missions, however, the high clergy of the Gregorians assumed a decidedly hostile attitude, with the result that the American missionaries at once began to inaugurate a system of proselytism. In this way arose the so-called American Protestant Mission congregations, the combined membership of which, in 1890, aggregated 12,000 adults, with 17,000 children being taught in the schools.

The American posts extend throughout every portion of Anatolia and Armenia, and include even Northern Syria and Mesopotamia. They consist of about 180 central and branch stations, with 117 churches, 5 Colleges, 26 high-schools for boys, 18 for girls, and several hundred common schools. The more important American centres in the interior are Sivas, Kaisariyeh, Charput, Aintab, Marash, Urfa, Bitlis, and Wan. Of these, Charput, near the confluence of the two sources of the Euphrates, and Aintap, upon the southern declivity of the east Cilician Taurus, contain the two principal colleges; all buildings being erected in modern style.

When I recall the hospitality and the variety of information received at the hands of the men and women of the American mission stations during my last trip through Armenia, I become doubly conscious of the responsibility assumed in attempting to criticize the life-work of these noble and pious people. I make this statement in order to remove any possible misconception as to my motives if, in the course of this paper, I venture to criticize certain phases of the American work. Whatever may be said, however, it must be admitted that the influence exerted by America upon the intellectual life of the Armenian nation deserves a very high estimate.

The political and social changes thus promoted have been followed by the conditions embraced in the term "The Armenian Question." In a word, the national consciousness of Armenia having been aroused, the school and the press found rapid and universal extension. Young men from the Turkish as well as from the Russian provinces thronged to obtain an education abroad; and, most important of all, there arose among the millions of Armenians scattered throughout the world a strong sense of national unity. This sentiment found its visible embodiment in the National Church; and so striking is this symbolization with Armenians that converts to other forms of Christianity are by them no longer recognized as compatriots. This explains the impossibility of ever making a successful propaganda in behalf of a foreign creed, and consequently applies to the American mission work, which, apart from its meritorious achievements, has caused a schism in the Armenian body social which will be extremely difficult if not impossible to heal. It is equally true that, in consequence of this intimate relationship between the Armenian and his National Church, the intellectual and religious endowment bestowed by the American missionaries upon their Protestant converts can never become a useful possession of the nation at large.

During the seventh decade of the present century, the contrast between the condition of the Armenians in Russia and those in Turkey was particularly marked, inasmuch as the latter, owing to their remoteness, were completely hidden from the gaze of civilized Europe, and were consequently subjected to greater injustice and oppression than were any other Christian subjects of the Sultan. Particularly atrocious were the acts of violence committed by the Kurds (already referred to as constituting one of the nationalities of Turkish Armenia) against the property, life, and honor of their Armenian neighbors; and these barbarities naturally aroused in the hearts of the Christian population of the country a strong desire to see Russia victorious in a war against the Turkish oppressor. To such a war, if successful, they confidently looked for an amelioration of their condition, for had not Russia for centuries been regarded as the guardian of the Christian communities in the Orient? Moreover, this powerful conviction that the Czar would come to their assistance was designedly encouraged from various quarters of Russia.

The war of 1877-78 was, as we know, attended by only a partial success of the Russian arms. When the conquest of the Turkish armies had finally been achieved—a conquest which entailed an enormous sacrifice of time, money, and men—the resources of Russia were so completely exhausted that she was compelled to submit, when the European Powers, and notably England, at the Congress of Berlin (1878), prevented her from fully reaping the fruits of victory. Russia was compelled to surrender the territory of Armenia, already occupied by the Muscovite forces; the Armenians, on the other hand, receiving a guarantee that the European Powers would secure from Turkey an improvement of their condition. This guarantee is embodied in Article 61, Acts of the Congress of Berlin of 1878, which reads as follows:

> The Sublime Porte assumes the obligation of immediately establishing the necessary improvements and reforms demanded by the local conditions of all provinces inhabited by Armenians, *and guarantees security against the Circassians and Kurds.* The Porte further pledges itself to advise the Powers, at stated intervals, of the reforms introduced; *and the Powers will exercise surveillance as to their proper execution.*

This document bears the signatures of the European Powers as well as of Turkey. Yet to the Armenians it has not had the value of the paper upon which it is written; and to it we must directly ascribe all the terrible misery that has fallen to their lot within the last few years. The complete disregard of the Armenian complaints cannot be looked upon as nearly so serious an evil as the unkept promise of the European Powers to exercise surveillance over the proper execution of the Turkish reforms.

In 1898 I took an extensive trip through Turkish Armenia as well as through the strongly Armenian provinces of Anatolia and Kurdistan, and I can assure the reader that no adequate conception can be formed as to the actual conditions in those provinces. Two hundred thousand Armenians have either been murdered or have succumbed to wounds, sickness, and hunger. Over 100,000 children have been robbed of one or both parents, and have been left helpless upon the world. Over 50,000 fugitives have crossed over the Russian and Persian borders, barely escaping with their lives. From the Sea of Wan to the Euphrates, I found but a single village which had not been plundered and devastated by Kurds or Turks. In every other community a large number of the young men had either been murdered or had sought safety in flight, while women and girls had been kidnapped. These atrocities would never have been perpetrated to such an awful extent had not the European Powers in 1878 bestowed upon the Armenians that baneful gift, Article 61.

Despite the guarantee of the Powers, the question of reforms for Armenia, during the years following upon the Congress of Berlin, was scarcely touched upon by the Turkish Government, which soon became convinced that none of the European nations was interested in pressing the matter beyond an occasional energetic diplomatic protest. Consequently, the Government at Constantinople soon began to instigate a series of vexatious intrigues against the Armenians, using as its agents, first, the provincial representatives of the Government, then the Kurds, and, finally, the Mohammedan population generally; and these persecutions obtained additional virulence from the fact that the Armenians were known to have had a hand in the war of 1877–78.

Throughout a period of seventeen years (1878–95) these unfortunate conditions, due to Article 61 and various other unfulfilled pledges of the Powers, gradually brought the educated and politically informed classes of the Armenian population to the brink of despair. With fanatical zeal the youth of the land maintained the validity of Article 61, and sought upon every possible occasion to convince the people that they were being defrauded of a sacredly guaranteed right. Said they: "Europe is obliged, before God and man, to redeem its pledge in behalf of our interests against Turkey, either by diplomatic negotiations or by the intervention of arms!" It was to England, particularly, that the people looked for the fulfillment of this moral obligation; and certainly no other nation ever gave the Armenians greater encouragement to sustain their cause than did England.

Secret societies of every description were now organized for the purpose of preparing the people for the fulfillment of that "sacred duty" which, it was held, the European nations would sooner or later fulfill. These agitators, inspired partly by an honest belief, and partly by the hope of more successfully manipulating the people, eventually went so far as to announce European intervention for the near future. Nay, some of the members of these revolutionary societies proceeded to actual threats, and occasionally to deeds of violence, against the Turks, in order to stir the authorities and the Mohammedan populace to bloody reprisals against the Armenians. They hoped, in this way, to promote difficult complications which would necessitate the armed intervention of Europe, and justified these desperate measures with the words: "It is better that a few should die in sacrifice than that a whole people should decay."

Naturally, nothing could have embittered the Turks more than this constant agitation, which was openly designed to bring about foreign interference on Turkish soil. Apart from this, another circumstance here deserves consideration. During my visit to Anatolia I was told by Turks of irreproachable character—and the matter is no secret to those familiar with the affairs of the Palace at Constantinople—that a number of persons in the *entourage* of the Sultan, in order to carry favor with that ruler, continually picture to him all manner of imaginary dangers, in order that they may pose as the guardians and saviours of his Majesty. These methods were practised with considerable success with regard to the Armenian revolutionists. Frightened at the reports conveyed to him, the Sultan finally decided upon orders of death against the Armenian insurgents; and these orders, with the disturbance and discontent created by the menacing attitude of the Armenians themselves, together with religious fanaticism, lust of gain, and a desire to appease the rebellious Kurds, all conspired to bring about the terrible events of 1895-96.

Even from a Turkish point of view the massacres were regarded as pure insanity. They depopulated and devastated as extensive territory as completely as if a war had swept over it, and contributed to reduce the revenue of whole provinces to a minimum. The actual purpose of rendering Armenians harmless might easily and expeditiously have been effected by a general and imperative order of disarmament—more particularly, as the majority of the Armenian population were without guns. Selfishness, blind rage, and silly thoughtlessness were here responsible for the heaviest blow sustained by the Turkish Government since the war of 1877.

In addition to England, it is likely that Russia and France would have been inclined to favor intervention. Yet two circumstances cooperated to frustrate these good intentions. In the first place, England, in the event of a serious engagement of France and Russia in the Orient, would at once have utilized her opportunity in other parts of the world for the furtherance of selfish purposes; while Germany, owing to her friendly relations with Turkey, would have been unable to participate. In this regard Germany's policy has been severely condemned from the standpoint of Christianity and humanity; but this harsh criticism is frequently based upon ignorance of the motives governing the action of German statesmen.

Owing to the tremendous increase of her population and the comparative worthlessness of the colonies hitherto acquired, Germany, for very self-preservation, is compelled to secure markets offering raw material in exchange for manufactures; and of these Turkey has now become one of the most important. As an illustration I need here cite but a single instance, viz., the Bagdad railroad, extending from Constantinople to the Persian Gulf. This enterprise, conducted under the supervision of Germans and eventually to be controlled by them, will ultimately secure industrial and commercial employment to hundreds of thousands and perhaps millions of people throughout the German Empire. As an anti-Turkish attitude would have destroyed these prospects, we can readily understand why the German Emperor and his advisers considered it incumbent to place the interests of their own people above those of the Armenians.

What, then, will be the future of the Armenian nation? Although enthusiasts may dream of a future kingdom of Armenia, I believe it probable that, politically speaking, the Armenians, in the event of an ultimate dissolution of Turkey, will, for the greater part, become subjects of the Czar. But a discussion of this political side of the question is not my purpose; and it therefore remains for me to consider only the prospects of the Armenian nation from an ethical point of view.

The European and American benefactors of Armenia have, during the past four or five years, contributed over $3,000,000 to alleviate the suffering of the people; and it may be safely asserted that it was largely the assistance thus offered which enabled the Armenians to tide over the terrible period of poverty and famine immediately following upon the massacres. Nevertheless, of the 100,000 orphans that survived the massacres a great number afterward succumbed to privation and want. Some were dragged into Mohammedan houses, while others are still living amid misery and want. Fifty thousand, however, are now safely housed in the orphan asylums built for these children by contributions from Germany, England, America, and elsewhere, and these institutions may be attended with infinite blessing provided education be so conducted that the children, instead of becoming estranged, shall be fitted to work as a leaven among their own people. To this end, two conditions are requisite: (1) the children must not be converted to Protestantism, but must be permitted to remain within their own National Church; and (2) inasmuch as the children will probably pass their lives in the Orient, all branches of secular education must be so conducted as to prepare the graduate for Oriental conditions.

In this connection, I am compelled to assume a somewhat critical attitude toward the practice of my esteemed American friends in Turkey. True, it has now been decided to permit the students to attend the Gregorian Church, while so instructing them at the asylums that they shall nevertheless eventually become Christians in the evangelical sense. But this aim has not been everywhere realized; and I have further observed that certain schools give instruction in branches which, while useful, and perhaps needful, to English and American children, will only tend, in a country like Turkey, to arouse views and sentiments in complete discord with actual conditions. The reader will readily understand why I cannot here be more explicit; and I trust, further, that my words will not occasion doubt as to my sincere conviction that the American mission-institutions, during the past few years, have proved the most important factor in the redemption of the Armenian people.

Finally, we should not forget that within the fold of the National Church itself, and particularly at Etchmiadzin, the seat of the Patriarch, sound reforms have now been successfully instituted, aiming at the vitalization of clerical life and a more thorough scientific training of the ministry. In view of this fact, it devolves upon us as a sacred duty to do our utmost to secure amicable relations between these Gregorian reformers and the evangelical missions from abroad. Above all, we must strive to convince the Armenian clergy that we have no intention of making proselytes, and that we shall be content to leave the religious and national unity of the Armenian people undisturbed.

NOTES

1. Dietrich Jung and Wolfgang Piccoli, *Turkey at the Crossroads. Ottoman Legacies and a Greater Middle East* (London and New York, 2001), 39.
2. Bernard Lewis, *The Middle East. A Brief History of the Last 2000 Years* (New York, 1995), 323–24.
3. Lord Kinross, *The Ottoman Centuries. The Rise and Fall of the Turkish Empire* (New York, 1977), 475–76.
4. *Ibid.*, 553–54.
5. Article 16, Treaty of San Stefano, as quoted in *Turkey* (London), no. 22 (1878): 262.
6. *Turkey* (London), no. 36 (1878): 5–6.
7. *Turkey* (London), no. 38 (1878): 384.
8. T. Peterson, "Turkey and Armenians," *The Catholic World* 61 (1895): 667; R. Davey, "Turkey and Armenia," *The Fortnightly Review* 63 (1895): 205; S. Shahid Bey, *Islam, Turkey, and Armenia and How They Happened* (St. Louis, 1898), 198–99.
9. "Lord Rosebery's Deliverance," *The Spectator* 77 (17 October 1896): 504.
10. *Turkey* (London), no. 1 (1895): 29.
11. "Armenia and the Powers," *The Contemporary Review* 69 (1896): 635–37.
12. Turkey (London), no. 1 (1895): 66.
13. *Ibid.*
14. *Ibid.*, 73.
15. "The Armenian Policy of France," *The Spectator* 77 (1896): 634.
16. A. J. Kennedy, *Salisbury, 1830–1905. Portrait of a Statesman* (London, 1953), 256–57.
17. *Turkey* (London), no. 2 (1896): 127.
18. *Turkey* (London), no. 1 (1895): 206.
19. J. Kirakossian, *The Armenian Genocide. The Young Turks before the Judgment of History* (Madison, 1992), 63.
20. S. Shahid Bey, *Islam, Turkey, and Armenia and How They Happened* (St. Louis, 1898), 201.
21. G. W. E. Russell, "Armenia and the Forward Movement," *The Contemporary Review* 71 (1897): 11–12; E. Pears, *Life of Abdul Hamid* (New York, 1917): 234–35.
22. Blue Book, Turkey, no. 2 (1896), 325; E. M. Bliss, *Turkey and Armenian Atrocities* (Philadelphia, 1896), 428–34, 475–76.

23. Blue Book, Turkey, no. 2 (1896), 320–22; E. M. Bliss, op. cit., 425, 451–57, 478.
24. Blue Book, Turkey, no. 2 (1896), 323–30.
25. J. Bryce, *Transcaucasia and Ararat* (London, 1896), 510.
26. Blue Book, Turkey, no. 2 (1896), 116.
27. A. Nazarbek, "Zeytun," *The Contemporary Review* 69 (1896): 528.
28. "Lord Salisbury and Armenia," *The Nation* 61 (1895): 193.
29. R. Taylor, *Lord Salisbury* (London, 1975), 168.
30. "The Constantinople Massacre," *The Contemporary Review* 70 (1896): 459–60.
31. "The Massacres," *The Spectator* 77 (1896): 292.
32. M. Gulesian, "The Armenian Refugees," *The Arena* 17 (1897): 652.
33. G. Papadopoulos, *England and the Near East, 1896–1898* (Thessalonica, 1969), 111.
34. *Ibid.*, 112.
35. J. De Novo, *American Interests and Policies in the Middle East, 1900–1939* (Minneapolis, 1963), 16.
36. *Ibid.*, 8, 11–12.
37. *Ibid.*, 9; P. Rohrbach, "The Contribution to the Armenian Question," *The Forum*, 29 (May 1900): 486–87.
38. Cyrus Hamlin (1811–1900), an American missionary. He served on various missions in Turkey from 1837 to 1859, then founded and was President of the Robert College in Constantinople from 1860 to 1876. He returned to the United States and briefly was President of the Middlebury College (1880–1885). He wrote extensively on Turkey.
39. J. De Novo, op. cit., 14.
40. *Ibid.*, 16.
41. R. Mirak, "Armenian Emigration to the United States to 1915," *Journal of American Studies* 1 (Autumn 1975): 33–34.
42. E. L. Godkin, "The Armenian Resolutions," *The Nation* (30 January 1896): 93.
43. "The Death Warrant of Armenia," *The Spectator* 75 (21 December 1895): 885–86.
44. *Ibid.*, 886.
45. "Americans and Armenians," *The Spectator* 76 (1 February 1891): 156–57.
46. E. L. Godkin, "The Armenian Resolutions," *The Nation* (30 January 1896): 93.
47. *Ibid.*
48. *Hayk* (New York), no. 23 (15 December 1893): 357.
49. Alexander Terrell was the U.S. Minister in Turkey.
50. *Hayk* (New York), no. 23 (15 December 1893): 357.
51. L. J. Gordon, *American Relations with Turkey (1830–1930)* (Philadelphia, 1932), 26.
52. *Ibid.*, 24.
53. *Ibid.*, 24.

NOTES

54. United States Congressional Record, U.S.S., December 3, 1894.
55. "Rational Sympathy," *The Nation* 61 (1895): 384.
56. *Papers Relating to the Foreign Relations of the United States, with the Annual Message of the President, transmitted to Congress December 2, 1895, Part I-II* (Washington, DC, 1896), xxxiv.
57. A. W. Terrell, "An Interview with Sultan Abdul Hamid," *The Century Magazine* 55 (1897): 134.
58. *Ibid.*, 134.
59. L. J. Gordon, op. cit., 26.
60. *Papers Relating to the Foreign Relations of the United States, with the Annual Message of the President, transmitted to Congress December 7, 1896, Part I-II* (Washington, DC, 1897), xxviii.
61. A. W. Terrell, op. cit., 134.
62. J. De Novo, op. cit., 4–5.
63. *Ibid.*, 22–23.
64. *Nor Dar* (Tiflis) (11 January 1895).
65. R. Mirak, *Torn between Two Lands. Armenians in America, 1890 to World War I* (Cambridge, MA, 1983), 213–14.
66. *Ibid.*, 364.
67. Edwin M. Bliss (1848–1919), an American missionary and journalist. Born in Erzerum, he graduated from the Robert College in Constantinople. He served as an assistant to the representative of the American Bible Society from 1872 to 1875, and traveled extensively in Turkey, Persia, and Egypt. He was the editor of the "Missionary Encyclopedia" (1889–1891), and editor of *Independent* (1891–1901). His works include "Turks in Armenia, Crete and Greece," "Turkey and the Armenian Atrocities," and others.
68. *Hayk* (30 November 1894): 236–38.
69. *Nor Dar* 3 (6 January 1895).
70. *Nor Dar* 7 (13 January 1895).
71. *Nor Dar* 97 (3 June 1895).
72. M. H. Gulesian, "England's Hand in Turkish Massacre," *The Arena* 17 (1897): 271–82; "The Armenian Refugees," *The Arena* 77 (1897): 652–62.
73. *Nor Dar* 97 (3 June 1895).
74. *Hayk*, no. 14 (15 March 1895): 197–98.
75. *Ibid.*, 199.
76. *Nor Dar* 59 (8 April 1895).
77. R. Mirak, op. cit., 219–20.
78. U.S. Congressional Record, U.S. Senate, February 12, 1896; R. Mirak, op. cit., 220.
79. R. Mirak, op. cit., 223.
80. "Aid for Armenia," *The Outlook* 53 (1895): 93.
81. *Nor Dar* 31 (22 February 1895).
82. *Nor Dar* 33 (24 February 1895).
83. *Nor Dar* 34 (25 February 1895).

84. "An American Heroine in the Heart of Armenia," *The Review of Reviews* 13 (1896): 449.
85. R. Mirak, op. cit., 225.
86. E. M. Bliss, op. cit., 504.
87. *Ibid.*, 512–14.
88. *Ibid.*, 514.
89. *The Catholic World*, a Roman Catholic monthly published in New York City.
90. First Earl of Beaconsfield, or Benjamin Disraeli (1804–1881). British politician who served as prime minister (1868 and 1874–1880) and was instrumental in extending the power and scope of the British Empire.
91. William Ewart Gladstone (1809–1898), British political leader who served as Liberal prime minister four times (1868–1874, 1880–1885, 1886, and 1892–1894).
92. Pyotr Skobeloff was a general in the Russian army.
93. The term Giaour (there may be spelling variations of the word), in general, means "an infidel," i.e., a non-Muslim who was typically subject to harsher taxation and enjoyed lesser rights than the Muslims.
94. *The Nation*, a weekly founded in 1865 and edited until 1902 by Edwin Godkin, a prominent American journalist. The periodical covered foreign policy, as well as political and economic issues.
95. Edwin Lawrence Godkin (1831–1902) was a well-known American journalist. Born in Belfast, he achieved prominence as a reporter at the *Daily News* of London during the Crimean War, and covered the American Civil War for the *Daily News* and *the New York Times*. He founded and edited *The Nation* from 1865 until his death in 1902. He was also the editor of *Evening Post* from 1882 until his death.
96. Fifth Earl of Rosebery, or A. P. Primrose, (1847–1929) was a British politician who served as prime minister (1894–1895) and supported imperialist policies.
97. Robert Arthur Talbot Gascoyne Cecil. Third Marquis of Salisbury (1830–1903), British politician who was Foreign Minister under Benjamin Disraeli and prime minister of England (1885–1892 and 1895–1902).
98. Belgian politician and reviewer. He served as Belgian Minister of the Interior from 1878 to 1884. He was also the Secretary General of the Institute of International Law.
99. *The Outlook*, a New York-based political magazine.
100. A Turkish general, Commander of the Fourth Army Corps in the Ottoman army.
101. MacColl was a British clergyman and a public figure. He was a member of the Grosvenor House Association (the British-Armenian Society) and wrote numerous articles on the Armenian Question in the British and French press.
102. The Turkish Grand Vizier at the time.
103. James Bryce, or First Viscount of Dechmont (1838–1922), was a British

lawyer, politician, and historian. He was a Liberal M.P. since 1874, and occupied several Cabinet-level positions, including Trade Secretary from 1894 to 1895 and Secretary for Ireland from 1905 to 1906. He was the Ambassador to the United States, authoring the famous *American Commonwealth*. Having traveled extensively, he also wrote on Armenia and the Armenian Question (see bibliography).

104. Loris Melikoff, Lazaroff, and Gugasoff were prominent nineteenth-century Russian army generals of Armenian descent.
105. *The Century Magazine* was a New York-based magazine.
106. Cyrus Hamlin (1811–1900), an American missionary. He served on various missions in Turkey from 1837 to 1859, then founded and was president of the Robert College in Constantinople from 1860 to 1876. He returned to the United States and served as president of the Middlebury College (1880–1885). He wrote extensively on Turkey.
107. Henry Hyvernat (1858–1941). Hyvernat was an Orientalist and professor of Assyrian and Egyptian studies at the Catholic University. He spent a year in Western Armenia as part of a French scientific expedition. In 1889 he became Chair of the Semitic and Egyptian Literature Department at Catholic University.
108. Note: in reality, the Armenian language is a separate branch of the Indo-European family of languages.
109. William James Stillman (1828–1901). An artist and writer, Stillman worked in Britain and the United States. He was the special correspondent for the London *Times* in Italy and Greece from 1878 to 1898. He was also the editor of the *Photographic Times*.
110. Full name Clarissa Harlowe Barton (1821–1912). American administrator and nurse who did battlefield relief work during the Civil War and founded the American Red Cross in 1881.
111. Sir George Hamilton Seymour was Her Majesty's Ambassador to the Court of Nicholas I from 1851 to 1854.
112. Frederick Greene, an American missionary, was the Secretary of the National Armenian Relief Fund, and worked extensively to assist the Armenian population in the Ottoman Empire during the massacres of 1894 to 1896.
113. *Review of Reviews* was a monthly digest of news items founded in London in 1889 by the prominent British journalist William Stead and published until 1936. The American edition of the journal appeared simultaneously and soon became an independent publication.
114. Emil Dillon was the reporter for the *Daily Telegraph* in 1895 and covered the Armenian massacres. Born in Dublin and educated in Philosophy and Oriental languages in France and Germany, Dillon moved to Russia, receiving a Master's degree from St. Petersburg University. He also studied Old Armenian (Grabar) and translated Armenian historian Yegishe's fifth-century *Vardanank* (The War of Vardan) into Russian. He wrote extensively on the subject of Armenia, Armenian language, and the Armenian Question.

115. Henry Lynch was a member of the Royal Geographic Society and the author of a series of articles on the Armenian Question in 1894–1896. He later published a book on Armenia.
116. Grace Kimball was an American missionary in the Van area who did humanitarian work during the massacres.
117. *The Forum* was published in New York from 1886 to 1940, when it was absorbed by *Current History*.
118. M. M. Mangasarian was a graduate of Robert College in Constantinople and Princeton Theological Seminary. An ordained minister, he renounced the pulpit for ethical culture and free thinking, and was for many years affiliated with the independent Religious Society of Chicago. Mangasarian's publications include "A New Catechism: What Is Christian Science," "Morality without God," "The Truth about Jesus—Is He a Myth," "What Is the Trouble with the World," "What Has Christ Done for the World," and many others.
119. A Greek consular officer.
120. William Stead (1849–1912) was the publisher of the *Review of Reviews*. He also authored such books as *United States of Europe* and *Americanization of the World*.
121. Aleksey Borisovich Lobanov-Rostovski (1824–1896). Prince Lobanov served as Russia's ambassador to Austria-Hungary from 1882 to 1895 and as Foreign Minister from 1895 to 1896.
122. Lyman Abbott (1835–1922). A clergyman by training, he left religious practice in 1869 and devoted himself to journalism. He became the editor of the *Outlook* in 1887.
123. Founded in 1889, *The Arena* was published in Boston.
124. Moses Gulesian was the secretary of the Boston-based Friends of Armenia. A prominent Armenian American businessman from Boston, he put up the jobless refugees from Armenia in his factory. His provision of food, clothing, and instruction in English and "American customs" eased the transition for many Armenian refugees.
125. Samuel John Barrows (1845–1909) was an American public figure and journalist best known for his efforts to promote reforms of the penitentiary system. He was the editor of the *Christian Register* from 1880 to 1896. As a member of the Friends of Armenia society, he visited U.S. Secretary of State Walter Gresham in 1894 to discuss the Armenian Question.
126. An American poet and translator. She translated and published Armenian poems in various magazines and was an Armenian advocate during the 1894–1896 massacres.
127. Professor Rendel Harris (1852–1941) was a professor of paleontology at Cambridge University from 1893 to 1903. He and his wife Helen were sent to Armenia in March 1896 by the British Friends Society to conduct humanitarian work for the Armenian population.
128. *The Century Magazine* was a New York-based monthly.

NOTES

129. *The Atlantic Monthly* was founded in Boston in 1857 and continues to publish political and scientific critique.
130. A United States Foreign Service officer in Turkey.
131. German scientist and political analyst who studied the economic and political problems of the Ottoman Empire. Rohrbach advocated expansion of German interests in the Middle East and assumption of "protector's status" by Germany for the Christian population of the Ottoman Empire.

Bibliography

Abbott, L. "Armenian Question." *The Outlook* (5 December 1896): 1036–38.
"Agitation against Turkey: Is War Inevitable?" *The Spectator* (19 September 1896): 356–58.
"Aid For Armenia." *The Outlook* 53 (January 1895): 93–94.
"An American Heroine in the Heart of Armenia." *The Review of Reviews* 13 (April 1896): 444–49.
"Americans and Armenians." *The Outlook* (18 February 1896): 156.
"Anarchy in Turkey." *Harper's Weekly* 39 (16 November 1895): 1098.
Argyll, G. D. C., Duke of, *Documentary and Historical Evidence of England's Responsibility for the Horrors Inflicted upon the Armenian People.* Manchester, 1896.
———, *Our Responsibilities for Turkey: Facts and Memories of Forty Years.* London: J. Murray, 1896.
"Armenia and the Powers: From behind the Scenes." *The Contemporary Review* (January 1896): 628–43.
"The Armenian Claim on Europe." *The Spectator* (15 December 1894): 839–40.
"The Armenian Crisis." *The Review of Reviews* 11 (January 1895): 45–54.
"The Armenian Debate." *The Spectator* (18 July 1891): 85–87.
"The Armenian Massacres." *Harper's Weekly* (28 December 1895): 1249–50.
"The Armenian Meeting." *The Spectator* (11 May 1895): 642–43.
"The Armenian Policy of France." *The Spectator* (7 November 1896): 633–34.
"The Armenian Question." *The Spectator* (27 July 1895): 105.
"The Armenian Reforms." *The Spectator* (18 May 1895): 674–75.
Arthur, P. *Map of Territorial Tyranny of the Turk.* London: G. Phib, 1896.
Azhderian, A. *The Turk and the Land of Haig; Or Turkey and Armenia.* New York: The Merschon & Co., 1898.
Baldwin, E. F. "The Turks and the Armenians." *The Outlook* (8 February 1896): 240–43.
Barkley, H. C. *A Ride through Asia Minor and Armenia, Giving a Sketch of the Characters, Manners, and Customs of Both Mussulman and Christian Inhabitants.* London: J. Murray, 1891.
Barrows, J. C. "Der Herr Graf." *The Outlook* (22 August 1896): 329–30.
Basmajian, K. H. *Social and Religious Life in Orient.* New York: American Tract Society, 1890.
Beheznilian, K. *Armenian Home-Life. An Address to the Boys and Girls of England.* London: n.p., 1896.

Benjamin, S. G. W. "Armenians and the Porte." *The Atlantic Monthly* (April 1891): 524–30.

Bell, M. S. "Around and About Armenia." *Scottish Geographical Magazine* 6 (1890).

Bent, J. T. "Notes on the Armenians in the Asia Minor." *Journal of Geographical Society* 6 (1890).

———. "The Two Capitals of Armenia (Sis and Etchmiadzin)." *Eastern and Western Review* (1892).

———. "Travels amongst the Armenians." *The Contemporary Review* (November 1896): 695–709.

Bishop, I. L. B. "The Shadow of the Kurd." *The Contemporary Review* (May–June 1891): 642–54.

Bishop, J. B., and E. L. Godkin. "Armenian Horror." *The Nation* (14 January 1897): 24–25.

Bliss, E. M. "Kurds, Armenians, and Turks." *Harper's Weekly* (29 December 1894): 1242.

———. *Turkey and Armenian Atrocities. A Reign of Terror. Centuries of Oppression.* London: Unwin, 1896.

Blunt, W. S. "Turkish Misgovernment, with Discussion." *The Nineteenth Century* 40 (November 1896): 838–48.

Bryce, J. "The Armenian Question." *The Century Magazine* (November 1895): 150–54.

———. *Transcaucasia and Ararat.* London: Macmillan, 1896.

Burgin, G. B. "The Armenian at Home." *Cassel's Family* (May 1897).

Capper, S. G. *The Haunting Horrors in Armenia, or Who Will Be Damned for This.* London: Clowes, 1896.

Claden, P. W. *Armenia: The Case against Lord Salisbury.* London: n.p., 1897.

Clinch, B. J. "The Christians under Turkish Rule." *American Catholic Quarterly Review* XXI (1896).

"The Compromise in Constantinople." *The Spectator* (19 October 1895): 508–9.

Conder, C. R. "Sultan's Greatest Danger (excerpt)." *The Review of Reviews* 13 (March 1896): 337–38.

Cons, E. "Armenian Exiles in Cyprus." *The Contemporary Review* 70 (December 1896): 888–95.

"Constantinople Massacre." *The Contemporary Review* 70 (October 1896): 457–65; also printed in *Living Age* (7 November 1896): 352–58.

Coode, G. B. M. "The Armenian Church, Its History, And Its Wrongs." *New Review* 9 (1893).

Correspondent, A. *The Armenian Troubles and Where the Responsibility Lies.* New York: Little Co., 1895.

"The Czar's Visit." *The Spectator* (26 September 1896): 389–90.

Davey, R. "Turkey and Armenia." *The Fortnightly Review* 63 (February 1895): 197–210.

———. *The Sultan and His Subjects.* London: Chapman and Hall, 1897.

"The Death-Warrant of Armenia." *The Spectator* (21 December 1895): 885–86.

Delegate, A. "Reminiscences of a Delegate to the Congress of Berlin." *L'Armenie* (15 August 1892).

Dillon (Lanin), E. J. "Armenia and the Armenian People." *The Fortnightly Review* 54 (August 1890): 258–73.

Dillon, E. J. "The Condition of Armenia." *The Contemporary Review* (August 1895): 153–89.

———. "The Condition of Armenia," exc. *The Review of Reviews* (February 1895): 331–32.

———. "The Fiasco in Armenia." *The Fortnightly Review* 65 (March 1896): 341–58.

"Evil of the Turk." *The Outlook* (24 August 1895): 301–2.

"Eyewitness to the Armenian Horrors." *The Catholic World* (May 1896): 279.

"The Fate of Constantinople." *The Spectator* (26 September 1896): 390–91.

Filian, G. H. *Armenia and Her People; Or the Story of Armenia by an Armenian*. Hartford: American Publishing Co., 1896.

Foreign Office. *Turkey 1890–1891, No. 1, 1892, No. 2, 1895, No. 1, 1896, No. 1, 3, 5, 6; Correspondence Respecting the Condition of the Population in Asiatic Provinces of Turkey*. London: Harrison, 1890–1896.

———. *Turkey 1896, No. 2, Correspondence Relative to the Armenian Question and Reports from Her Majesty's Consular Officers in Asiatic Turkey*. London: Harrison, 1896.

———. *Correspondence Respecting the Introduction of Reforms in the Armenian Provinces of Asiatic Turkey*. London: Harrison, 1896.

Gabrielian, M. S. *The Armenians or the People of Ararat*. Philadelphia: Allen, Lane & Scott, 1892.

———. *Facts about Armenia*, New York: Rewell & Co., 1895.

———. *Christian Armenia and the Christian Powers. An Address to American Churches*. New York: Rewell & Co., 1897.

Geffcken, F. H. "The Eastern Question: Turkish Reforms and Armenia." *The Nineteenth Century* (December 1895): 991–1000.

Ghulam-us-Saghlain. "The Mussulmans of India and the Armenian Question." *The Nineteenth Century* (June 1895): 926–39.

Gladstone, W. E. "The Armenian Question." *Christian Literature* 14 (1896).

———. "The Massacres in Turkey." *The Nineteenth Century* 40 (1896).

———. *The Eastern Crisis. A Letter to the Duke of Westminster*. London: J. Murray, 1897.

Godkin, E. L. "Armenian Trouble." *The Nation* (17 January 1895): 44.

———. "Armenian Resolutions." *The Nation* (30 January 1896): 93.

———. "Turkey in Extremis." *The Nation* (30 January 1896): 172–73.

Greene, F. D. *The Armenian Massacres; Or the Sword of Mohammed, Containing a Complete and Thrilling Account of the Terrible Atrocities and Wholesale Murders Committed in Armenia by Mohammedan Fanatics (The Mohammedan Reign of Terror in Armenia)*. Philadelphia: National Publishing Co., 1896.

———. *The Armenian Crisis in Turkey; The Massacre of 1894, Its Antecedents and Significance, with a Consideration of Some of the Factors which Enter into Solution of This Phase of the Eastern Question*. New York: Putnam's Sons, 1895.

Gregory, D. S. *The Crime of Christendom (The Armenian Crisis and Massacres)*. New York: Abbey Press, 1900.

Guinness, R. J. "The Massacres in Turkey." *The Nineteenth Century* (1896).

Gulesian, M. H. "The Armenian Refugees." *The Arena* (March 1897): 652–62.

———. "England's Hand in Turkish Massacres." *The Arena* (January 1897): 271–82.

Hamlin, Cyrus. "The Armenian Massacres." *The Outlook* (7 December 1895): 944–45.

Hamlin, C. "The Martyrdom of Armenia." *The Missionary Review of the World* 9 (1896).

———. "The Genesis and Evolution of the Turkish Massacre of Armenian Subjects." *American Antiquarian Society Proceedings* XIII (1899).

Harris, J. R., and H. B. Harris, *Letters from the Scenes of the Recent Massacre of Armenian Subjects*. London: Nisbet Co., 1897.

———. Review of *Armenia's Desolation and Woe: Review of Letters from Armenia*. *The Review of Reviews* 15 (May 1897): 626–27.

Harris, W. B. "An Unbiased View of the Armenian Question." *Blackwood's Magazine*. (October 1895): 483–92.

Havenmeyer, J. C. *The Relation of the U.S. to Armenia. An Open Letter to the President*. New York: Yonkers, 1896.

Haweis, E. A. B. "A Persian on the Armenian Massacres." *The New Century Review* I (1897).

Hepworth, H. *Through Armenia on Horse Back*. London: Isbister Co., 1898.

Hodgetts, E. A. B. "Armenian Massacres: Russian Policy." *The Nineteenth Century* (1895).

———. *Round about Armenia. The Record of Journey across the Balkans through Turkey, the Caucasus, and Persia in 1895*. London: Low, Marston Co., 1896.

Howard, W. W., *Horrors of Armenia: the Story of an Eye-witness*. New York: Armenian Relief Association, 1896.

Hyvernat, H. "Armenia: Past and Present." *The Catholic World* (December 1895): 312–26

Information Bureau. Armenia. London: n.a., n.p., 1896.

Kalopothakes, D. "The Constantinople Massacres." *The Nation* (8 October 1896): 265–67.

Khalil, Khalid. "The Armenian Question." *The Atlantic Quarterly Review* 10 (1895).

Kimball, G. N. "Massacres at Van." *The Review of Reviews* (October 1896): 468.

———. "Situation in Armenia." *The Outlook* (21 November 1896): 905–6.

———. "Dr. G. Kimball and Her Relief Work at Van." *American Review* (1896).
Knapp, G. H. "The Story of an Armenian Refugee." *The National Magazine* (1897).
Lepsius, J. *Armenia and Europe* London: Hodder and Stoughton, 1897.
Lidgett, E. S. *An Ancient People. A Short Sketch of Armenian History*. London: J. Nisbet, 1897.
"Lord Salisbury in Turkey." *The Spectator* (7 December 1895): 808.
"Lord Rosebery's Deliverance." *The Spectator* (17 October 1896): 504.
"Lord Salisbury and Armenia." *The Spectator* (8 February 1896): 193.
Lynch, H. F. B. "Armenian Question 1. In Russia." *The Contemporary Review* (June 1894): 847–65.
———. "Armenian Question 2. In Russia." *The Contemporary Review* (July 1894): 91–107.
———. "Armenian Question 3. In Turkey." *The Contemporary Review*. (September 1894): 435–56.
———. H. F. B. "The Armenian Question: Europe or Russia?" *The Contemporary Review* (February 1896): 270–76.
MacColl, M. *England's Responsibility toward Armenia. With a Letter from the Duke of Westminster*. London: Longmans Green, 1895.
———. "The Constantinople Massacre and Its Lesson." *The Contemporary Review* (November 1895): 744–60.
———. *The Sultan and the Powers*. London: Longmans Green, 1896.
———. "Armenia and Transvaal." *The Fortnightly Review* LIX (1896): 1–16.
Macdonald, A. *The Land of Ararat*. London: n.p., 1893.
Malcolm, J. A. "Armenian's Cry for Armenia." *The Nineteenth Century* (October 1890): 640–47.
Mangasarian, M. "Armenia's Impending Doom: Our Duty." *The Forum* (June 1896): 449–59.
"The Massacres." *The Spectator* (5 September 1896): 292.
"Massacres in Turkey: October 1, 1895–January 1, 1896." *The Review of Reviews* (February 1896): 197–98.
Maunsell, F. R. "Eastern Turkey in Asia and Armenia." *Scottish Geographical Magazine* XII (1896).
McDermot, G. "The Great Assassin and the Christians of Armenia." *The Catholic World* (December 1896): 295–305.
"Mr. Gladstone on Armenia." *The Spectator* (10 August 1895): 164.
National Armenian Relief Committee. *How To Save Alive the Orphan Children of Martyrs in Armenia*. New York: 1896.
Nazarbek, A. "Zeitun." *The Contemporary Review* (April 1869): 513–28.
———. *The Voice of the Armenian Revolutionists upon the Armenian Problem and How to Solve It*. London: n.p., 1895.
Northrop, H. D. *The Mohammedan Reign of Terror in Armenia*. Washington, DC: American Oxford Publishing Co., 1896.
Nubar, B. *A Practical Scheme for the Solution of the Armenian Question. Memorandum*. Manchester: Manchester Guardian Printing, 1890.

Ogden, R., and G. Hunt. "Lord Salisbury and Armenia." *The Nation* (15 August 1895): 110–11.

Old Indian. Historical Sketch of Armenia and the Armenians in Ancient and Modern Times, with Special Reference to the Present Crisis. London: n.p., 1896.

O'Shea, J. "Unhappy Armenia." *The Catholic World* (January 1895): 553–61.

Otteley, H. B. *Map of the Massacres.* London: n.p., 1896.

"Our Duty in Armenia." *The Spectator* (25 May 1895): 709.

"Our Failure in Turkey." *The Spectator* (14 December 1895): 844.

"Our Obligations to Armenia." *Macmillan's Magazine* 71 (1895).

Papazian, G. "The Past and the Present of the Armenians." *The Christian Register* (1891).

Papers Relating to the Foreign Relations of the United States, with the Annual Message of the President Transmitted to the Congress, December 7, 1893. Washington, DC: Government Printing Office, 1894.

Papers Relating to the Foreign Relations of the United States, with the Annual Message of the President Transmitted to the Congress, December 3, 1894. Washington, DC: Government Printing Office, 1895.

Papers Relating to the Foreign Relations of the United States, with the Annual Message of the President Transmitted to the Congress, December 2, 1895, Part I and II. Washington, DC: Government Printing Office, 1896.

Papers Relating to the Foreign Relations of the United States, with the Annual Message of the President Transmitted to the Congress, December 7, 1896, and *Annual Report of the Secretary of State.* Washington, DC: Government Printing Office, 1897.

"Peasant Life in Armenia." *The Outlook* (20 April 1895): 671.

Pierce, W. F., and L. F. Pierce. "The Armenian Church." *The Review of Reviews* (April 1897): 455–56.

Peterson, T. "Turkey and the Armenian Crisis." *The Catholic World* (August 1895): 665–76.

Pitkins, T. "Turkish Grievances and the Bloodtax." *Harper's Weekly* (26 December 1896): 1275.

"The Policy of Russia in Turkey." *The Spectator* (22 February 1896): 262–63.

"The Possible Extirpation of the Armenians." *The Spectator* (30 November 1895): 752–53.

Rafiüddin, Ahmad. "A Moslem's View of Abdul Hamid and the Powers." *The Nineteenth Century* 38 (1895).

Ramsay, W. M. *The Historical Geography of Asia Minor* London: J. Murray, 1890.

———. "Two Massacres in Asia Minor: Diocletian and the Massacre of the Armenians." *The Contemporary Review* (September 1896): 435–48; excerpts also published in *The Review of Reviews* (October 1896): 466.

———. *Impressions of Turkey during Twelve Year's Wanderings.* London: Hodder and Stoughton, 1897.

Rassam, H. "The Armenian Difficulty. Results of a Local Inquiry." *The Asiatic Quarterly Review* 9–10 (1895).

"Rational Sympathy." *The Nation* (28 November 1895): 384.

Rawnsley, H. D. *The Darkened West. An Appeal to England for Armenia.* Keswick: Bakewell, 1896.
Roberts, Ch. "Mother of Martyrs." *The Atlantic Monthly* (January 1899): 90–96.
Rohrbach, P. "The Contribution to the Armenian Question." *The Forum* XXIX, No. 4 (1900): 481–92.
Rojers, J. G. "Massacres in Turkey." *The Nineteenth Century* (October 1896): 654–80.
———. *The Living Age* (14 November 1896): 393–96.
Rolin-Jaeuemyns, M. G. *The Armenia, the Armenians, and the Treaties.* London: John Heywood, 1891.
"The Rumors about Turkey." *The Spectator* (12 December 1896): 846–47.
Russell, G. W. E. "Armenia and the Forward Movement." *The Contemporary Review* (January 1897).
Ryan, R. M. "Why We Catholics Sympathize with Armenia." *The Catholic World* (November 1895): 181–85.
Sadik Effendi. "The Armenian Agitation: A Reply to M. F. S. Stevenson." *The New Review* 9 (1893).
Sadik, Shahid Bey. *Islam, Turkey, and Armenia, and How They Happened. Turkish Mysteries Unveiled.* St. Louis: Woodward, 1898.
Safir. "The Armenian Question." *The Asiatic Quarterly Review* 9 (1895).
Salmone, H. A. "The Massacres in Turkey." *The Nineteenth Century* 40 (1896).
Schweiger-Lerchenfeld, A. F. *Armenia and the Armenians,* Vol. XXII. Mendville: Chautauquan, 1896.
"The Situation of To-Day." *The Spectator* (3 October 1896): 420–21.
Stanley, H. M. *My Early Travels and Adventures in Armenia and Asia.* London: n.p., 1895.
Stead, W. T. "Eastern Ogre; or St. George to the Rescue, 1878 and 1896." *The Review of Reviews* (November 1896): 576–81.
Stein, R. "Armenia Must Have a European Governor." *The Arena* (May 1895): 368–90.
Stevenson, F. S. "Armenia." *The Contemporary Review* (February 1895): 201–9.
———. *England, Turkey, and Russia: A Historical Retrospect.* London: Anglo-American Association, 1896.
———. "The Armenian Agitation: A Rejoinder to Sadik Effendi." *The New Review* 9 (1893).
———. *The Case for the Armenians.* London, 1896.
Stillman, W. J. "Eastern Question." *The Nation* (9 January 1896): 27.
———. "Germany and the Armenians." *The Nation* (11 May 1899): 351–52.
Stride, W. K. "Immediate Future of Armenia." *The Forum* (November 1896): 308–20.
"The Sultan of Turkey. By One Who Knows Him." *The Review of Reviews* 13 (April 1896).
"The Suspense in Constantinople." *The Spectator* (12 October 1895): 476–77.

Svoboda. "Among Kurdish Brigands in Armenia." *World Magazine* IV (1899).
Telfer, J. B. "Armenia and Its People (Country, Inhabitants, Social Customs)." *Journal of Society of Arts* 39 (1891).
Ter-Gregor, N. *History of Armenia, from the Earliest Ages to the Present Time.* London: J. Heywood, 1897.
Terrell, A. W. "An Interview with Sultan Abdul Hamid: With a List of Armenians in the Turkish Civil List." *The Century Magazine* (November 1897): 133–38.
Terzian, D. *Mathematics of Religion. The Recent Massacres in Turkey Foretold in the Bible.* Boston: n.p., 1897.
Troshine, Y. "Bystander's Notes of a Massacre. The Slaughter of Armenians in Constantinople." *Scribner's Magazine* (January 1897): 48–67.
"The True Danger in Armenia." *The Spectator* (13 September 1890): 329–30.
Tupper, H. A. *Armenia: Its Present Crisis and Past History* Baltimore and New York: J. Murphy Co., 1896.
"A Vanishing Treaty." *The Spectator* (9 August 1890): 172–73.
Vartooguian, A. P. *Armenia's Ordeal. A Sketch of the Main Features of the History of Armenia and an Inside Account of the Work of American Missionaries among Armenians and Its Ruinous Effect.* New York, 1896.
Watson, W. *The Year of Shame.* London: J. Lane, 1897.
White, G. E. "Morning Light in Asia Minor." *Missionary Review of the World* XI (1898): 9.
Williams, A. W., and M. S. Gabrielian. *Bleeding Armenia, Its History and Horrors.* New York, 1896.
Wintle, W. J. *Armenia and Its Sorrow, With an Additional Chapter Bringing Record to September 1896.* London: Melrose, 1896.
Woods, H. Ch. *The Truth about Asia Minor.* London: n.p., 1890.
"What Must Be Done in Armenia." *The Review of Reviews* 13 (1895): 337–38.
"Who Is Responsible." *The Review of Reviews* 13 (April 1896).
"Why the Sultan Is Responsible for the Armenian Massacres." *The Outlook* (15 February 1896): 283–84.
Zimmerman, B. *The Armenian Church.* London: n.p., 1894.
———. *The Breviary of the Armenian Church.* London, 1895.

INDEX

Abbott, Lyman, 296
Abdul, Aziz, 95, 96, 136, 204
Abdul, Hamid II, 15, 19, 23, 25, 28, 30, 36, 39, 40, 45, 69, 96–99, 128, 136, 138, 149, 166, 172, 179, 180, 187, 207, 214, 252, 260
Abdul, Medjid, 65, 95–96, 136, 256, 257, 268
Abraham, 108
Adana, 244, 279
Aderbaijan. *See* Azerbaijan
Adrianople, 204
Aegean Sea, 228
Aesop, 229
Africa, 128, 166, 261
Agopian/Agop, 257, 268–69
Aintab, 35, 43, 118, 140, 164, 279, 284
Ak-Shair, 138
Alashgird. *See* Alashkert
Alashkert, 22, 24, 69
Albania, 130
Alexander II, 71, 75
Alexander the Great, 102, 131, 165, 280
Alexandretta. *See* Alexandrette
Alexandrette, 21, 34
Alexandria, 236, 240
Alfred the Great, 282
Algiers, 128, 232
Allan, William, 198
Allen, Henry, 41
Amalfi, 212
America, 73, 82, 87, 90, 98, 109, 113–14, 140, 156, 159, 162, 165–66, 171–73, 175, 188, 226, 232–34, 246, 257, 268, 279, 289

America Board for Foreign Missions, 34, 116, 156, 234
American Bible Society, 293
American Commonwealth, 295
American Protestant College, 35
American Red Cross Society, 11, 42–43, 45, 116–18, 295
Anatolia, 146, 217, 284, 286, 288
Anatolian College, 35, 36
Anglo-Russian Agreement, 1878, 22
Anglo-Turkish Convention. *See* Cyprus Convention
Angora, 125, 126, 140
Ani, 100
Antiochus III, 280
Arabia, 47, 127, 152, 165, 261
Araks, 72, 82, 100, 101, 167, 278, 280
Ararat, 51, 73, 83, 101–9, 130, 167, 175, 241, 278, 279, 280, 281
Aras. *See* Araks
Araxes. *See* Araks
Ardashir, 280
Ardavatz. *See* Artavazd
Arena, 44, 236
Aristotle, 150
Arius, 261
Armenia, 19, 21–23, 31, 36–37, 40, 43, 45, 47–48, 50–53, 55, 56, 58–60, 64, 67–69, 75, 77–81, 89, 92–94, 98, 100–110, 116–17, 123–24, 127, 130–32, 146–47, 150, 151–54, 155, 157, 164, 167–70, 175, 178, 190, 192, 194, 200–201, 203, 205–6, 211, 217, 219–21, 226, 233, 236, 246, 248, 276, 278, 280–82, 284–85, 287, 289–90, 291, 292, 293, 294, 295, 296

Index

Armenian Genocide, 11, 33
Armenian National Alliance, 13
Armenian Province, 19
Armenian Question, 13, 19, 21, 22,
    23, 24, 26, 27, 28, 31, 32, 33,
    35–36, 39–41, 44–45, 60, 65,
    68, 75, 77, 82, 85, 149, 151,
    169, 194, 225, 249, 274, 277,
    278–79, 284, 292, 294, 295,
    296,
Armenian Relief Committee, 42,
    117, 162, 238
Armenian Relief Fund, 116, 295
Armenian Sea. *See* Van Lake
Arsace the Great. *See* Arshak the
    Great
Arsacidae. *See* Arshakides
Arshak the Great, 102
Arshakides, 102
Artashat, 280
Artashes, 280
Artavazd, 102
Artaxata. *See* Artashat
Artaxias. *See* Artashes
Artin Pasha, 257
Asia, 19, 48, 60, 70, 75, 79–80, 82,
    91, 108, 125, 128, 129, 153,
    166, 167, 168, 171–72, 199,
    203, 204, 213, 214, 220, 239,
    257, 261, 279
Asia Minor, 48, 49, 60, 73, 83, 85,
    93, 94, 103, 105, 114, 124, 125,
    126, 127, 130, 137, 140, 151,
    152, 215, 217, 218, 219, 220,
    222, 248, 250, 253, 255, 258,
    274, 278, 280, 281
Assyria, 100
Athens, 32, 179, 270
Atlantic Monthly, 44
Austria-Hungary, Austria, 21, 22,
    26, 93, 196, 232, 259, 274, 276,
    277, 278, 279, 296
Ayntab. *See* Aintab
Ayrarat, 280
Ayvazian, Dr., 42, 238
Azerbaijan, 278

Babylon, 280
Bagdad. *See* Baghdad
Baghdad, 34, 103, 127, 289
Bagrat, 103
Bagratides, 100, 103–4, 280
Bahdje-Kapou, 180
Bahri Pasha, 185
Bailiwick of Brandenburg, Johan-
    niter, 217
Baker, Mrs., 239
Baku, 19, 279
Balians, 257
Balkans, 18–19, 20–21, 23–24, 26,
    220, 274, 276
Balmoral, 194
Baltimore, 232, 248
Bangor, 155
Baptist Philadelphian, 42
Barnum, Dr., 142
Barrows, Samuel J., 41, 239, 296
Barsumas of Nisibis, 78
Bartholomew, 102
Bartlett, Ashmead, 188, 255
Barton, Clara Harlowe, 42–43,
    116–17, 295
Barton, James, 234
Barton, Stephen E., 116
Batum, 19, 279
Bayazid, 22, 168
Bazarid, 69
Beaconsfield. *See* Disraeli
Beirut, 27, 34, 35
Belfast, 294
Berlin, 22, 54, 144, 170, 190, 196,
    200, 274
Berlin Congress, 22, 24, 133, 190,
    285–87
Berlin Treaty, 22–23, 28, 31, 37, 41,
    59, 64–67, 75, 124, 132–33,
    176, 200–201, 203, 221
Bern, 270
Berne. *See* Bern
Bible, 103, 131, 149, 242, 256, 279,
    282
Bismarck, Otto, 53
Bithynian Olympus, 125, 261

Bitlis, 41, 50, 63, 81, 116, 157, 158, 284
Black Sea, 21, 25, 100, 102, 172, 204, 209, 219, 261, 278, 280
Blackwell, Alice, 41, 238–39
Blackwell, Henry, 41
Blanchard, Newton, 37
Bliss, Edwin, 41, 43, 242, 247, 293, 294
Bosnia, 11, 21, 89
Bosphorus, 67, 74, 76, 81, 104, 123, 166, 168, 173, 190, 193, 213, 219, 257, 261, 265
Bosporus. *See* Bosphorus
Boston, 40, 41, 42, 43, 44, 237, 238, 242, 296, 297
Boston Herald, 40
Brewer, David, 42, 117
Brighton, 240
Britain. *See* Great Britain
British Friends Society, 296
British Guyana, 35
British Woman's Relief Committee, 43
Brusa. *See* Bursa
Bryce, James, 67, 212, 294
Bucharest, 269
Bulgaria, 21, 32, 48–52, 60, 69, 126, 128, 167–68, 185, 191–92, 199, 228, 236, 250, 277, 279
Bull, John, 193
Burke, Edmund, 87, 213
Burnaby, Colonel, 218
Bursa, 126
Byzantine Empire, 83, 103, 105, 107
Byzantium. *See* Byzantine Empire

Cabell, Mr., 267
Caesar, 64, 172
Cairo, 168
California, 167
Calvinism, 229
Cambodia, 11
Cambridge University, 296
Canada, 275

Canning, Stratford, 96
Carlyle, 215
Caspian Sea, 100
Catherine de Medici, 228
Catholic University, 100, 295
Catholic World, 44, 47, 67, 77, 291, 294
Catholicism, 78
Central America, 36
Central Asia, 52, 66–67, 105, 125–26
Central Turkish College, 35
Century Magazine, 44, 82, 252, 295, 296
Cesarea, Cesaria. *See* Kayseri
Chalcedon, 106–7, 131, 261
Charles V, 128
Charput. *See* Kharberd
Chester, 58, 60
Chicago, 41, 177
Chicago Tribune, 40
Chichli, 267
China, 118
Chios. *See* Khios
Christendom, 49, 55, 74, 106, 148, 211, 213, 216, 225, 231, 281
Christian Herald, 42, 43, 161, 162, 163
Christianity, 45, 48–49, 61, 66, 71, 73–74, 82, 102–3, 105, 107, 111, 114, 131, 165, 168, 205, 208, 229, 246, 258, 280, 285, 288
Christian Register, 40, 41, 42, 296
Cilicia, 30, 73, 83, 104, 105, 279, 280
Clarke, James Freeman, 228
Cleveland, Grover, 36–41, 93, 113–15
Cogswell, Dr., 247
Commonwealth, 42
Conder, Major, 152
Confucius, 256
Congregationalist, 42
Constantine, 128, 165

Index

Constantinople, 20, 24, 26, 29, 32–33, 35, 36, 38, 39, 43–44, 63, 80, 84, 88, 90, 91, 95, 96, 98, 99, 107, 110, 123–24, 126, 127, 128, 131, 136, 138, 141, 156, 166, 168, 169, 172–73, 176, 177, 178, 179, 182, 192, 196, 197, 203, 205, 208–9, 212, 220, 223, 226, 236, 252–53, 256, 263, 267, 270, 274, 276–77, 279, 280
Constantinople Woman's College, 35
Contemporary Review, 146, 151, 252
Crete, 33, 52, 176–78, 259, 293
Crimea, 127, 173
Crimean Khanate, 128
Crimean War, 96, 128, 132, 294
Crispi, 274
Cunaxa, 280
Current History, 296
Currie, Phillip, 44
Curzon, Lord, 213
Cyprus, 22, 54, 127, 190–93, 196, 199, 200, 203, 217, 221
Cyprus Convention, 22–23, 31, 75, 191, 193–94, 199, 203
Cyrus the Great, 131, 261, 280

Dadian, Mr., 256–57
Daily News, 40, 294
Daily Telegraph, 146, 295
Damascus, 68, 228, 259
Dante, 125
Danube, 168
Dardanelles, 21, 81, 99, 138, 149, 190, 193, 197–99, 204, 219, 275–76
Davey R., 291
Day, William R., 40
Deir-el-Kamar, 167
Delaware, 41
Delyannis, 277
Diarbekir. *See* Diyarbakir
Dillon, Emil J., 146, 147, 148, 295
Diocletian, 226

Disraeli, Benjamin (Lord Beaconsfield), 48, 54, 128, 146, 189–90, 192–93, 195, 294
Diyarbakir, 141, 169
Dodge, William, 39
Dorpat. *See* Tartu
Dover, 29
Dublin, 295
Dufferin, Lord, 133
Duke of Alva, 226, 228, 230
Duke of Queensbury, 230

East, 19, 20, 45, 48, 69, 79, 85, 164, 166, 169, 171, 174, 196, 197, 202, 211, 214, 216, 223, 225, 245, 249, 281, 285, 288
Eastern Armenia, 19
Eastern Europe, 47
Eastern Mediterranean, 18, 22, 217
Eastern Question, 112, 113, 116, 152, 200, 203, 220, 258
Eastern Roumelia, 199
Eastern Turkey, 145
Echmiadzin, 100, 103, 108, 111, 281, 290
Echmiazin. *See* Echmiadzin
Eckford, Mr., 95
Egin, 164
Egypt, 24, 28, 53, 71, 80, 95, 105, 113, 124, 126, 127, 128, 145, 171, 220, 236, 240, 254, 278, 279, 281, 293
Elizabeth, 128
Ellis Island, 234, 237
Emin, Pasha, 158
England. *See* Great Britain
English Society of Friends, 248
Erevan/Erivan. *See* Yerevan
Erzerum/Erzeroum. *See* Erzurum
Erzincan, 83, 148
Erzinghian/Erzinghan. *See* Erzincan
Erzurum, 34, 59, 63, 83, 116, 136, 141, 148, 151, 156, 293
Euphrates, 51, 72, 82, 100, 130, 167, 202–3, 278, 284, 286

Euphrates College, 35
Europe, 19, 20, 29, 33, 36, 42, 44, 48, 51, 55, 59–60, 73, 75, 79, 80, 83, 85, 86 87, 93, 109, 112, 114, 120, 123, 126, 128–29, 131–32, 140, 143–44, 147, 149, 151 152, 165, 166, 167, 168, 170–74, 178, 187–88, 189, 190, 191 193–94, 199–201, 203, 204, 206, 212, 214–17, 220–21, 224, 225, 227, 232, 233, 238, 239, 253, 254, 255, 261, 262, 267, 277, 287
European Turkey, 26, 176, 214
Eutyches, 106–7, 261
Evangelical Alliance, 42, 116
Evening Post, 294
Exeter College, Oxford, 218

Far East, 25, 153
Feri-Koi, 180, 181
Fessenden, Mrs., 239
Finland, 283
Fisk, Pliny, 34
Forum, 44, 164, 211, 278
France, 17, 24–27, 87, 97, 124, 172–74, 201, 224, 232, 236, 259, 288
Francis I, 128
Freeman, Mr., 87
Friends of Armenia, 41, 296

Gabrielian, M. S., 42
Galata, 181, 270
Galata-Serai, 180, 181, 182, 184
Gallipoli, 126, 192, 197
Gargiulo, 252
Gateshead, 198
Gemereg, 164
Geneva, 217
Genghis Khan, 165
Georgia, 127, 278
Germany, 25–26, 28, 53, 166, 172–73, 176, 178, 213, 216, 224, 226, 232, 259, 274, 275, 277, 278, 288–89, 295, 296

Girl's Boarding and Day School, 156
Gladstone, William, 48, 50, 58–60, 192, 195, 213, 224, 294
Godfrey, Duke, 259
Godkin, Edwin Lawrence, 120, 292, 294
Golden Horn, 265
Gomer, 102
Great Britain, 13, 17–18, 21–22, 24, 25, 26, 31, 35–36, 43, 45, 47–48, 53, 54, 58, 59, 69, 75, 79, 85, 89, 90, 96, 97, 98, 99, 112–15, 124, 128–29, 132–33, 135, 145, 146, 152, 153, 159, 162–63, 172–74, 181–82, 189–99, 201, 202, 206, 211, 216–18, 221, 224, 226, 230–32, 245, 246, 249, 259, 274–77, 285, 287–89
Greater Armenia, 104
Greece, 127, 199, 220, 232–33, 236, 276–77
Greek Empire. *See* Byzantine Empire
Greek-Turkish War, 32
Green, Frederick D., 42, 134
Gregory the Illuminator, 80, 103, 131, 165, 283
Gresham, Walter, 41, 296
Griscom, Lloyd, 40
Grosvenor House Association, 294
Gugassoff, 71, 295
Gulesian, Moses H., 41, 292–93, 296
Gumushgerdan, 257
Gurun, 141

Hafiz, 166
Haik, 130, 244, 279
Hamid. *See* Abdul Hamid II
Hamilton, Caroline F., 43, 118
Hamlin, Cyrus, 35, 43, 187, 258, 267, 295
Hammer, Van, 68
Hannibal, 280

Index

Harberd, Harpoot. *See* Kharberd
Harris, Rendel J., 248–51, 296
Hassankaleh, 148
Hastings Warren, 77
Hatt-e-Humayun, 17, 144
Hatt-e-Sherif of Gulhane, 15, 17, 144
Hawaii, 231
Herzegovina, 21, 128
Hoar, George Frisbie, 37, 93
Holland, 228
Holland, T. E., 220
Holocaust, 11
House of Commons, 213
House of Lords, 31
Howe, Julia Ward, 41
Hubbell, Dr., 116
Hugo, Victor, 69
Hungary, 127, 213
Hussein Pasha, 158

Independent, 42, 258, 293
India, 73, 77, 89, 124, 126, 278, 279
International Woman's College, 35
Iran. *See* Persia
Ireland, 78, 295
Islam, 45, 50–51, 61–62, 64, 66, 88, 98, 104–5, 125, 129, 133, 143–44, 168–69, 205, 212, 228–29, 256, 281
Ismael Pasha, 254
Israel, 225
Istanbul, 19
Italy, 26, 53, 115, 166, 196, 216, 224, 259, 274, 295
Izmirlian, Patriarch, 137, 248
Izmit, Izmid, 138

Japan, 79
Japhet, 130
Jerusalem, 34, 212, 213, 216, 217
John Hopkins University, 248
Judas Machabeus, 79
Jude, 102
Justinian, 261

Kaisariyeh, *See* Kayseri
Kallay, Count, 89
Kars, 71
Kavash, 159
Kayseri, 140, 164, 218, 284
Kentucky, 40
Kharberd, 34–35, 116, 141–42, 188, 218, 223, 251, 284
Kharput. *See* Kharberd
Kherson, 128
Khios, 52, 69, 167
Khizan, 158
Khorasan, 125
Kimball, Grace N., 43, 155–57, 163, 185, 187, 296
Kinross, Lord, 19
Konjieh. *See* Konya
Konya, 105
Koran, 61, 69, 72–73, 98, 105, 136, 149, 168–69, 229, 256
Ku Klux Klan, 230, 255
Kuetzgrolian, Mr., 257
Kurdistan, 145, 219, 278, 286

Labouchere, 223
Larnaca, Larnica, 195
Layard, A. H., 22, 60
Lazarew Institute for Oriental Languages, 283
Lazaroff, 71, 295
Lebanon, 22, 68–69, 89, 128, 133, 153, 228
Lemme, Mr., 266, 268
Lend a Hand, 185
Lennep, Van, 167
Leo X, 128
Leon de Lusignan, 105
Lesser Armenia, 104
Lincoln, Abraham, 166
Livonia, 283
Lobanoff-Rostovski, Aleksey, 194–96, 296
London, 22, 24, 112, 193, 204
Louis XVI, 260
Louisiana, 37
Lynch, Henri F. B., 151, 296

INDEX

MacColl, Malcolm, 64, 133, 294
Macedonia, 93, 130, 177, 189, 190, 202
Machiavellianism, 48
Madeh, 218
Maine, 155
Malta, 21, 216–17, 223
Mamelukes, 105
Manelian, Mr., 269
Manelian, Mrs., 268–69
Mangasarian M. M., 296
Marash, 35, 118, 140, 141, 188, 244, 284
Marblehead, 38
Mardin, 249
Marlboro, 40
Marmora Sea, 21, 219, 261, 265
Marseilles, 32, 236, 245, 265, 270
Marzvan, Marzovan, 35, 143
Massachusetts, 40, 43, 247
Massachusetts Legislative Assembly, 35
Massis, *See* Ararat
Maximoff, Mr., 265
McKinley, William, 39
Mecca, 127, 229
Medina, 127
Mediterranean Sea, 26, 100, 124, 151, 209, 220, 231, 232, 278
Mehmet Ali, 95, 149
Melikoff, Loris, 71, 295
Mersin, 244–45
Mesopotamia, 100, 111, 127, 209, 220, 259, 284
Mesrob, Mashtots, 103, 131
Michael Protocol Effendi, 257
Middlebury College, 295
Middle East, 39, 44, 291, 292, 297
Midhat Pasha, 136
Milton, 233
Minneapolis, 292
Mirak, Robert, 292–94
Mithridates, 102
Mohammed the Conqueror, 127, 166
Mohammedanism. *See* Islam

Moks, 159
Monroe, James, 34, 35, 120, 124
Montenegro, 21, 128
Moscow, 128, 194, 283
Mosul, Mosoul, 41, 69
Munier, Pasha, 252, 260
Murad, V, 128
Mush, Moosh, Moush, 60, 73, 147
Mussa Bey, 64
Mustapha Pasha, 157

Nagin Pasha, 185
Nagin-Pacha. *See* Nagin Pasha
Naples, 261
Napoleon, 172
Napoleon III, 173
Napoleon, Louis, 96
Nation, 36, 44, 53, 112, 120, 176, 179, 274, 294
National Armenian Relief Committee Fund, 42
Navarino, 128
Nazarbek, A., 292
Near East, 15, 24, 26, 28, 33, 34
Nejib Pasha, 68
Nestorius, 106–7
New Hampshire, 40, 155
New Orleans, 123
New York, N.Y., 40–44, 117, 156, 163, 225, 237, 238, 248
New York Herald, 40
New York Red Cross Hospital, 116
New York Times, 40, 294
Newcastle Daily Leader, 198
Nicholas II, 196
Nicholas I, 128, 167, 295
Nicomedia. *See* Izmit
Nineveh, 80, 102, 167
Noah, 101, 244, 279
Noe. *See* Noah
Nonconformist Unionist Association, 31
North American Review, 187
Northern Asia, 105
Novikoff, Madame, 194, 200

Odessa, 279
Ohio General Assembly, 42
Olney, Richard, 35–37, 39, 99, 120, 254
Oorsha. *See* Urfa
Orient. *See* East
Osman, Pasha, 254, 260
Othman, Osman, 105, 125–26, 128
Ottoman Bank, 264
Ottoman Empire, 11, 15–18, 20–22, 25–32, 34–35, 37–44, 47–51, 58–60, 64–65, 67, 70, 75, 80–81, 84, 86–90, 92, 95–96, 106, 108, 111, 113, 118, 120, 123, 125–31, 133, 134, 140, 141, 144, 148, 152–53, 156, 165–66, 168, 170–77, 187, 190–95, 202–3, 206–9, 213–14, 218, 220–21, 223–25, 227, 231–32, 234, 236–37, 244, 246, 252–58, 260, 262, 276, 278, 281, 284–93, 295–97
Ottoman Porte. *See* Sublime Porte
Outlook, 42–44, 61, 95, 125, 163, 205, 225, 293–94, 296
Oxford, 220

Palestine, 217, 279
Palu, 138
Pan-Islamism, 18
Paris, 69, 96, 105, 170, 270
Parseeism, 78
Parsons, Levi, 34
Patras, 179
Patrick, Mary Miles, 35
Patriotic Federation of Armenians, 42
Peabody, Professor, 41
Pennsylvania, 278
Pera, 137, 179, 181, 183
Perozes, 78–79
Persia, Persian Empire, 19, 51, 78–79, 83, 103, 106–7, 125–26, 130, 134, 151, 165, 171, 185, 209, 278, 280–81
Persian Armenia, 131, 282

Persian Gulf, 151, 220, 289
Peter the Hermit, 213, 216
Petrus Mechitar, 282
Pharisaism, 192
Philadelphia, 40–41
Photographic Times, 295
Piccoli, Wolfgang, 291
Piraeus, 32, 179, 184
Plymouth, 235
Poland, 78, 219, 231, 279
Pompeius, 280
Porte, *See* Sublime Porte
Potter, Alonzo, 42
Poughkeepsie, N.Y., 210
Prince Islands, 21
Princeton Theological Seminary, 296
Protestantism, 34
Providence, 41, 94
Prusso-French War, 1870–1871, 18
Psamatia, 266, 268, 271

Reformation, 281
Religious Society of Chicago, 296
Republic of Armenia, 12
Rever, 238–39
Review de Paris, 149
Review of Reviews, 43–44, 140, 149, 155, 294–96
Revue de Droit International, 59
Rhodes, 215, 217, 223
Riddle, Mr., 267
Robert College, 35, 292–93, 295–96
Rohrbach, Carl Albert Paul, 292, 297
Rolin-Jacquemyns, M. G., 59
Roman Empire, 106
Romania, 126, 128, 269
Rome, 100–101, 105–7, 111, 113, 115, 217, 280, 282
Roopenians, 104
Rosebery, Lord, 24, 27–28, 54, 291, 294
Royal Geographic Society, 296
Rumania/Roumania. *See* Romania

INDEX

Russia, 17–19, 21–22, 24–28, 48, 53–54, 70–71, 75–79, 83–84, 87–89, 93, 95–99, 106, 108, 110, 112, 114, 123–24, 126–28, 130, 132, 134–35, 145–46, 151, 153, 170, 172–74, 178, 185, 188, 190, 192, 194–97, 201–2, 204, 209, 216, 219–20, 226, 231, 259, 276–79, 281, 283, 285, 288, 295–96
Russian Armenia, 108, 131–32
Russo-Persian War, 1826–1828, 19
Russo-Turkish War, 1877–1878, 20, 128
Rustchuk, 168
Rwanda, 11

Sabbas, John, 80
Sadi, 166
Sadik, Shahid Bey, 291
Said, Pasha, 65
Saladin, 105, 259
Salisbury, Lord, 27–32, 54, 58–60, 87, 112–14, 144, 169, 176, 178, 190, 192, 214–15, 274–77, 291–92
Salonica. See Thessaloniki
Salvation Army, 238
Sanders, Mr., 120
San Lazzaro, 282
San Stefano Treaty, 21–22, 75, 84, 132–33, 170, 190, 291
San-Francisco, 38
Sardinia, 173
Sassanids, 102–3, 280
Sasun/Sassoun/Sassun, 24–25, 28, 37, 41–42, 63, 67–69, 86, 90, 134, 148, 162, 215, 223
Savfat, Pasha, 22
Scet, 80
Schuyler, Eugene, 167
Scio, Scios. See Khios
Scobeloff. See Skobeloff
Scotland, 190, 249
Scottish Review, 152
Scutari, 261

Selucia, 28
Sennacherib, 131
Senner, Dr., 237
Seraglio, 129
Serai, 182–84
Serbia, Servia, 52, 126, 128
Seymour, George Hamilton, 128, 295
Shadagn, 159
Shah Abbas, 165
Sherman,
Sivas, 34, 140, 143, 164, 284
Skobeloff, Pyotr, 48, 294
Smith College, 118
Smyrna, 34–35, 43, 162, 259, 274, 279
Sofia, 168
Somerset, Henry, 236
South Caucasus, 12, 19
Spain, 216, 226
Spectator, 31, 36, 196, 291–92
St. James Gazette, 224
St.Petersburg, 27, 108, 196, 295
Stamboul. See Constantinople
Stead, William T., 137, 295–96
Stillman William James, 295
Strauss, Oscar, 39, 40
Sublime Porte, 16–17, 21–25, 28, 33, 36, 40, 43, 48–51, 53, 55, 59–60, 67, 77, 80, 93, 108–9, 111, 117–18, 123, 125, 129, 132–33, 136–37, 152, 176, 178, 201, 214, 220–21, 255–56, 286
Suez Canal, 17
Sugat, 125
Suleiman the Magnificent, 127–28
Switzerland, 100, 270
Syra, 179
Syria, 126–27, 152–54, 220, 279, 281, 284

Talmud, 256
Tamerlane, 126, 141
Tanzimat, 15, 18
Tarsus, 244
Tartu, 283

Taurus, 31, 279, 284
Terrell, Alexander, 37–40, 93, 99, 254
Terzian, Nina, 13
Terzian, Rouben, 13
Thaddeus, 102, 131
Therapia, 263–64
Thessaloniki, 49
Thogormah, 102
Thomas, 102
Thrace, 130
Tiflis, 19
Tigranes I, 131
Tigris, 51, 82, 100, 130, 167, 228
Times, 295
Tiridates, King, 103, 106, 165, 280
Torquemada, 226, 228, 230
Tozer, 218–19
Trabzon, 140–41, 148, 164
Transcaucasia, 47, 83, 220, 292
Transylvania, 127
Trebizond. *See* Trabzon
Tribune, 92–93
Tripoli, 128
Tripple Alliance, 26, 201, 224, 274, 276–77
Turkey, Turkish Empire. *See* Ottoman Empire
Turkish Armenia, 111, 130, 205, 226, 285
Turkmenchai, 19
Turpin, Dick, 191

Ulfilas, 131
United Friends of Armenia, 41
United States of America, 11, 13, 33–36, 39–41, 43–45, 82, 85, 99, 113, 115, 138, 144, 224, 231–33, 237, 248, 252, 255, 258, 261, 269, 275, 292–93, 295–96
Unkiar-Skelessi, 128
Urartu, 279–80
Urfa, 118, 251, 279, 284

Valarce, 102
Van City, 20, 24, 41, 43, 81, 111, 116, 155–59, 185, 284, 296
Van Lake, 43, 83, 100–101, 109, 130, 278–79, 286
Varna, 168
Vaspurakan, 24
Vassar College, 157, 210
Venezuela, 35–36, 113, 231, 275–76
Venice, 282
Victoria, Queen, 27–28
Vienna, 127, 220, 282
Vincent, Edgar, 265
Voltaire, 215

Wallace, Lew, 254
Wallachia, 127
Walter the Penniless, 213
Wan. *See* Van City, Lake
Washburn, 255
Washington, D.C., 12–13, 55, 116–17, 264, 293
Waterloo, 172
Watson, William, 174
Webster, Daniel, 233
West, 19, 45, 79
West Bournemouth, 274
Western Armenia, 19–21, 23–25, 27, 29–31, 33, 42, 44
Western Europe, 178
Westminster Gazette, 194
Westminster, Duke, 58
White House, 36–37, 41, 92
White, Peregrine, 155
Willard, Frances E., 236
William of Orange, 228
Williams, Major, 187
Winans, Henry, 225
Woman's Armenian Relief Committee, 162–63
Woman's Christian Temperance Union, 238–39
Woman's Journal, 41
Woman's Medical College, 156
Worcester, 40

World War I, 33
Wyoming, 123

Xenophon, 52, 131, 261
Xerxes, 280

Yegishe, 295

Yerevan, 132, 280

Zableh, 167
Zeitun (also Zeytun, Zeitune, Zeitoun), 20, 24, 30, 65, 143
Zeki, Pasha, 63, 65
Zoroastrianism, 51, 78